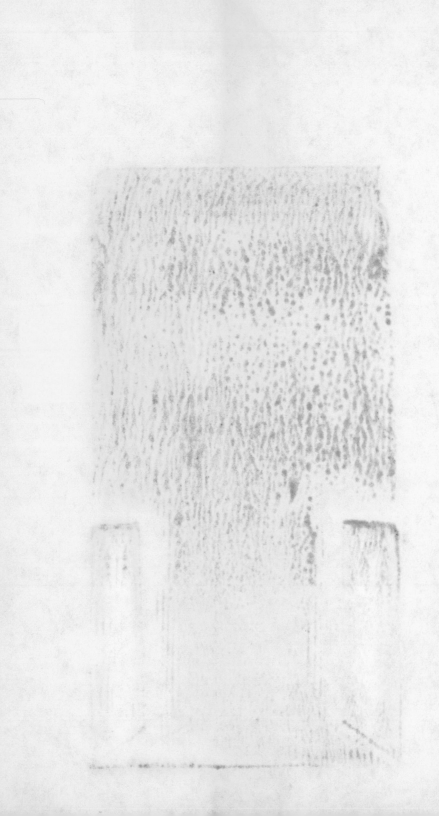

O, THOSE
EXTRAORDINARY
WOMEN!

or the joys of literary lib

Books by Seon and Robert Manley
Beaches: Their Lives, Legends and Lore
Islands: Their Lives, Legends and Lore
The Age of the Manager: A Treasury of Our Times

Books by Seon Manley
My Heart's in the Heather
My Heart's in Greenwich Village
Nathaniel Hawthorne: Captain of the Imagination
Long Island Discovery
James Joyce: Two Decades of Criticism
Rudyard Kipling: Creative Adventurer
Adventures in the Making: The Romance of Crafts Around the World
Teen-Age Treasury for Girls
Teen-Age Treasury of Good Humor
Dorothy and William Wordsworth: The Heart of a Circle of Friends

Books by Seon Manley and Gogo Lewis
Ladies of Horror: Two Centuries of Supernatural Stories by the Gentler Sex
To You With Love: A Treasury of Great Romantic Literature
The Oceans: A Treasury of the Sea World
Teen-Age Treasury of Our Science World
Teen-Age Treasury of the Arts
Teen-Age Treasury of Imagination and Discovery
High Adventure: A Treasury for Young Adults
Mystery! A Treasury for Young Readers
Merriment! A Treasury for Young Readers
Magic! A Treasury for Young Readers
Suspense! A Treasury for Young Readers
Polar Secrets: A Treasury of the Arctic and Antarctic
Shapes of the Supernatural
A Gallery of Ghosts

O, *THOSE EXTRAORDINARY WOMEN!*

or the joys of literary lib

SEON MANLEY AND SUSAN BELCHER

Chilton Book Company / Philadelphia / New York / London

Copyright © 1972 by Seon Manley and Susan Belcher
First Edition   All Rights Reserved
Published in Philadelphia by Chilton Book Company
and simultaneously in Ontario, Canada,
by Thomas Nelson & Sons, Ltd.
Library of Congress Cataloging in publication Data
Manley, Seon.
    O, those extraordinary women!
    1. Authors, Women. 2. Authors, English—
Biography. 3. Authors, American—Biography.
I. Belcher, Susan, joint author. II. Title:
PR111.M24 820'.9'9287 [B] 72–8061
ISBN 0–8019–5636–1
Designed by Warren Infield
Manufactured in the United States of America

The quotation at the front of the book is from
Granite and Rainbow by Virginia Woolf and is
quoted by permission of Harcourt Brace Jovanovich, Inc.
The quotation on the last page of the book is
from A Room of One's Own by Virginia Woolf and is
quoted by permission of Harcourt Brace Jovanovich, Inc.

For our mothers
Carolyn McLean and Susan Lockhart
and our daughters
Shivaun Manley and Allyson Belcher

CONTENTS

O, THOSE EXTRAORDINARY WOMEN!

or the joys of literary lib

The extraordinary woman depends on the ordinary woman. It is only when we know what were the conditions of the average woman's life, the number of her children, whether she had money of her own, if she had a room to herself, whether she had help in bringing up her family, if she had servants, whether part of the housework was her task—it is only when we can measure the way of life and the experience of life made possible to the ordinary woman that we can account for the success or failure of the extraordinary woman as a writer.

Virginia Woolf

THE WOMAN OF MIND.

My wife is a woman of mind,
  And Deville, who examined her bumps,
Vow'd that never were found in a woman
  Such large intellectual lumps.
"Ideality" big as an egg,
  With "Causality"—great—was combined;
He charg'd me ten shillings, and said,
  "Sir, your wife is a woman of mind."

She's too clever to care how she looks,
  And will horrid blue spectacles wear,
Not because she supposes they give her
  A fine intellectual air;
No! she pays no regard to appearance,
  And combs all her front hair behind,
Not because she is proud of her forehead,
  But because she's a woman of mind.

She makes me a bushel of verses,
  But never a pudding or tart,
If I hint I should like one, she vows
  I'm an animal merely at heart;
Though I've notic'd she spurns not the pastry,
  Whene'er at a friend's we have din'd,
And has always had two plates of pudding,
  Such plates! for a woman of mind.

Not a stitch does she do but a distich,
  Mends her pen too instead of my clothes;
I haven't a shirt with a button,
  Nor a stocking that's sound at the toes;
If I ask her to darn me a pair,
  She replies she has work more refined:
Besides, to be seen darning stockings!
  Is it fit for a woman of mind?

The children are squalling all day,
  For they're left to the care of a maid;
My wife can't attend to "the units,"
  "The millions" are wanting her aid.
And it's vulgar to care for one's offspring—
  The mere brute has a love of its kind—
But *she* loves the whole human fam'ly,
  For *she* is a woman of mind.

Every thing is an inch thick in dust,
    And the servants do just as they please;
The ceilings are cover'd with cobwebs,
    The beds are all swarming with fleas;
The windows have never been clean'd,
    And as black as your hat is each blind;
But my wife's nobler things to attend to,
    For she is a woman of mind.

The Nurse steals the tea and the sugar,
    The Cook sells the candles as grease,
And gives all the cold meat away
    To her lover, who's in the Police.
When I hint that the housekeeping's heavy,
    And hard is the money to find,
"Money's vile filthy dross!" she declares,
    And unworthy a woman of mind.

Whene'er she goes out to a dance,
    She refuses to join in the measure,
For dancing she can't but regard
    As an unintellectual pleasure:
So she gives herself up to enjoyments
    Of a more philosophical kind,
And picks all the people to pieces,
    Like a regular woman of mind.

She speaks of her favourite authors
    In terms far from pleasant to hear;
"Charles Dickens," she vows, "is a darling,"
    "And Bulwer," she says, "is a dear;"
"Douglas Jerrold," with her "is an angel,"
    And I'm an "illiterate hind,"
Upon whom her fine intellect's wasted;
    I'm not fit for a woman of mind.

She goes not to Church on a Sunday,
    Church is all very well in its way,
But she is too highly inform'd
    Not to know all the parson can say;
It does well enough for the servants,
    And was for poor people design'd;
But bless you! it's no good to her,
    For *she* is a woman of mind.

Mary Wollstonecraft, from the portrait by John Opie, courtesy, National Portrait Gallery, London. "Something resides in this heart that is not perishable." From *Letters Written During a Short Residence In Sweden, Norway, and Denmark.*

A HYENA IN PETTICOATS
MARY WOLLSTONECRAFT

The Wollstonecraft order . . . . do infinite mischief; and, for my part, I do not wish to have anything to do with them.

Harriet Martineau, 1878

Those who are bold enough to advance before the age they live in, and to throw off, by the force of their own minds, the prejudices which the maturing reason of the world will in time disavow, must learn to brave censure. We ought not to be too anxious respecting the opinion of others.—I am not fond of vindications.— Those who know me will suppose that I acted from principle.—Nay, as we in general give others credit for worth, in proportion as we possess it—I am easy with regard to the opinions of the *best* part of mankind.—I *rest* on my own.

Mary Wollstonecraft, 1797

See Wollstonecraft, whom no decorum
  checks,
Arise, the intrepid champion of her sex;
O'er humbled man assert the sovereign
  claim,
And slight the timid blush of virgin fame.
  "Go, go (she cries) ye tribes of melting
    maids,
Go, screen your softness in sequester'd
  shades;
With plaintive whispers woo the uncon-
  scious grove,
And feebly perish, as despis'd ye love.
What tho' the fine Romances of Rousseau

Bid the frame flutter, and the bosom glow;
Tho' the rapt Bard, your empire fond to
  own,
Fall prostrate and adore your living throne,
The living throne his hand presum'd to
  rear,
Its seat a simper, and its base a tear;
Soon shall the sex disdain the illusive sway,
And wield the sceptre in yon blaze of
  day; . . .
Surpass their rivals in the powers of mind
And vindicate *the Rights of womankind.*"
"Unsex'd Females," Richard Polwhele,
  1798

EVEN as a girl she had been overwhelming. She overwhelmed her sisters, her employees, her lovers and, finally, her readers. She always gave too much, rather than too little, felt too keenly rather than not enough, was always far more ready for her times, and the times to come, than the times were ready for her. She had an extraordinary sense of her own worth, for what she was to do and how she was to prepare herself to do it. She was extraordinarily sensitive, painfully dominating, given to ghastly depressions, witty in conversation, gentle in friendship, but always completely and totally overwhelming.

She was Mary Wollstonecraft.

In a life rich and full, in a public life at a public time, dominated by revolution and new ideas, in an age of turmoil, discontent, constant revision of the past and a far too great expectation of the future, Mary Wollstonecraft, a really quite slight figure, strutted admirably through the streets of London, the foreign capitals of the world, the society of Dublin, through country houses and country places, never missing a thing.

Her daughter, Mary Shelley, was to have the mind of a poet, the deep imaginative drive of the novelist. Mary Wollstonecraft had the mind of a computer. She stocked it with the information of her day, programmed it with her own excess energy, was once the talk of London and after her death and some of the more private details of her life were known—courtesy of her husband—the despair of the moral world.

So to describe her:

When the great Tallyrand came to have tea with her after she had dedicated *The Vindication of Rights of Women* to him she served, alas, tea and claret in the same glass. No social arbitrator, she!

Madame Roland. The great revolution-ist who was a friend of Mary Wollstone-craft during the latter's stay in Paris.

Consumed by grief at the erosion of one tempestuous love affair with Gilbert Imlay, she quietly calculated the spot which would be most suitable for suicide, walked along in the rain until her garments were no longer buoyant, then threw herself into the Thames. But she did not drown; how could she? The Thames in those days was as polluted as are the waters of our own country today. She floated, was rescued, went on greater than ever.

Once an extremely bedraggled creature with no concern for appearance, hair dank and unkempt, black limp stockings and fusty clothing, a beaver cap on her head, she presented an all too universal picture of the "intellectual woman." Only at thirty did she find her

Samuel Taylor Coleridge. The poet and philosopher who once asked William Hazlitt "If I had ever seen Mary Woll-stonecraft, and I said, I had once for a few moments, and that she seemed to me to turn off Godwin's objections to something she advanced with quite a playful, easy air. He replied, that this was only one instance of the ascendancy which people of imagination exercised over those of mere intellect."

BLOODY News, laſt Night's Packet. bloody News.—Here's the Monthly Magazines,. and all the neweſt Publications

FRESH Herrings, large Dublin-bay Herring. alive here'—Here's a large freſh Cod alive here.—Here's large Soles or Places alive, or fine Boyn Salmon.

BUYE the dry Turf; bøye Turf; buye the dry Turf—Here's the dry Bog-a-Wood.—Here's the Chips to light the Fire; Maids!

NINE o'Clock' Nine o'Clock! paſt Nine o'Clock, and a dark cloudy Night.

Dublin Street Cries. From an illustrated broadsheet published in Dublin about 1775 reproduced in *The Journal of the Royal Society of Antiquaries of Ireland (1924)*. Typical street ballads of Ireland that were current during Mary Wollstonecraft's stay in Ireland.

voice and came into her own in personal beauty and attractiveness; she dressed carefully and became one of the lovely women of the world.

Concerned deeply with human rights, not just women's rights, she was attacked by the intellectual women of her day. Hannah Cowley: "I protest I know nothing about politics;—will Miss Wollstonecraft forgive me—whose book contains such a body of mind as I hardly ever met with—if I say that politics are *unfeminine?*—I never in my life could attend to their discussion." The great bluestocking, Hannah More, was not concerned with the theory of the book; she was simply determined never to read it. "There is something fantastic and absurd in the very title." Mary's own sisters commiserated with each other. "Did I tell you how much the gentry of Pembroke is shocked at Mary's book? Everyone declares it the most indecent rhapsody that ever was penned by man or woman." She was, Horace Walpole said, "a hyena in petticoats." But there were others: Aaron Burr, who brought up his glorious daughter Theodosia on its principles; Southey, who was reluctant to admire anybody, said quite frankly that he had praise for no living being except Mary Wollstonecraft.

With the mind of a computer she often distilled the purple passion prose of a hothouse flower. "Perhaps in the education of both sexes, the most difficult task is to adjust instruction as not to narrow the understanding whilst the heart is warmed by the generous juices of spring just raised by the electric fermentation of the season nor to dry up the feelings by employing the mind and investigations remote from life." Mary was indeed supplied with generous juices. Too generous.

Self-taught, self-educated, her innovation and independence of thought astounded Tom Paine, Coleridge, Godwin, Wordsworth —all the greats were, in effect, to suckle on some of her wisdom. But all of them knew only the public woman; the private woman was something quite apart. As with all women with such tremendous drive, she was often lonely. Over and over again she tried to find what she needed: a companion of her own worth, a world that she thought she deserved and, if necessary, a world that she would make. Her thinking was so vainglorious that it led her to strange beds. Her

Robert Southey. Poet Laureate of England who wrote to his friend, Joseph Cottle, on March 13, 1797, "Have you ever met with Mary Wollstonecraft's *Letters from Sweden and Norway?* She has made me in love with a cold climate, and frost and snow, with a northern moonlight." This was the book about which William Godwin said, "If ever there was a book calculated to make a man in love with its author, this appears to me to be the book." As such, Mary was a precursor of the romantic revival.

passions were so powerful that they led her to immortality.

For years her name and her importance dwindled into nothingness, not because what she had to say was unimportant, but rather because her private life dictated that terrible obscurity into which a writer who is too familiarized in his or her own day sometimes fades after death. The vultures of literary history will say the writer was not a genius; the works were not quite that good; he was not original, his writing went downhill; he has nothing to say to us today. Literary reputations suffered from that terrible slide into the nowhere, which was the public reaction to a public life. For Mary, who after her death slid into a public mire, the dissolution of her reputation was almost complete. The famous Mrs. Wollstonecraft, once indeed the wittiest woman in London, was nothing, they were to say twenty-five years after death, nothing but a whore, a prostitute. She became not only a symbol of the free woman, but also the too-free woman who gave unremittingly and too overwhelmingly to the men she loved.

She was hated by the Tory press, occasionally even despised by friends she had known. Reviewers who attacked her memoirs published posthumously by William Godwin accused her of mistreating her family, satirized her attempts at suicide, indicated that she had shown no respect for her parents, that her students had been neglected, that she was perpetually in debt, that her books debased their readers, most of all that she was immodest and indeed, *what*

The Roman matron was often a political hostess, less frequently a writer. She often, however, kept elaborate diaries, an art form that allowed expression for women. She was, as well, a great letter writer, also an acceptable form of communication.

immodesty! She had, for example, shown too much interest in such fields as botany, that gentle, immodest activity. She was indecent because women should be healthy, give some thought to their bodies for the preservation of soundness and life. She was indelicate; she wanted woman to be known as "a human creature." They depicted her in novels as a woman of corruption. They attacked her in reviews, they satirized both her and her husband in vindictive poems.

Why? Because in London in 1791, Mary Wollstonecraft, an auburn-haired beauty of thirty-two sat down with all her wits about her and wrote a book entitled *Vindication of the Rights of Women.* She had not forgotten the other side of the coin. She had already published a tract entitled *Vindication of the Rights of Men*—a bellowing cry for liberty in government and society, a scream for reform. A personal attack on Edmund Burke, it was highly emotional and, the reviewers said, peppered with "elegant and nervous language." As a tract it was highly influential; as yesterday's literature, it is long forgotten. Not so *Vindication of the Rights of Women.* Neglected for nearly a hundred years after her death, it became, and has continued to be, a rallying cry in the "feminist" movements. Yet she wanted so little; no supremacy of women, no castration of men—just simple mutual respect between man and woman, a respect that she felt could only be obtained by the proper education of women. "The neglected education of my fellow creatures," she cried, "is the grand sour of the misery I deplore."

She knew whereof she spoke. An educated woman might even be able to read the writings of the times that decreed, as did Lord Chesterfield, that women were only children of a larger growth. "A man of sense only trifles with them, plays with them, humours and flatters them, as he does with a sprightly, forward child, but he neither consults them about, not trusts them with serious matters, though he often makes them believe that he does both; which is the thing in the world that they are proud of; for they love mightily to be dabbing in business (which by the way they always spoil); and being justly distrustful, that men in general look upon them in a trifling light, they almost adore that man, who talks more seriously to them and who seems to consult and trust them; I say who seems, for weak men really do, but wise ones only seem to do it." (*Letters to His Son.*)

Mary had seen that trifling light on many a face: for years she had been a woman who wrote—shock enough—but worse she was, as she said herself, a new genus, a woman who wrote for her livelihood. It was an incredible undertaking, even for a man.

The literary world was slowly moving from the quixotic imprimatur of the private patron to the pugilistic Grub Street. Since the beginning of the eighteenth century there had been a growing demand for books, and the fact book; the book that would make news was growing in importance. First, stately, impregnable, now almost dust to the hand if you pick up those old editions, were the encyclopedias. The first had been the *Lexicon Technicon* in 1710, then *Chamber's Cyclopaedia* in 1728, and the grand publishing venture of the *Encyclopedia Britannica* in 1771. Originally none of them was the hardbound book of today. Instead they appeared serially in pamphlet form to take advantage of the widest possible market. One might be well read in the vicissitude of the auk without ever reaching the trials of zoology unless there were enough pence in the pocket. The well-to-do could afford the world from *A* to *Z*, and with staggering self-satisfaction bound their sequels into leather and the stately private libraries of England, Ireland and Scotland grew plump with fatted calf.

The author, however, waxed thin. Printers and publishers could afford, for the first time, a publishing program. The working author grubbed away on talk and tea. Genius brought in little—a state that has not changed for the better—but hard work, tedium, eye strain—stamina helped. Publishers looked then, as they look now for the book that would "sell"—investments were heavy. Originality was discouraged; the publishers' ideas were casually submitted to the working writer, and the "bread-and-butter books," as they were called then and are still called, piled up on the shelves like so many stale sandwiches. But people were hungry for guidance. Ill-wrought books of guidance preceded the sex guides of the twentieth century, but it was the soul rather than the body that was submitted to self-voyeurism, self-castigation and self-satisfaction. Devotional books abounded, almanacs were as plentiful as the coffee-table books of today, and children's books, now that the child was considered a "human creature" (the way Mary Wollstonecraft hoped the world would consider a woman), abounded. The hack writer could try his hand at any or all. The woman writer dared only at devotional or children's books. They were the back door to personal expression, and if a woman carefully wiped her feet on the mat as she entered the publishing domain, she might be heard.

Mary, for her own reasons, had no devotion. A spinster at thirty-two (with adamant ideas against marriage, again for her own reasons), she had no children. That did not matter. Her first professional effort was a children's book. She had tried being a governess, she had tried a "little school," the only outlets at that time for the talented woman; but, as she said, "the monies did not answer." She needed money and she needed answers, not only to the overwhelming social problems of her own day, but also to some of her own drive. Her first book was *Thoughts on the Education of Daughters: With Reflections on Female Conduct, in the More Important Duties of Life*. A raging potboiler (it brought her ten much-needed guineas), it was a cry for an improvement of the home environment, a put down on the world of cosmetics and fine clothes that Mary currently

Destruction of the Bastile.

spurned, and a passing insight into Mary's own life as she cried:
"The heart is very treacherous, and if we do not guard its first
emotions, we shall not afterwards be able to prevent its sighing for
impossibilities."

It was her own childhood that she must have had in mind.

She had been born on April 27, 1759, in the London that she
loved, but her parents promptly pulled up stakes, as they would do
frequently, and settled for a while in Epping Forest. One of her
earliest memories was sitting in front of a fireplace together with
her sisters and brothers in total silence. There, on order from their
vindictive father, they would stare into the flames. But there in the
family she had little opportunity for solitude at all, for solitude
requires a respect on the part of the parents that neither father nor
mother seemed determined to give. Those who fear their own
thoughts are inclined to be suspicious of the thoughts of others, and
Mary during her childhood learned to keep her thoughts to herself.

There were no books; she did not particularly long for them
as long as she could keep the impressions of the world around her
fresh and vital in her mind. Her early education was haphazard, in
day schools as the family moved from spot to spot. It did not matter

that the girls had no education, just as long as the boys might have some vocation. Her brother, Edward, who appeared to her as tyrannical as her father, prepared for the law and later Mary took her brother James in hand and prepared him for the navy.

In 1774 Edward Wollstonecraft moved outside of London to a village called Hoxton. There for the first time Mary was to know the pleasure of a friend nearly her own age, Frances, or Fanny, Blood, who was three years older, but who had accomplishments that Mary realized would be useful to her. Women, perhaps more often than men, seem to be able to prepare for the practicality of the future even in the confines of genius. Mary knew that she must educate herself for some kind of role in the world. As a matter of fact she was very determined that she have a role and, as she grew older, that she would have a voice too, and it was a voice that was going to be heard. She would not speak up against her father. The thought of it did not terrify her, but any open rebellion on her part antagonized him. He allowed no comment, no idle conversation and certainly no back talk. He now openly and regularly beat her mother.

Edward Wollstonecraft was the true tyrant of the period. He ranted, raved, and then demanded complete silence from the chil-

An English Pilgrim. The earliest autobiography in English was created by a woman, Margery Kempe, who made a tour of the Holy Land in the Middle Ages.

dren that he raved at. It was not strange that Mary's mother had, as she called it, "an indolence of character." Certainly all spunk, drive, even effectiveness, had been completely erased from her life. She had little or no interest in her children and, to Mary's great shock, almost no interest in their education.

The children, too, were too ingrown to enjoy one another's company. There was only the neighboring heath with its healthy breezes that Mary remembered with any pleasure. And even that heath and open-air freedom that she called paradise was threatened.

Wollstonecraft, who had been a master weaver in London, evidently yearned for something better: the ambiguous life of a country gentleman. He came upon a small inheritance and began the moves that were to make him more disagreeable and more impecunious as time went on. His craft had taught him nothing about the exigencies of farming. Each farm was to be the ideal one, each new location was to contain a treasure in the ground, and each new house was to know the same misery.

The moving from house to house, from place to place, made young Mary unusually observant. She grew familiar with the problems of the rural England that was so rapidly changing, in the niceness of communication with the tradesmen, in idle solitude, such as Wordsworth was to be so inspired by in his own Cumberland during his childhood. Mary was not a solitary, indeed in a large family she felt inundated, and hiding in the hay with her brothers and sisters, she tried to stifle the sound of her mother's cries as the latter was regularly beaten.

"At fifteen," she wrote, "I resolved never to marry for disinterested motives, or to endure a life of dependence."

With unusual insight, one of her commentators in the latter nineteenth century, Mrs. Oliphant, commenting on *Vindication*, wrote, "We have said that society is too much vexed and irritated even yet by this subject to be able to permit it to be discussed with calmness: and still more was the case in the end of the last century, when for the first time a woman ventured to complain of the inequality of her day." Her background, Mrs. Oliphant suggested, explained a great deal.

William Godwin, who said after Mary's death, "The partner of my life was too quick in conceiving resentments; but they would dignify and restrain; they left no hateful and humiliating remembrances behind them, and we were as happy as is permitted for human beings."

She was a woman who had already experienced many hard struggles and much sorrow. She had been in some degree the bread-winner, in every way the support and guide of a family, neither so amenable to her influence nor so grateful for her exertions as would have been seemly, the members of which were in the habit of criticising their sister somewhat sharply in the letters which passed between them behind her back. Her father was an entirely disreputable person, from whom his children derived neither help nor countenance. To be brought up under such a shadow, or rather to struggle towards a better and higher life, in the depressing presence of

A. Pope. After reading Alexander Pope's epistle *On the Character of Women,* Mary Wollstonecraft called him "a snarling poet" who found "every woman is at heart a rake" and that, indeed, "most women have no characters at all."

a hopeless and degraded parent, is the breeding of all others which most revolts the mind of a high-spirited girl. Indeed, we might almost venture to say that the strong protestations in favour of something, varying from age to age, which is called the Rights of Women, with which society has been vexed and disturbed to an extent which has made it incapable of judging what is just in them—have risen almost invariably from women compelled by hard stress of circumstances to despise the men about them. Exception will probably be taken to this assertion both by the women themselves who utter these protestations and by the critics; but yet we hold by what we have said. Women, no more than men, are exempt from the painful action of contempt; but when they are obliged to despise those to whom they would naturally look up, the irritation and misery of the sentiment is magnified tenfold. To say that her drunken father was the reason why Mary Wollstonecraft wrote the *Rights of Women* would be too strong an accusation; but this circumstance evidently brought a painful struggle into her life. And one of her sisters, the pretty one, the beauty of the family, poor Bess, made an unhappy marriage, and had to be taken out of her husband's clutches almost in a state of frenzy by Mary herself. Thus degraded by the besotted folly of one man, and driven into energetic action by the unkindness of another, she certainly was. And it was not till after nearly ten years' experience of the slings and arrows of outrageous fortune that she put forth the book which was the first word of a long controversy. For the greater part of that time she had been engaged in teaching, and when in 1787 she came to London to a little house in a street near Blackfriars Bridge to endeavour, with the favour of good Mr. Johnson, the publisher, to get her living by translations from the French and little books for children, she was a woman nearly thirty, at an age when the deprivations of life and the spurns which patient merit of the unworthy takes are felt most keenly. Here she made a home for her brothers and sisters, supported her father in his village, and was the head of all the family concerns; and it was here that the *Vindication of the Rights of Women* was produced.
(*Literary History of England 1790–1825*, Margaret Oliphant.)

Mary had an uncanny ability to be able to educate herself and to know the manner in which to do so. She took great chances with places, with books, frequently reading far beyond that which her simple education had made easy. And she took enormous chances with people. She was a thorn in the side of her first employer, Mrs. Dawson, to whom she was a companion, but she learned much from her sojourn in Bath and in time her name was to be spoken with respect in that famous watering place.

She was later to be a threat to Lady Kingsborough in Ireland where she took a job as a governess. She embarrassed her ladyship by her ability to talk so well and brilliantly, but soon she held almost command performances as an entertainer for the society that frequented the great houses of Ireland. She talked, she read, and she watched. In Bath she had seen idle society; she was, as she constantly admitted, no woman of quality. In Ireland, she found that poor Lady Kingsborough had the unfortunate little conceit of talking too intimately to her dogs and, complained Mary wisely, too little to her children. Mary held her in careful disdain. It was a world in which no one did anything, no one really had anything important to say except about clothes and hunting and drinking fine wines. They knew indeed which glass for the tea and which for the claret. To hell with that. Mary didn't need it. There was life to be drunk in one great quaff. Tea and claret could all be mixed together in one piece of chipped crystal.

Her stay with Mrs. Dawson had been interrupted by the illness of her mother and, in a complaining mood (she could upon occasion be one of the world's greatest complainers), Mary went back and faithfully nursed the dying woman. Her father had taken a new paramour, to the shock of the family, and once again Mary felt that she and only she could hold the family to some semblance of sanity. Indeed one sister had married and, in what would appear to be a post-partum depression, felt herself vilified by her husband. Mary absconded with her sister and for the first time knew the public taunt. She had indeed broken up a marriage. Well, she would do more. As the sister regained clarity of mind, Mary set up a school with her. It was successful until her old friend Fanny Blood, who had married (which Mary had nicely managed, perhaps even to the extent of making the reluctant bridegroom finally pop the question), and who was living in Lisbon, sent for her.

Fanny was dying. Once again Mary sat by the sickbed; once again she managed a bereaved household. She was able even in her grief to observe the countryside and Lisbon itself, tucking away in the corner of her mind observations on the Portugese that were as

Dean Swift, who antagonized Mary Wollstonecraft by his comment that woman was "a sort of Species hardly a degree above a Monkey." From copperplate engraving by Pierre Fourdrinier after a painting by Charles Jervas.

trenchant as any sociological studies of the time. She returned home exhausted, broken, defeated. She had lost her best friend. It was apparent that the school was bankrupt. She was already hopelessly in debt. Then she found her voice.

"Mr. Johnson," wrote Mary to her sister, "assures me that if I exert my talents in writing, I may support myself in a comfortable way. I am then going to be the first of a new genus. . . . This project has long floated in my mind."

The new idea was that a *woman* might write for a living, always, of course, a precarious undertaking for either man or woman. But she started on a decade of enormous productivity and her life as a professional writer had begun. The end result was seven very original works and some important translations. When she died at thirty-eight there were still four volumes to be projected.

Her writing career immediately made her acquainted with the great minds of her age. She was to meet and know Tom Paine, to marry William Godwin, have "a platonic" affair with Henry Fuseli, to know William Blake, Brissot, the Rolands. She was to know revolutionary France, England, Wales, Ireland, and Scandinavia. She was to know that tyranny could exist for all, that radicalism meant the support of rights for all and only in part was she concerned with "the misery and oppression peculiar to women that arise out of the partial laws and customs of society."

No, this struggle was certainly not, as some would like to suggest, men against women. It was a more basic struggle, the struggle of the person against the institution, the struggle against establishments and ways of thought that oppress the intellect.

Perhaps one of her most extraordinary innovations was her use of *I*. She knew that the propagandist *I* could sway and move. When she called out for the liberty of reason in *Vindication of the Rights of Men* which preceded *Vindication of the Rights of Women*, she said, "I war not with an individual when I contend for the rights of men and the liberty of reason. You see, I do not condescend to cull my words to avoid the invidious phrase. Reverencing the rights of humanity, I shall dare to assert them."

Through trial and error she had acquired her own voice. The *I* was important for the time. Only the individual could sway some of the lethargy of the period. "A person has the right," she said, "when amused by a witty or amusing egotist to talk of himself. . . . Whether I deserve to rank among this privileged, my readers alone can judge. And I give them leave to shut the book if they do not wish to become better acquainted with me." She said not long before she died, "I am compelled to think there is something in my writings more valuable than the productions of some people on whom you bestow warm eulogisms, [she is writing to Godwin] I mean more of the observations of my own senses, more of the combining of my own imagination, the effusions of my own feelings and passions."Mary was not a simple writer and, indeed, upon occasion she could be a remarkably nongraceful one. But something about everything she said and the way she said it makes one want to, in her own words, become better acquainted with her.

And to know her, one had to know some of the passion that controlled her mind and, less successfully, her senses. It was inevitable that this intellectual woman, the propagandist, this witty talker, this remarkable woman with the sense of her own *I*, should fall completely and madly in love, not only once, but indeed twice and, finally happily, for the third time.

The first was Henry Fuseli and what an extraordinary choice, if one considers his personal appearance: white haired, ugly, with a thick accent and a snarling tongue, he was no beau. He was, however, the greatest genius in art of his time, as the eminent historical painter Benjamin Haydon maintained:

> Fuzeli was undoubtedly the greatest genius of that day. His Milton gallery showed a range of imagination equal to the poet's; his Satan bridging Chaos, his Uriel watching Satan, his Shepherd's Dream, his Fairies from Shakespeare, and his Ghost in Hamlet, announce him as . . . being the greatest inventor in art since Julio Romano. But in the modes of conveying his thoughts by form, colour, light, and shadow, and above all, nature, he was a monster in design; his women are all strumpets, and his men all banditti, with the action of galvanized frogs, the dress of mountebanks, and the hue of pestilential putridity. No man had the power like Fuzeli of rousing the dormant spirit of youth; and there issued from his inspiration the nucleus of painters, who have been the firmest supporters of the British school.

Caroline Lucretia Herschel, a contemporary of Mary Wollstonecraft's, published one of the first scientific books by a woman, the *Catalogue of the Stars,* sponsored by the Royal Society. A brilliant mathematician, she was described in the mid nineteenth century as "one of those women who occasionally come forth before the world, as in protest against the commonly accepted ideas of men regarding the mental capacity of the gentler sex. Of all scientific studies one would suppose mathematics to be the most repulsive to the female mind."

But Fuzeli, as a painter, must be a warning to all. Had he taken the trouble to convey his thoughts like the great masters, his pictures would have risen as time advanced; yet as time advances, his pictures, from having no hold on our feelings like the simplicity of nature, must sink.

Today, like Mary, Fuseli had been vindicated as the great artist he was.

It was a one-sided courtship—all on Mary's side. Fuseli was happily married, but that did not faze Mary. After all her love was "platonic," and she found no embarrassment in suggesting to Mrs. Fuseli that they maintain a *ménage â trois.* Mrs. Fuseli demurred and with sinking spirits Mary took off for France . . . a country as much in revolt as herself.

Immediately she was initiated into the pain of a country struggling for liberty. All that she saw she could not condone, as she wrote in a letter to her publisher: "About nine o'clock this morning, the king passed by my window, moving silently along (excepting now and then a few strokes on the drum, which rendered the stillness more awful) through empty streets, surrounded by the national guards, who, clustering around the carriage, seemed to deserve their name. The inhabitants flocked to their windows, but the casements were all shut, not a voice was heard, nor did I see any thing like an insulting gesture.—For the first time since I entered France, I bowed to the majesty of the people, and respected the propriety of behaviour so perfectly in unison with my own feelings. I can scarcely tell you why, but an association of ideas made the tears flow insensibly from my eyes, when I saw Louis sitting, with more dignity than I expected from his character, in a hackney coach, going to meet death, where so many of his race have triumphed. My fancy instantly brought Louis XIV before me, entering the capital with all his pomp, after one of the victories most flattering to his pride, only to see the sunshine of prosperity overshadowed by the sublime gloom of misery. I have been alone ever since; and, though my mind is calm, I cannot dismiss the lively images that have filled my imagination all the day. Nay, do not smile, but pity me; for, once or twice, lifting my eyes from the paper, I have seen eyes glare through a glass-door opposite my chair, and bloody hands shook at me. Not the distant sound of a footstep can I hear. . . . I wish I had even

Edmund Burke. The British statesman whose book, *Reflections on the Revolution in France*, so antagonized Mary that she wrote *Vindication of the Rights of Men*—a plea that all humanity was entitled to govern itself. It was he who coined the phrase, "O, those extraordinary women!"

kept the cat with me!—I want to see something alive; death in so many frightful shapes has taken hold of my fancy.—I am going to bed—and, for the first time in my life, I cannot put out the candle."

She was in Paris when England declared war on France on February 1, 1793, and for two months lived in terror and poverty. Then in April, in a Paris spring, she fell in love.

Gilbert Imlay was an American. He had served in the American Revolution, he had explored the West, he was the author of a reasonably well-known book, *Topographical Description of the Western Territory of North America: Containing a Succint Account of its Soil, Climate, Natural History, Population, Agriculture, Manners and Customs.* He was as exotic as a cowboy and as free ranging.

Mary found herself a cottage at Neuilly, and Imlay, who had registered her as his wife in Paris so she could avoid deportation, little knew how soon he would be overwhelmed by her love.

On June 13 she wrote to her sisters that she was "now at the house of an old gardener, writing a great book and in better health and spirits than I have enjoyed since I came to France." The gardener, a gentle man who doted on Mary, brought her fresh grapes and fruits from the garden as they came into season, but of course neither the great book nor the sweet grapes were what enticed Mary. It was being infatuated with Imlay. He came from Paris frequently. Imlay, if not deeply in love with her, found her attractive and told her so. It was a new experience and she doted upon it. The book, too, would be great, what book about the French Revolution would not be? She felt inspired and at peace. The inspiration, or perhaps just being too close to the scene of action, or even her own happiness worked against this book which was the least successful or meaningful book she had undertaken or was to undertake. It was not a first-hand report on the Revolution, but concerned itself only with the events leading up to three years prior to her visit. She, who had always written with *I*, who spoke out with a private voice and private affirmation, no longer wrote *I*, but in the third person, a rather dull and tedious book that was shortly superseded by all the other works on the Revolution. Still it did not matter to Mary; she was in love.

Sometimes it was difficult for Imlay to come from Paris; the Terror made even leaving the toll gates difficult, and then Mary would meet him at the barrier gate. Those seemed to have been the happiest moments of her life up until that moment. She loved, she wrote later to Imlay, his "barrier face" that looked upon her for a while with unadulterated affection, and it was there while they stayed at an inn at the barrier gate that they conceived the child Fanny whom Mary called her "barrier child."

There were other barriers in the love between Imlay and Mary which had nothing to do with the torment in the City of Paris. Imlay was, quite frankly, a man who enjoyed being footloose and fancy free. Mary was tired and certainly during her pregnancy, neither footloose nor fancy free. But she was still content. She wanted more support, however, she wanted to see more of Imlay, to know that at this time, at least for once in her life, she would be protected. She fell into her old demanding pattern. She, who would receive so little but would demand so much, began to grate on the nerves of her lover. He disappeared more and more frequently. She disliked, she said, his business face, contrasting it with the barrier face and now when he came to the cottage the business face seemed to be more and more omnipresent.

She looked forward to returning to Paris and living with Imlay intimately. "You can scarcely imagine with what pleasure I anticipate the day when we begin almost to live together and you would smile to hear how many plans of employment I have in my head now that I am confident my heart has found peace in your bosom. Cherish me with a dignified tenderness which I have only found in you and your own dear girl will try to keep a quickness of feeling that has sometimes given you pain. Yes, I will be good that I may deserve to be happy and whilst you love me I cannot again fall into the miserable state which rendered life a burden almost too heavy to be borne."

The public woman had become his own dear girl, but more than anything else that quickness of feeling, that too great need, was to rip them apart. They moved to Paris and lived quite simply as man and wife. Although Mary began to call herself Mrs. Imlay, she preferred the fact that her marriage was quite unconventional, indeed no true marriage at all and that she did not have to clog her soul "by promising obedience, etc., etc."

Taste À La Mode: The Rotunda Gardens in 1790. From Walker's *Hibernian Magazine,* July, 1790.

She was not unconventional enough, however, to be able to accept Imlay's constant disappearances. "Of late," she wrote, "we're always separating, crack, crack and away you go. Bear with me," she cries, "a little *longer."* There was some talk that they would throw up everything and go to live in America. Although she was able to appreciate that fantasy for a while, Imlay would disappear again and she would write once more, "Well! but, my love, to the old story —am I to see you this week, or this month?" It seemed to her that Imlay was struggling to make money. It wasn't money that she loved, it was he. "I hate commerce," she said. "You will tell me that exertions were necessary. I am weary of them. The face of things public and private vexes me."

But she was never so low that she could not look the political situation clearly in the face. In the same letter she says, "I really believe that Europe will be in a state of convulsion during half a century at least. Life is but a labor of patience. It is always rolling a great stone up a hill. Before a person can find a resting place, imagining it is lodged, down it comes again and all the work has to be done over ever anew."

Certainly she seemed to feel that she had to re-create her love over and over again.

Then she let an incautious sentence slip into a letter to this man whom she loved. She shouted blindly, "A man is a tyrant." The voice of the public Mary began to creep into her personal life. She was filled, she said with perilous humors, but she could not accept being "treated with coldness." She followed him to Le Havre (she yearned for her poor books, but her child was soon to be born), only to find that Imlay had once again been called back to Paris "on business." It was a lament as modern as today.

The child was born and she was happy. "My little girl begins to suck so manfully that her father reckons saucily on her writing the second part of *The Rights of Women,"* writes Mary. But the war raged on. "The French will carry all before," she said, "but my God how many victims fall beneath the sword and the guillotine? My blood runs cold and I sicken at the thought that the revolution would cause so much blood and bitter tears." Her letters to Imlay, who even now disappeared time and time again, grew more petulant, and when he was called to England on business for two months she stayed in Paris, which she had grown to love. Engrossed in her own work, her manuscript completed and sent to London, she did not realize that quite frankly her love affair had evaporated. She wrote to Imlay that he had been embruted by trade and the vulgar enjoyment of life. "Bring me back," she cried, "then, your barrier face. . . ."

She began working again, however, making sure that she would have enough money to support her child. By January 9, 1795, she was desperately lonely. She would, indeed, run away. What should she do? Imlay said he was going to return to Paris. In the next letter he said, Why didn't she come to London? She was confused and bewildered. She became ill. "The more I think, the sadder I grow."

She could wait no longer and sought him out in London. A simple woman would have realized it was all over, but Mary simply could not accept it. With unusual perspicacity Imlay knew that perhaps only a separation and one that appealed to her mind could get her over what was now obviously a deep concern for him, a love that he could neither respond to nor really appreciate. He sent her

Samuel Johnson was an admirer of Mary Wollstonecraft. His feeling, however, about intellectual women were ambiguous. He said, "Nature has given women so much power that the law has wisely given them little." One of the laws of the period declared, "All women of whatever age, rank, profession or degree, whether virgin, maid or widow, that shall from and after such Act impose upon, seduce, and betray into matrimony any of His Majesty's subjects by means of scent, paints, cosmetics, washes, artificial teeth, false hair, Spanish wool, iron stays, hoops, high heeled shoes or bolstered hips, shall incur the penalty of the law now enforced against witchcraft and like misdemeanors and that the marriage upon conviction shall stand null and void."

on business to Scandinavia, where, despite the enormous heartache from which she was suffering, she wrote an enchanting book entitled *Letters Written During a Short Residence in Sweden, Norway, and Denmark.* It was a book that William Godwin was to say later made one fall in love with the author.

Now her point of view changed. It wasn't that she needed Imlay any longer, she told herself, but Fanny, the child, needed a father. She must convince Imlay. She appeared to enjoy her own suffering. "For God's sake," she wrote, "spare me the anxiety of uncertainty. I may sing under the trial, but I will not complain." It was a period in which she quite frankly did nothing *but* complain.

Imlay wrote that their minds were not congenial. She agreed, "Certainly you are right," she said, "I have lived in an ideal world and forced its sentiments that you do not comprehend or you would not treat me thus. . . . I am not, I will not, be merely an object of compassion."

On October 4 she was back in Dover. Shortly after she realized what she should have long suspected not once but several times, that Imlay had "found a new attachment." In any case she sat down and wrote a painful letter describing the disposition of her child, her clothes, crying out, "I would encounter a thousand deaths, rather than a night like the last." For Mary had once more entered a household and found another woman.

She had thought of suicide once before but had been rescued from it. This time she would allow herself no chance of rescue. She chose a bridge on the Thames that was hardly frequented, then walked in the rain until her clothes were so drenched that she would instantly sink. She jumped and was almost immediately rescued.

Still she could not give Imlay up. Her letters continued, sometimes complaining, sometimes threatening, sometimes filled with terrible anxiety, but at least in one she knew what she needed. "On examining my heart, I find that it is so constituted that I cannot live without some particular affection. I am afraid not without a passion." The need was so exquisite that of course she would find one. Imlay had effaced her infatuation with Fuseli, now that strange, dour, radical William Godwin would erase the landscape of Imlay.

William Godwin, the author of *Political Justice,* was riding high. That was just where he wanted to be—the closer to God the better—but William wasn't really sure he *believed* in God. He had no such doubts about Godwin. Once a dissenting minister, he was sure that he, and he alone, knew not only the necessity for dissent, but the way to the good, the beautiful and the true. If all those ingredients had to be paid for from someone else's purse, the more the better. He was the great financial director of the spiritual ennui of the age. He had worked hard, putting out books and pamphlets, using that curiously abrasive, pedantic mind to explore the political injustices of his time. So he had arrived. He was a member of the literary salons in London and although there were those who would refer to him derisively as "just one of the Cockney group" it did not bother him. Social justice had come; he was lionized.

Mary Wollstonecraft had met him once before in his struggle for respectability. She was not impressed. She found him arrogant; he found her impossible. When they met again in 1796 he was at the top of his form; she, too, was at the top of hers. But she had crammed into her years far more living than poor Godwin was ever to see. There was something about the excitement of this new woman (a woman who, it was rumored, had lovers) that began to attract his eye. Of course marriage was out of the question. He looked for some sort of a companion and even thought about marriage, but in his books he had argued against it. It was a convention that would yoke anyone to disaster. On the other hand, the loneliness of his rooms and the prospect of his life stretching ahead of him at forty made him wonder. He was not unattractive to women, quite the contrary. Something about his terrible aloofness and dedication and the fact that part of him always ignored women attracted them. Mary had met Godwin years before, now Mary was quite a different woman. Quite frankly she had been through hell. She didn't like it, but she liked the ones who had led her through it. She found men very attractive indeed, and had suggested in *Vindication of Rights for Women* that there was a place for an honorable man in a woman's life. Godwin filled the bill.

They were an unlikely couple, but both of them melted under

In the early eighteenth century, newspapers in England were so rare they were dispatched by hand only, and the lord of the manor read them aloud to generally illiterate women and servants.

a strange aura they did not understand. The world of the literary salons watched in astonishment. Was this the Godwin who was the leading radical social philosopher of an age of upheaval? Was this the man, who, said William Hazlitt, had given a philosophical blow to the mind of the country? Was this the man about whose work Wordsworth had said, "Throw aside your books of chemistry and read Godwin, 'On Necessity' "; well, it was indeed. Some chemistry in Godwin's body was quite amazingly aroused by this woman who called out for rational, intellectual rights and who had become mired in love. But Mary was determined that if love was what she needed, love was what she would have. Godwin seemed to be the God-given choice.

A Hyena In Petticoats

They wrote lovely letters to each other—coy, sentimental. No, they would not live together. They must keep separate quarters. After all, were they not the spokesman and spokeswoman of a new age? And then, like many a woman before and after, Mary got pregnant and married Godwin. The news hit literary London like a bombshell. It was a matter of amusement, reflection and occasionally downright bewilderment. But the marriage was good. It was better than good, they were both radiantly happy. Both worked happily, Mary in her own quarters, William for his part had engaged rooms about twenty doors down "for literary occupation." All morning he wrote, afternoons he visited.

Mary was in her prime. She was having her portrait painted, she was pregnant. "I feel," she said, "great pleasure at being a mother." An occasional headache was all that disturbed her. They engaged a midwife for her confinement. She was ready. They entertained happily those last few days before her labor began. They were almost childishly excited. The boy —because it would be a boy— would be called William.

Mary awakened at five o'clock on August thirtieth; she was calm. The midwife was sent for and Godwin settled down to read his wife's autobiographical novel, *Mary*, which gives us what little material we have about her early life. It was a long labor, the child was not born until past eleven. Godwin waited for three hours and then the midwife came down to say that a doctor must be fetched, the placenta had not been properly expelled. There seemed to be no cause for alarm. Guests entertained William and "my alarms wore off as time advanced" he wrote later. He even devoted some time to business.

There were now doctors in charge as well as nurses. Mary seemed to be making some little advance and then suddenly she had a relapse. She had one shivering fit after another. The child, the young Mary, or baby Mary as she was called, was removed from the breast. Puppies were brought to draw off the milk. By Thursday night Mary felt better, at least the fits had stopped, but she had an idea of death, she said, and the following Saturday, she had lost, said Godwin, "any effort to follow any train of ideas with force or any accuracy of connection." On Sunday she was dead.

Grub Street in London, the working area for journalists and hacks, sometimes offered women a place to work, but only anonymously.

The following year Godwin placed an inscription above her grave:

> Mary Wollstonecraft Godwin,
> Author of
> A Vindication
> Of the Rights of Woman:
> Born 27 April, 1759:
> Died 10 September, 1797

Many years later, Virginia Woolf wrote her epitaph:

She whose sense of her own existence was so intense, who had cried out even in her misery, "I cannot bear to think of being no more—of losing myself—nay, it appears to me impossible that I should cease to exist," died at the age of thirty-six. But she has her revenge. Many millions have died and been forgotten in the hundred and thirty years that have passed since she was buried; and yet as we read her letters and listen to her arguments and consider her experiments, above all that most fruitful experiment, her relation with Godwin, and realise the high-handed and hot-blooded manner in which she cut her way to the quick of life, one form of immortality is hers undoubtedly: she is alive and active, she argues and experiments, we hear her voice and trace her influence even now among the living.

She left another legacy, the voice of her daughter, Mary Shelley.

2

FRANKENSTEIN'S MOTHER
Mary Shelley

I was as lonesome as a Crusoe.

Mary Shelley

They say that thou wert lovely from thy birth,
Of glorious parents, thou aspiring Child:
I wonder not—for One then left this earth
Whose life was like a setting planet mild,
Which clothed thee in the radiance undefiled
Of its departing glory; still her fame
Shines on thee through the tempests dark and wild
Which shake these latter days; and thou canst claim
The shelter, from thy Sire, of an immortal name.

Percy Bysshe Shelley

Women are not informed (he writes) for great cares themselves but to soothe and soften ours; their tenderness is the proper regard for the toils we undergo for their preservation; and the ease and cheerfulness of their conversation our desirable retreat from the labours of study and business. They are confined within the narrow limits of domestic offices, and when they strive beyond them they move eccentrically and, consequently, without grace.

Dr. Gregory

OUTSIDE there is a landscape of gaping cemeteries, strange shapes scurryings about in the black night, a piercing rain, a cacophony of lightning, a flash, and then one moves inward, into the salon. There all is peaceful and quiet, the fire blazes. Mary Shelley, alias Elsa Lanchester, a figure of early nineteenth-century decorum, sits gently inscribing the future on her needlework while Shelley and Byron, typical dandies of the period, strut and posture, casting shadows against the wall.

Everything is over life-size, the blacks superbly Gothic black, the whites fading into chalklike clarity. It is, of course, the world of cinema. Before us rests the landscape of *Frankenstein*, outside the cold graveyard, inside the heat of creativity. For many readers, the extraordinary films *Frankenstein* and *The Bride of Frankenstein* were the introduction to Mary Shelley's great novel. Hollywood, with its superb Gothic arrogance of the early thirties produced a lingering masterpiece filled with vignettes, Boris Karloff, the monster, Elsa Lanchester, first the subdued Mary and then the electrifying bride. Hollywood, as usual, took liberties, but not too many because the story that Mary had to tell and the way she chose to tell it was perhaps even more dramatic than even Hollywood could envision. So let us go back to the real story. She was a woman, who liberated herself by the pen, and not only liberated herself but also the whole world of storytelling. The most original novel of the nineteenth century, indeed of any century, was written, they discovered in shock, by a woman.

It is the dawn of the nineteenth century; women will write many a novel. Jane Austen will sweetly seclude herself from childhood, gathering bits and phrases the way, she said, a bird must collect the twigs and grasses for a nest. Her first two novels will simply be signed "by a lady." But by the time her third novel will

"Swift as a light and as cheering was the idea that broke in upon me. I have found it! What terrified me will terrify others; and I need only describe the spectre which had haunted my midnight pillow. On the morrow I announced that I had *thought of a story."* (Mary Shelley.) From a painting by Richard Rothwell. Courtesy, National Portrait Gallery, London.

Paris Fashion at the time (1800) when Monsieur D'Arblay, Fanny's husband, was exiled from France.

have been written she will have changed her mind. She decided then, she said, that "I shall become a monster," and signed her own name.

No such compunction bothered Mary Shelley. Print was second nature to her, stories had been in her head since childhood, ideas kept her awake. And yet, as the story opened on July 15, 1816, one could not predict the outcome of the evening. There were four characters in the drama, four characters and the weather. It was a stormy night in Geneva. The four characters were all exiles: Lord Byron, completely self-appointed, arrogant, already successful, somewhat patronizing; Percy Bysshe Shelley, in exile with the woman he loved intensely, Mary Godwin, only eighteen years old; and perhaps one of the greatest catalysts of all, Dr. Polidori, whose temperament was as extreme as the weather that howled outside the Villa Diodoti on the shores of Lake Geneva.

In the background there was another—Claire, Mary's half-sister, described in the early biographies as "a female relative," to be perhaps called today more suggestively, "that woman." She was the self-proclaimed mistress of Byron, a thorn in his bed and a lifelong blister to both Mary and Percy. Claire was given to the sulks; she appears somewhere vaguely offstage, creating another chord in the supernatural background music.

This intense group had only been together for a short time, but the ingredients were all there—passion, creative excitement and the landscape. The friends were drawn inwards by conversation, outwards by the call of the lake. It was the time of the bise, or northeast wind, when the waters of the lake drive toward the town, while the waters of the Rhone join in the same direction and a current sets up high waves "in spiriting." "We are all animated by our contest with the elements."

The Ridiculous Philosopher. From a drawing by Maclise. By the time this caricature was made the "great Godwin" had become a figure of fun.

35

Polidori, the Shelleys and Byron went boating almost every day. Once they propelled themselves into the current on the lake and were almost engulfed in waves. " 'I will sing you an Albanian song,' cried Lord Byron. 'Now be sentimental and give me all your atten-

Percy Bysshe Shelley. Painted by Amelia Curran in 1819. Courtesy, National Portrait Gallery, London.

A contemporary silhouette of Dr. Charles Burney and his family. Young Fanny is knitting at the far right.

tion.' It was a strange wild howl that he gave forth, but such as he declared was an exact imitation of the savage Albanian mode." (*Letters and Journals of Lord Byron with Notices of his Life*, Sir Thomas More.)

Polidori, the least well known of the group was also subject to hysteria. Polidori was accompanying Lord Byron as a medical advisor. In part he supervised Byron's extraordinary diet, a thin slice of bread with tea at breakfast, a light vegetable dinner with a bottle or two of seltzer water tinged with *vin de grave,* and for the evening a cup of green tea without milk or sugar, aided and abetted by an enormous wad of chewing tobacco.

The rivalry between Polidori and Byron was immense. The arrogance of the doctor seemed to fascinate the good lord which only added to Polidori's provocations.

"After all," he said, "what is there you can do that I cannot?"

"Well, since you force me to say it," said Byron, "I think there

Villa Diodati in Switzerland where Shelley, Byron and Mary Shelley decided to write ghost stories and where Mary first had the idea for *Frankenstein*.

are three things that I can do which you cannot. I can swim across that river, I can snuff out that candle with a pistol shot at the distance of twenty paces and I have written a poem which fourteen thousand copies were sold in one day."

This strange relationship became further distorted by Shelley's presence. In the space of a brief week Polidori had acquired such an antipathy for the young poet that he had already challenged him to a duel, simply because Shelley had bested him in a sailing match. Shelley, perhaps the most sensitive in the household, had known sentiments against dueling, but Lord Byron had none. "Recollect" he shouted to Polidori, "that though Shelley has some scruples about dueling, I have none and shall be ready at all times to take his place."

Mary and Percy had a cottage of their own but each evening when the weather was fit for sailing they joined Byron. It was a tempestuous summer and they often stayed overnight at his villa because the rain was too torrential. Drying off from the sail they would sit in front of the fire and talk well into the early morning. There was never any lack of subjects, they said, "and grave or gay, we were always interested." One subject was Shelley's and Mary's intense interest in metaphysics. Or they might discuss the state of

38

Shelley's last home, Casa Magni.

literature, or even the quality of friendship. Always there was the joy of reading books together. That week the group had read German ghost stories—why shouldn't they each write one? "You and I," said Lord Byron to Mary, "will publish ours together."

Mary, although she could talk and talk well, had a difficult time competing with the extraordinary torrent of conversation that erupted from Shelley and Byron. But Mary now was not one to keep things to herself. She had kept them to herself for too long.

She had always been a spectator. Her father, William Godwin, one of the greatest figures in London and one of the greatest talkers, had at least allowed her that. She knew the conversation of giants. She knew how to listen. She had heard every great author from Charles Lamb to Wordsworth declaim in her father's parlor.

That evening in Geneva, however, she was unusually quiet. Byron took the stage first. Inspired by too much of his evening green tea and perhaps an overwhelming packet of chewing tobacco, he spun out his outline for a story to be called "The Vampire."

For his part, Polidori settled for a skull-headed lady, a peeping ghost who looked through keyholes. Mary said nothing, for she had grown cautious. Earlier that evening when they had been reading

HOW
I PLAY
WITH MY
DOLLIES.

"A woman is a doll herself," said Rousseau, the French philosopher. *How I play with my dollies. St. Nicholas Magazine, 1889.*

a particularly frightening story, Shelley had blanched. Then Byron began majestically the wonderful words of Coleridge's *Christabel*, his voice boomed the line, "Behold her bosom." It was too much for Shelley. He gave a wild British shriek, particularly piercing with his high voice (not for him an Albanian cry), jumped to his feet, almost electrified, and was propelled as "by another force from the salon."

This was a highly susceptible group of persons indeed. Mary followed him to his room, bathed his face and gave him a dose of that early nineteenth-century cure-all, laudanum.

There was a simple enough explanation, Shelley said, for his distress. He had been casting a look at Mary's bosom while Byron had intoned the line beginning "Behold . . ." and suddenly he had seen eyes in her breast. So, rattled by Mary's décolletage, Shelley contributed nothing to the evening and no fanciful ghost story emerged from his pen.

Mary, too, was distressed. She could think of nothing to write; perhaps the climate was just too exciting, perhaps the rain was too threatening, perhaps Lord Byron's voice was just too omnipresent. In any case, worn out, she took to her bed but, alas, not to sleep. Fortunately for us it was a creative insomnia. The next few nights she was restless. She wrote later:

"I busied myself *to think of a story*—a story to rival those which had excited us to this task. One which would speak to the mysterious fears of our nature and awaken thrilling horror—one to make the reader dread to look round, to curdle the blood, and quicken the beatings of the heart. If I did not accomplish these things, my ghost story would be unworthy of its name. I thought and pondered—vainly. I felt that blank incapability of invention which is the greatest misery of authorship, when dull Nothing replies to our anxious invocations. 'Have you thought of a story?' I was asked each morning, and each morning I was forced to reply with a mortifying negative.

"Every thing must have a beginning, to speak in Sanchean phrase; and that beginning must be linked to something that went before. The Hindus give the world an elephant to support it, but they make the elephant stand upon a tortoise. Invention, it must be humbly admitted, does not consist in creating out of void, but out of chaos; the materials must, in the first place, be afforded: it can give form to dark, shapeless substances, but cannot bring into being the substance itself. In all matters of discovery and invention, even of those that appertain to the imagination, we are continually reminded of the story of Columbus and his egg. Invention consists in the capacity of seizing on the capabilities of a subject; and in the power of moulding and fashioning ideas suggested to it.

"Many and long were the conversations between Lord Byron and Shelley, to which I was a devout but nearly silent listener. During one of these, various philosophical doctrines were discussed, and among others the nature of the principle of life, and whether there was any probability of its ever being discovered and communicated. They talked of the experiments of Dr Darwin (I speak not of what the doctor really did, or said that he did, but, as more to my purpose, of what was then spoken of as having been done by him), who preserved a piece of vermicelli in a glass case till by some extraordinary means it began to move with voluntary motion. Not thus, after all, would life be given. Perhaps a corpse would be reanimated; galvanism had given token of such things: perhaps the component parts of a creature might be manufactured, brought together, and endued with vital warmth.

"Night waned upon this talk, and even the witching hour had gone by before we retired to rest. When I placed my head on my pillow, I did not sleep, nor could I be said to think. My imagination, unbidden, possessed and guided me, gifting the successive images that arose in my mind with a vividness far beyond the usual bounds of reverie. I saw—with shut eyes, but acute mental vision—I saw the pale student of unhallowed arts kneeling beside the thing he had put together. I saw the hideous phantasm of a man stretched out, and then, on the working of some powerful engine, show signs of life, and stir with an uneasy, half-vital motion. Frightful must it be; for supremely frightful would be the effect of any human endeavour to mock the stupendous mechanism of the Creator of the world. His success would terrify the artist; he would rush away from his odious handiwork, horror-stricken. He would hope that, left to itself, the slight spark of life which he had communicated would fade; that

Byron after riding. A contemporary cut-out by Mary's friend, Mrs. Leigh Hunt.

this thing which had received such imperfect animation would subside into dead matter, and he might sleep in the belief that the silence of the grave would quench forever the transient existence of the hideous corpse which he had looked upon as the cradle of life. He sleeps; but he is awakened; he opens his eyes; behold, the horrid things stands at his bedside, opening his curtains and looking on him with yellow, watery, but speculative eyes.

Percy Bysshe Shelley. A bust by Mrs. Leigh Hunt, etched by William Bell Scott.

Lord Byron at the age of nineteen. Engraved by W. Finden.

Sara Coleridge the daughter of Samuel Taylor Coleridge. A contemporary of Mary Shelley's, an intellectual and a beauty, she wrote the following observations to her friend, Aubrey de Vere: To AUBREY DE VERE, Esq.: *Chester Place, August 20, 1847.*—I had a very interesting talk last night with Mr. H. T., who is looking remarkably well. He put in a strong light the unattractiveness of intellectual ladies to gentlemen, even those who are themselves on the intellectual side of the world—men of genius, men of learning and letters. I could have said, in reply, that while women are young, where there is a pretty face, it covers a multitude of sins, even intellectuality; where there is not that grand desideratum to young marrying men, a love of books does not make the matter much worse in one way, and does make it decidedly better in the other: that when youth is past, a certain number of persons are bound to us, in the midst of all our plainness and pedantry; these old friends and lovers cleave to us for something underneath *all that*, not only below the region of good looks, skin, lip, and eye, but even far deeper down than the intellect, for our individual, moral, personal being, which shall endure when we shall be where all will see as angels ken, and intellectual differences are done away: that as for the *world of gentlemen at large*—that world which a *young* lady desires, in an indefinite, infinite way, to charm and smite—we that are no longer young pass into a new, old-womanish, tough state of mind; to *please* them is not so much the aim as to set them to rights, lay down the law to them, convict them of their errors, pretenses, superficialities, etc., etc.; in short, tell them a *bit of our mind.* This, of course, is as foolish an ambition as the other, even more preposterous; but it is so far better that even where the end fails, the means themselves are a sort of end, and a considerable amusement and excitement. So that intellectualism, if it be not wrong in itself, will not be abandoned by us to please the gentlemen."

Mary Shelley. From a contemporary miniature.

"I opened mine in terror. The idea so possessed my mind that a thrill of fear ran through me, and I wished to exchange the ghastly image of my fancy for the realities around. I see them still: the very room, the dark parquet, the closed shutters with the moonlight struggling through, and the sense I had that the glassy lake and white high Alps were beyond. I could not so easily get rid of my hideous phantom; still it haunted me. I must try to think of something else. I recurred to my ghost story—my tiresome, unlucky ghost story! Oh! If I could only contrive one which would frighten my reader as I myself had been frightened that night!

"Swift as light and as cheering was the idea that broke in upon me. 'I have found it! What terrified me will terrify others; and I need only describe the spectre which had haunted my midnight pillow.' On the morrow I announced that I had *thought of a story*. I began that day with the words, 'It was on a dreary night of November,' making only a transcript of the grim terrors of my waking dream.

"At first I thought but of a few pages—of a short tale, but Shelley urged me to develope the idea at greater length. I certainly did not owe the suggestion of one incident, nor scarcely of one train of feeling, to my husband, and yet but for his incitement it would never have taken the form in which it was presented to the world."

Mary was fortunate in the fact that she had always been allowed to write:

"It is not singular that, as the daughter of two persons of distinguished literary celebrity, I should very early in life have thought of writing. As a child I scribbled; and my favourite pastime during the hours given me for recreation was to 'write stories.' Still, I had a dearer pleasure than this, which was the formation of castles in the air—the indulging in waking dreams—the following up trains of thought, which had for their subject the formation of a succession of imaginary incidents. My dreams were at once more fantastic and agreeable than my writings. In the latter I was a close imitator— rather doing as others had done than putting down the suggestions of my own mind. What I wrote was intended at least for one other eye—my childhood's companion and friend; but my dreams were all my own; I accounted for them to nobody; they were my refuge when annoyed—my dearest pleasure when free."

William Godwin considered writing a form of breathing and he was in sharp contrast to most of the early nineteenth-century fathers who rarely encouraged a girl to express herself or, if she did, often teased her unmercifully, or worse, destroyed all young efforts in a pet of peeve.

We know little about those secret ingredients that make up the creative process for any artist, but a warm glance at the households that produced the great women writers of the nineteenth century reveals a great deal of the literary furniture of their minds.

In the background there always seemed to be Papa in a big chair. Sometimes the Papas were benevolent, often tyrants, sometimes kind, but they were a distinct presence in the young girl's life. Mary Wollstonecraft's father had been intensely cruel, but certainly he had been significant. If she later raged against tyranny, it was a healthy rage that could only help humanity. And there seemed to be, too, only a most conciliatory tone in her writings, so that in the very understanding of tyranny, she made some reconciliation to that towering figure that had so tormented her childhood. For her daughter, Mary Godwin, a father was something else again. Despite his painful eccentricities, Godwin gave her a taste for print, access to books, and a kind of benign neglect that seems extremely productive creatively.

In those early years, when education for girls was so rare, exceptional fathers made valiant efforts to educate their daughters. But often it was a tyranny of education that proved as painful as a whipping . . . and as unproductive. Aaron Burr, for example, one of the most officious of all parents, raised his remarkable daughter on the precepts of Mary Wollstonecraft's *Vindication*. His letters to Theodosia are filled with cultured cant:

Philadelphia, 7th January, 1794
When your letters are written with tolerable spirit and correctness, I read them two or three times before I perceive any fault in them, being wholly engaged with the pleasure they afford me; but, for your sake, it is necessary that I should also peruse them with an eye of criticism. The following are the only misspelled words. You write *acurate* for *accurate; laudnam* for *laudanum; intirely* for *entirely;* this last word, indeed, is spelled

both ways, but *entirely* is the most usual and the most proper.

Continue to use all these words in your next letter, that I may see that you know the true spelling. And tell me what is laudanum? Where and how made? And what are its effects?

—"It was what she had long wished for, and was at a loss how to procure *it.*"

Don't you see that this sentence would have been perfect and much more elegant without the last *it?* Mr. Leshlie will explain to you why. By-the-by, I took the liberty to erase the redundant *it* before I showed the letter.

I am extremely impatient for your farther account of mamma's health. The necessity of laudanum twice a day is a very disagreeable and alarming circumstance. Your letter was written a week ago, since which I have no account. I am just going to the Senate Chamber, where I hope to meet a journal and letter.

Affectionately, A. Burr

His daughter never wrote a creative line. A gracious hostess, and a learned woman, she was simply for her father an extension of his own overriding personality—she was the beautiful doll with a voice—but it was her father's.

Mary Godwin, for her part, had been superbly ignored.

The creator of *Frankenstein* was also fortunate in her husband. Shelley had that superb gift of genuinely being interested in other writers. *Frankenstein* screamed to be written, it's true, but Shelley was never threatened by Mary's voice. And what an extraordinary voice it was! Mary must have often felt that, like Frankenstein, she had created a monster.

Fortunately the age was ripe for such a book. The world opened it's arms to the horrid with almost depraved delight. It was as omnipresent on the bookshelves as sex-ridden books are today, and often as ridiculous. Frequently the books were just poorly concealed, long, sexual fantasies of lost maidens, sensual blackness, shadows in the night. Not surprisingly, later Victorian ladies in utter decorum and inner repression would spin out endless tales of horror for the hearthside. Indeed, although Mary's *Frankenstein* was innovative in every way, even she wrote in the shadow of that remarkable gentlewoman of letters, Mrs. Ann Radcliffe, who first fanned the Gothic

flame in a novel. (Even today the Gothic novel in the book trade
is held in poor repute . . . it is a so-called "woman's book," and more
than one booksalesman speaks of such disparagingly as he pockets
his commission. Fortunately, such writers as Daphne Du Maurier
pocket more).

No one, however, disparaged Mrs. Radcliffe. Now almost forgotten, she was the literary sensation of her day, yet very little was
known about her life. We know that she died in 1823 and a contemporary chronicler tells us, "This admiral writer had, in her youth,
the benefit of the society of Mr. Bentley, the well-known man of
letters and taste in the arts and of Mr. Wedgwood, the able chem-
ist." Somewhere or other this maid of the macabre, "distinguished
for her beauty," met and married William Radcliffe, editor of a
contemporary newspaper, the *English Chronicle.* Ann smelled printing ink and liked it. Her early novels sold adequately but with the
publication of *The Mysteries of Udolpho* Mrs. Radcliffe was a literary lioness. It was not a role she cared for. Instead she pocketed her
five hundred pounds, a completely unheard of sum for any novel,
let alone one written by a woman, and thereafter "studiously avoided
London society." She spent her time in excursions to favorite rural
resorts, and in the enjoyments of her quiet home.

Having so removed herself from the parlors of London, Ann
often became a subject of gossip. "It was said that, in consequence
of brooding over the terrors which she had depicted, her reason had
been overturned, and that the author of the *The Mysteries of Udolpho* only existed as the melancholy inmate of a private madhouse;
but there was not the slightest foundation for the unpleasing ru-
mour."

Sir Walter Scott, who incautiously admired too many lady
writers' turns of phrase the way his male contemporaries admired
a turn of ankle, breathlessly praised Mrs. Radcliffe's talents as of
"agitating and tremendous nature."

Today this greatly overpraised writer is unreadable. Mary Shelley's *Frankenstein,* however, is more popular than ever and is still
published in many editions. Mrs. Radcliffe's life, too, from the little
we know of it seemed relatively serene; Mary Shelley's, neé Godwin,

was anything but.

Mary Wollstonecraft had commanded her scene. Despite all the passions and reverses she had worked productively for the common good. Her daughter Mary was to be far different. Although eager and hungry throughout her life to track down friends of her mother's and to hear what they had to say about her, she was at no point "a feminist" and upon occasion derided the name. But she was, like her mother, enormously dramatic. Mary Wollstonecraft had made up her own drama and then cast herself in a major role. For Mary, the daughter, the role seems to have been cast for her by others from the very beginning.

Act 1, Scene I

A motherless child, desperately unhappy, she had acquired by the time she was three years old the traditionally cruel stepmother. William Godwin had married again, a woman with two children. One named (Mary) Jane was to change her name to Claire and be forever a thorn in the side of young Mary and a strange thistle in the complex garden of nineteenth-century literary history. From the beginning, Mary seemed to be in Jane's shadow. Turbulent and beautiful, she would have a leading role in Mary's life scenario. If it were to have a title it would be called *Our Circle of Tempests.* Indeed, Shelley said, they lived in such a circle, and there is probably no better title for such an extraordinary acting out of private passions.

Scene II

The child Mary grew ill from want of plain, ordinary affection. She was sent to Scotland and there she found not only contentment, but also what seemed to be inspiration. There she could do what she wanted, nothing, if that was what she chose. It was a time which she felt "my dreams were all my own, I accounted for them to nobody, they were my refuge when annoyed, my dearest pleasure when free." It was in Scotland that she began even as a child to think of writing. It wasn't surprising, she said, "that as the daughter of two persons of distinguished literary celebrity I should very early in life have thought of writing." She admitted she lived in waking

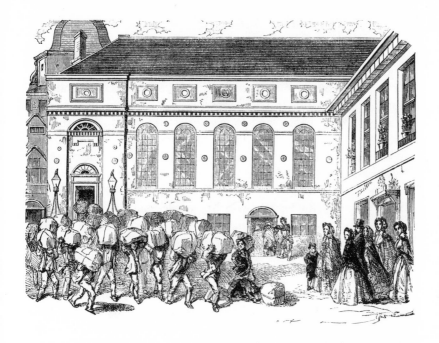

'Almanac Day' at Stationers' Hall. Throughout the nineteenth century, almanacs of all kinds were extraordinarily popular. They allowed a new outlet for the woman writer.

dreams and then she said, "I did not make myself the heroine of my tales." In fact she never seemed to play a leading role in her own life.

Scene III

June, 1814. Mary returned from Scotland to Skinner Street where the Godwins were living. After her solitude in Scotland Mary was overwhelmed by the activity of the house. The Godwin children were impossible. Mary's half-sister, Fanny Imlay, "the barrier child," was tyrannized by Jane who was determined to be an actress. Mary herself went around her so-called home with a long face, nearly always depressed, burdened by endless chores. The household was consumed by debt. The Godwins had entered into a publishing program, one of the first juvenile publishing houses in the world, but the creditors came faster than the book buyers. And then enter a new player: tall, almost beautiful, big boned, cramped into seemingly boy's clothes, came young Shelley, a genius, compressed into the world's style. Dead at thirty, he would always seem a slightly overgrown schoolboy, vainly trying to catch his genius with a butterfly net. For Godwin he was something else. He was the son of a baronet with a goodly inheritance; Godwin felt he could net him like a fish. But for once and forever in relation to Shelley and her father, Mary stole the scene. They fell hopelessly in love. With that painful and curious morbidity of a child that has lost her mother, Mary found some comfort in going to her mother's grave. And it was there one afternoon that her half-sister Jane led Shelley and where Mary and Shelley plighted their troth. Shelley gave her a copy of his *Queen Mab* and when she went home she wrote, "This book is sacred to me and there's no other creature shall ever look into it. I may write in it what I please. Yet what shall I write? That I love the author beyond all powers of expression and that I am parted from him, dearest and only love by that love we have promised to each other. Although I may never be yours, I can never be anothers, but I am thine, exclusively thine." For days she wandered around the house, her eyes bright with that "piercing look" that so many were to remember, dressed in the tartan gown she had brought back from Scotland. She saw little of Shelley in the next few days; he was too busy trying to raise money for Godwin, and when he succeeded he returned to the house to meet an enraged Godwin. He had discovered that Percy and Mary were in love. William, the advocate of free love, the nonconformist, the nonconventional, howled in distress. The girl was dispatched to her room. Both Shelley and Mary of course had overlooked the fact, or did not care to consider that he was already married to Harriet Westbrook. For Shelley, the explanation was simple. "You must know" he said to his friend Peacock, "everyone who knows me must know that the partner of my life should be one who can feel poetry and understand philosophy. Harriet is a noble animal but she can do neither."

ACT II, Scene 1

It was a dark night, Mary and naturally Jane (she was to play some part in the scene) crept slowly downstairs carrying one small bag with a change of clothing. They shut the door, dashed out into the London streets where Shelley waited in a post chaise. The driver cracked his whip, the chaise took off, the elopement was on. All three raced from the chaise to a ship that would take them to Calais. It was a bad voyage, the sea violent, a fierce thundersquall, rains almost engulfing the boat. Would they drown? "Mary did not know our danger," Shelley said later. "She was resting between my knees, but they were unable to support her. She did not speak or look, but I felt she was there." This young, mad lover with whom she had pledged her troth was to be always fascinated by the idea of death by drowning, but that morning when they landed, Mary was too exhausted to notice his strange, febrile excitement.

Scene IV

The indomitable Mrs. Godwin by sheer force of nerve arrived in Calais. At Shelley's hotel there was a scene with Jane. Mary is obviously no good, said her stepmother, she is a bad influence. Was she not the daughter of that frightful woman? Her daughter Jane must return to England. Jane for the moment, said yes. Mrs. Godwin turned on her heel and departed.

ACT III, Scene 1

Now Jane, Shelley and Mary were fugitives in earnest. Funds were almost nonexistent, but they managed continual traveling, frenetic movements, but move they must with a kind of constant moving that signaled the torment of their life together. A night in Boulogne, six days in Paris, a trip by mule to Switzerland, the girls in black silk gowns, Shelley, carrying a basket of fruit and bread, leading them by a rope. Shelley hurt his leg; Mary dismounted from the mule and gave him her perch. They must have a carriage. All the time they were in emotional flight. The land around them was also desolate. It had been burnt over by Napoleon in the winter and spring of 1814. The echoes of war bounced from the landscape, echoes that were to mean much to Shelley, but Mary, who was ill with what she called "one horrible spasm," grew more depressed. Still this was the man she loved and she would be with him. For Jane the whole thing was strictly glorious. Every place they saw was beautiful.

O, Those Extraordinary Women

For forty-two days this strange trio wandered by every means of conveyance across the Continent. When they rested, they wrote or read. Shelley and Mary read all of Mary Wollstonecraft together, Tacitus, all of Shakespeare. Mary and Jane started stories, Mary's was called "Hate." Later all three would describe this emotional hegira as "an inconstant summer of delight and beauty." By September 13, they were all back in London, penniless.

Scene II

But no, it is not a scenario. Human lives rarely are, and particularly if they are the lives of highly creative, tortured individuals, because this curious trio were all of that. Many books depicted the Shelleys as highly romantic. We need romantic figures and it is difficult at times to accept the fact that, in retrospect, their lives seemed vaguely sordid. In their eagerness to escape from convention, they were frequently escaping from themselves, or worse from creditors. It's a pathetic sight to see Shelley, still in his schoolboy clothes, scurrying around from place to place, avoiding bailiffs, avoiding creditors. They called him mad Shelley in school and he himself seemed to realize that he contained madness within him, but he also contained genius and during those years his genius ripened and flowered. He thought of himself not as the young Narcissus, but as an Apollo, tramping through the woods, a laurel wreath on his head. If not the king of the poets, he was rapidly becoming a prince of poetry. Mary was a precarious princess. Besides her entourage always contained Jane. It was Jane, now called Claire, who decided they all would go to Switzerland in May, 1816. The party was increased by one—Mary and Percy's baby, William, who had been born in January.

Why the trip? Nobody seemed to know. The Shelleys were just willing to go, but Claire had a very definite reason. She had decided to fall in love. The decision was well planned. Mrs. Godwin, who was called a born manager, had given Claire something of the kind. She, too, could be indomitable when pressed. If one were to fall in love on the grand, passionate scale that Claire demanded, whom would she choose? Yes, she would choose him; he need not choose her. The answer seemed obvious to Claire. Would it not be the

The cremation of Shelley as re-created by Louis Edward Fournier. In truth, however, Byron could not tolerate the scene and plunged into the sea. Courtesy, Walker Art Gallery, Liverpool, England.

greatest wit of the day, the handsome rake, the most talked-about man in England, Lord Byron? Of course. Neither Shelley nor Mary knew anything about this fantasy, and well aware of Claire's ability to get her way, would still have doubted that she would have carried this off as nicely as she did. She bombarded Byron with letters. At first he made no reply at all, then only tersely. He hated the women who ran after him, or so he said. Somehow or other Claire contrived a meeting and by the time they left for Switzerland, where Claire knew Byron had been planning to retreat, she was his mistress. It was this entourage that arrived on the shore of Lake Geneva for that extraordinary meeting of minds that produced *Frankenstein* on Mary's part; the great canto of *Childe Harold* on Byron's part; the strange, abortive manuscript by Polidori called *The Vampire,* and hardly a handful of poems by Shelley. Byron's personality seemed to be too commanding for Shelley and creatively he went underground. But the talk was superb. It reeled and cavorted around the lakes and through the dining rooms, Shelley's voice rising to a pitch of excitement, his generally waxy face burning with color. Mary was never to forget the sound of Byron and Shelley talking together: the sound of their voices seemed to haunt her. It seemed to be a Garden of Eden that summer in Switzerland, but as usual trouble hovered in the shrubbery. Claire confided in her usual histrionic way that

55

she was pregnant. Mary and Shelley were shocked. True, perhaps they had eloped unconventionally, but Shelley always found his own ideals high. Theirs and theirs alone had been a marriage of two, true minds.

Even a marriage of true minds, however, can mean turbulence, and until Shelley's death by drowning in 1822, Mary barely was to know a moment's peace. They moved constantly, were hounded by debts and despair—all but one of their children dying from the fevers of the day. Oppressed by her own sorrows, with a propensity toward deep melancholy, Mary wrote only erratically. Still she wrote; one wonders how. At the time of her own death, she had written six novels, several plays, short stories, two novellas, and, because she had to make a living after Shelley's death, the usual travel and biographical books that were standard fare for the day.

Only one other novel, *The Last Man* holds any excitement today. Here, once again, Mary Shelley was truly innovative. It was one of the first, and one of the most exciting of early science fiction novels. It is a story of the future; that desolate time that would know only the last man on earth. Curiously pertinent today, it was considered, when published 1820, the product of a "diseased imagination." She was to enjoy far more acceptance with her last novel, *Lodore,* based on those days with Lord Byron. The public welcomed it; but Claire, long since disenchanted with Byron, came to the attack:

Mrs. Hare admired *Lodore* amazingly; so do I, or should I, if it were not for that modification of the beastly character of Lord Byron of which you have composed Lodore. I stick to *Frankenstein,* merely because that vile spirit does not haunt its pages as it does all your other novels, now as Castruccio, now as Raymond, now as Lodore. Good God! to think a person of your genius, whose moral tact ought to be proportionately exalted, should think it a task befitting its power to gild and embellish and pass off as beautiful what was the merest compound of vanity, folly, and every miserable weakness that ever met together in one human being!

"Do not leave me alone with her," Mary said to her new daughter-in-law, the Lady Shelley, who would spend *her* lifetime preserving the legend of Percy Bysshe Shelley, "do not leave me alone with Claire. She has been the bane of my existence since I was three."

Mary finally had the last word.

3

BLUESTOCKINGS AND BON WITS

We go to these assemblies to sell our daughters, or corrupt our neighbor's wives. A ballroom is nothing more or less than a great market place of beauty.

Edward Bulwer-Lytton

The waltz is the only dance which teaches girls to think

Lord Byron

A name will sell any trash

Lady Holland

Run mad as often as you chose but do not faint. ·

Jane Austen

ＷE have next to bring to your notice a clever, somewhat frisky, débonnaire young person of the other sex, whom you should know—whom perhaps you do know; I mean Miss Frances Burney."

In such words the nineteenth-century American writer, Donald Mitchell, introduced the glorious Fanny to his readers; he dispatched her in a couple of pages, but not without explaining very simply how she had become a famous writer. "We have encountered her once before pushing her kindly way into old Dr. Johnson's anteroom when he was near death. The old gentleman had known intimately her father, Dr. Burney, and had always shown her a strong attachment. So did a great many of Dr. Burney's acquaintances, Garrick among them, and Burke, and it was probably from such men and their talk that she caught the literary bee in her bonnet and wrote a famous story of *Evelina.*"

The truth was, Fanny seemed to have been born with a hive of bees in her bonnet and a tongue as nimble as a hummingbird. Her name buzzes through the history of English literature, the joyous accent of early success, a happy marriage, a distinguished career, but a literary lady bee for all that.

By the time she was fifteen, Fanny Burney had already burned her first novel. The scrap heap made a distinguished fire because it also contained elegies, old plays, songs, stories, farces and a few tragedies.

Fanny was born into a world where society was all important. Her father, a fashionable musician, made it possible for all the Burneys to cross aristocratic thresholds that their somewhat modified circumstances would have not otherwise made possible. Good King George II was in his counting house counting up his vices, mourning the dead Queen Caroline and ignoring the world outside. Outside things were perilous. The political situation, not only in

Mrs. Thrale's Breakfast Table.

Frances Burney. Portrait by Edward Francesco Burney. Courtesy, National Portrait Gallery, London.

England but in France, would mean that soon there would be a French and English war, and by the time Fanny reached her majority there would be a French revolution. Across the sea a new nation would break away from Britain.

In Britain itself the great were even greater. Horace Walpole, "King of Strawberry Hill," counted up his rare collection of books; Dr. Johnson was, and would always be, in dire need of funds; Joshua

Reynolds, always with an eye for the ladies, was doing a new type of painting far different from the satirical lines of the good William Hogarth; Reynolds was a great cavalier. Fanny was to meet him and to cry into his ear trumpet—a necessity, he explained, because he had once caught cold in the drafty corridors of the Vatican. But he was never one to turn a deaf ear on a young girl.

The pace was leisurely. One rose late in the morning, met at the coffee house, talked and talked. Talking was the joy of life. Some say it came from the overstimulation of the coffee and tea that had been introduced into the eating pattern of Britain. Others thought that all the strange foods that were coming into Britain must, in all truth, account for the almost extraordinary stream of gossip and high talk that was constantly enveloping each person. If one did not talk, one gambled. Cards and dice were omnipresent. There was a touch of the exotic in the air. The strange foods, such as molasses, spices, nutmeg in particular, wafted a curious aroma over the coffee houses.

Homes were decorated with rare curios. Parrots and hummingbirds were found in stately mansions, and even a few black slaves gave an exotic touch to every salon. People smoked too much, and drank too much. Snuff and rich foods were counteracted by health waters and sweet air that one could obtain on the outskirts of London. Although London was a city, it had elements of a country town. A quarter of a mile from St. Paul's one could go into the green fields of Islington. It was a pleasure to walk around London. There were only two bridges, the old Westminster where one could stand and watch the ferrymen maneuvering beneath it, and the old London Bridge, thrust and crossbeamed, the very center of life.

All of London seemed to be a round of excitement. There was dancing at all times, and there were the clubmen. It was the age of the great clubs. Johnson had his own, Garrick had his, and even the women had theirs. Theirs was of a different type. It was more of a moveable salon (Hemingway would call his later, "a movable feast")—a feast of talk and high living. It was a society in which Fanny Burney was introduced very early—a society in which she played her role well. "I would never," said Mrs. Montagu, the queen of the bluestockings, "invite an idiot to the house." She never did.

O, Those Extraordinary Women

The term bluestocking, or a like epithet for "a lady of high literary taste," is nearly as old as the "literary woman." Indeed, it appears first in Greek comedy entitled *The Banquet of Plutarch*. Mill tells us in his *History of Chivalry* that it was reintroduced in fifteenth-century Venice when all writers and intellectuals were lumped together under a name "of some external sign of folly." The members, when they met in literary discussions, were distinguished by the color of their stockings. The colors were sometimes fantastically blended, and at other times, one color, particularly blue, prevailed.

History doesn't tell how "the female pedant," as she was called, suddenly took on this appellation, but from Venice the bluestocking crossed into Paris, then from Paris to England. In Boswell's *Life of Samuel Johnson* he explains, "About this time it was the fashion for several ladies to have evening assemblies where the fair sex might participate in conversation with literary and ingenius men, animated by a desire to please. These societies were denominated Bluestocking Clubs. One of the most eminent members of these societies, when they first commenced, was Mr. Stillingfleet, grandson of the bishop whose dress was remarkably grave, and in particular it was observed that he wore blue stockings. Such was the excellence of his conversation that his absence was thought so great a loss that it used to be said, 'We could do nothing without the Bluestocking.' And thus by degrees the title was established."

By the middle of the eighteenth century bluestocking clubs were flourishing, by the end of the Regency period they were downright florid. In London the salons were held by women of impeccable social position, close intimacy with the Court, and a taste for print and, often invective. Such women could be heard; indeed, it was difficult to shut them up. "They vie," said Horace Walpole, himself no mean manipulator of the malicious mot, "with one another till they are as unintelligible as the good folks at Babel."

Their voices were often strident, but they were heard. The Bluestockings had power enough and money to publish their own books and articles defending their right to have brains—even if upon occasion they seemed to have been addled. Their exploits reached the provinces where more than one lonely rural girl thought of herself as a bluestocking woman, a new type of woman, a woman with a right to an education, to her own voice.

Mary Wollstonecraft Godwin had been considered a bluestocking and traveled in such circles; her daughter Mary Shelley, although popular in such groups in the long years after Shelley's death, found such a movement "horrid." Even then there was a pattern of action and reaction on the part of women to single out their own identity—a kind of backlash seems almost inevitable after any concerted effort by women to reach a new plateau politically, socially, economically, or intellectually. The bluestocking period was to die out in the vacuity of Victorianism. Queen Victoria, like Mary Shelley, found them "horrid. They do not amuse us."

Some of them cannot help but amuse us however, even if occasionally we are smiling at our betters.

There was, for example, the incredible Swan of Lichfield—a very learned bird in a pond of strange ducks. The "Swan" was called Anna Seward at her birth in the charming town of Lichfield. While still a fledgling she had been tutored by her father, the canon of the cathedral, himself a minor literary eagle who had edited the plays of Beaumont and Fletcher. But Lichfield was a country town; London was the big city. The literary competiton between the two cultured spots was keen—made intensely keen by the fact that the good Dr. Samuel Johnson had been born in Lichfield where his father was a bookseller. Like any country boy with delusions of literary grandeur, Johnson had turned his back on his old hometown when he began to make dusty swaths through the salons of London. The local intelligentsia never forgave him, and Anna the Swan in particular never forgave him. She would put Lichfield on the map where the geniuses were many—if Johnson wouldn't recognize the literary of Lichfield, Anna remarked, it was only because *Johnson liked only worshippers.*

One of the geniuses of Lichfield to whom Anna often devoted her life, and her pen (she wrote his biography), was the extraordinary, eccentric Dr. Erasmus Darwin, the half-looped grandfather of the indomitable Charles. Dr. Darwin was a practicing physician and a malpracticing poet. He was, like his archenemy Samuel Johnson,

Cutout of Mrs. Montagu, the witty blue-stocking, by Mrs. Brown.

remarkably but commandingly unattractive: "His limbs too heavy for exact proportion; the traces of severe smallpox; features and countenance which, when they were not animated by social pleasure, were rather saturnine than sprightly, a form inclined to corpulence, a stoop in the shoulders, and the then professional appendage, a full-bottomed wig."

In the course of his poetic work, *Botanic Garden,* which included "The Loves of The Plants" and "Economy of Vegetation," that full-bottomed wig went often awry. Miss Seward frequently joined him on a flower bank as they wrote together, the good doctor often appropriating the Swan's verses for his own. She suffered only mild indignation at this masculine theft, and perhaps one can see why from a quick glance at the rural genius of the time.

> "But thou, whose mind the well-attempered ray
> Of Taste and Virtue lights with purer day,
> Whose finer sense each soft vibration owns
> Mute and unfeeling to discorded tones;
> Like the fair flower that spreads its lucid form
> To meet the sun, but shuts it to the storm:
> For thee my borders nurse the glowing wreath,
> My fountains murmur, and my zephyrs breathe,
> My painted birds their vivid plumes unfold,
> And insect armies wave their wings of gold."

When Dr. Darwin, however, took up his pen to write *The Loves of the Plants,* an equally windblown botanic escapade, the Swan of Lichfield would have none of it. Love, even between plants, was a darkly suggestive thesis, and she felt it was not "strictly proper for a female pen."

The Swan left us three volumes of poetry, all dreadful, but she was often a remarkably good literary critic and a fine witness to the remarkable men around: viz Dr. Darwin again, who in his role as innovative doctor, if not poet, was given to urgent needs to express his new ideas about health. Once on a boating expedition, and floating in a sea of claret, he plunged into the river, raced ashore, his wig akilter, his clothes drenched, and mounted a tub in the town square of Nottingham:

'Ye men of Nottingham, listen to me,' he said. 'You are ingenious and industrious mechanics. By your industry, life's comforts are procured for yourselves and families. If you lose your health, the power of being industrious will forsake you, *that* you know: but you may not know that to breathe fresh and changed air constantly is not less necessary to procure health than sobriety itself. Air becomes unwholesome in a few hours if the windows are shut. . . . I have no *interest* in giving you this advice. Remember what I, your countryman and a physician, tell you. If you would not bring infection and disease upon yourselves, and to your wives and little ones, change the air you breathe; change it many times a day by opening your windows.'

(*Literary History of England 1790–1825,* Margaret Oliphant.)

The frightened townspeople probably went home and locked windows and doors.

The Swan had started to write early in her life, but it wasn't easy. "At first my father encouraged it." But that didn't last long. "My mother threw cold water on the rising fires and even my father ceased to smile encouragement upon these attempts after my sixteenth birthday, in which Dr. Darwin unluckily told him that his daughter's verses were better than his—a piece of arch injustice to my father's muse which disgusted him with mine."

Nothing truly quenched the Swan's fires however, and soon like many a young poet she entered a literary contest as Edna St. Vincent

Henry Thrale. From an engraving by Scriven, after the painting by Sir Joshua Reynolds.

Millay and other girls were to do later. Edna St. Vincent Millay's introduction was into the fairly sedate literary world of the *St. Nicholas* magazine; Anna's was into a kind of bluestocking poetic bacchanal.

The queen of these revels was Lady Miller who had a literary salon in Bath. During the season she held it in the open air. The grounds were crowded with literati, but the focal point of interest was a large Etruscan vase in which poets deposited their classical lines. Then, having been gorged on food and wine, the assembled great chose a judge, the best poem was selected and the poet crowned. Our Swan received many such laurels. Never, however, from Dr. Johnson who, although he occasionally attended, was held in ill repute for having had an exchange with another lady poet who had given him a poem to read with the comment that she had, in addition, other irons in the fire.

"Then, Madame," said Johnson, "I advise you to put the poem with the irons."

But with Fanny Burney, Dr. Johnson was always gentle. She was so young when he met her, so attractive, so vivacious. Only he was aware that she was also incredibly industrious.

Dr. C. Burney. From an engraving by F. Bartolozzi, after Sir Joshua Reynolds.

By the time Fanny was seventeen, she was working every evening in her father's study. The candles burned on often until five o'clock in the morning, while she took a quill pen and wrote or scratched over every piece of spare paper she could find. She was composing a book that would put her on the map, propel her into society, make her at least the darling of the Blues, if not the queen. She was writing *Evelina.*

For a society in which it was still difficult for a girl to even read a novel, let alone write one, it was an activity filled with trepidation. Besides, despite her own debonair flippancy, there was a sincere side to Fanny, and, she complained, "an authoress is always supposed to be flippant, assuming and loquacious." She strongly feared censure and explained that was her principal motive "for wishing snuggship." Snuggship being the secrecy that she surrounded herself with when she wrote. Even at her own home, an unusually Bohemian one for the period, the fact that she wrote made her fear discovery. "The fear of discovery or suspicion in the house made the copying extremely laborious to me. For in the daytime I could only take odd

An elegant establishment for young ladies. Water-colour by Edward F. Burney, 1760–1848.

moments so that I was obliged to stay up the greatest part of my nights in order to get it ready."

Evelina was the history of a young lady's entrance into the world. It was written as a series of letters—ladies were allowed to write letters, if not novels, and such a device seems to have been comforting to the emerging lady novelists. Jane Austen's early version of *Pride and Prejudice* took the same form.

The book was considered exciting, even a little racy. The Bluestockings wondered how a young girl, barely out of her father's house, could have had such a view of the world.

"Where, Miss Fanny," she was asked, "where can or could you pick up such characters?"

"Oh M'am," she answered, "anybody might find, who thought them worth looking for."

Evelina today is, of course, unbearably old-fashioned, painful in its purple prose, but there is still an entertainment about it.

"We could wish it longer," Dr. Johnson said, while his bluestocking friend Mrs. Thrale demanded. "I wish it had been longer.

It is written by somebody that knows the top and bottom. The highest and lowest of mankind. It's very good language, and there is an infinite deal of fun in it."

Soon she was "our Fanny" and they began to make her, if not a wit, one of the witlings. She was kissed and adored by Dr. Johnson. Edmund Burke and Joshua Reynolds told her they were afraid she would put them in a book; so did the great Gibbon who was scribbling away on his own *The History of the Decline and Fall of the Roman Empire*. She was loved, and at the same time society was afraid of her; a dubious situation all too familiar to men and women writers. Her success, to her dismay, meant she was often lampooned in the press. She was never attacked as vitriolically as her friend Mrs. Montagu, the queen of the Blues, who evoked the following broadside:

> Yes, Smatter in the Muse's Friend,
> She knows to censure or commend
> And has of Faith & Truth such store
> She'll ne'er desert you—till you're poor.

Street Scene in Lichfield, including the birthplace of Johnson (being the under part of the lighted side of the large house on the right-hand side of the picture).

69

O, Those Extraordinary Women

> At Thirty she began to read,—
> At Forty, it is said could spell,—
> At Fifty, 'twas by all agreed
> A common school Girl she'd excell.
>
> This lady with study has muddled her head,
> Sans meaning she talk'd, & sans knowledge she read
> And gulp'd such a Dose of incongruous matter
> That Bedlam must soon hold the Carcase of Smatter.
>   With a down, down, derry, down.
>
> A club she supported of Witlings & Fools,
> Who, but for her dinners, had scoff'd at her rules;
> The reason, if any she had, these did shatter
> Of poor empty-Headed, & little-soul'd Smatter
>   With a down, down, derry, down.

Fanny was only too aware of how rapidly literary taste could turn against the Blues who were tolerated by the famous men of the day just as long as they remained charming hostesses. Mrs. Montagu became just a little too powerful in literary and political circles. A woman who shared the somewhat diverse talents of a contemporary Mary McCarthy *and* Bella Abzug was headed for a fall. Johnson urged Fanny to attack her:

Down with her, Burney!—down with her!—spare her not!—attack her, fight her, and down with her at once! You are a rising wit, and she is at the top; and when I was beginning the world, and was nothing and nobody, the joy of my life was to fire at all the established wits! and then everybody loved to halloo me on. But there is no game now; everybody would be glad to see me conquered: but then, when I was new, to vanquish the great ones was all the delight of my poor little dear soul! So at her, Burney—at her, and down with her!

Fanny, however, had warm feelings for her own sex, and was far too creative herself to need to be vindictive. By the time she wrote her third novel, *Camilla*, she was the greatest selling novelist of her day, and richer for that one book by some three thousand pounds, an unprecedented financial reward for a woman writer. Her celebrity brought her not only lampoons, but new duties.

David Garrick as Abel Drugger. From an engraving by F. Dixon, after Zoffany.

Jane Austen. From engraving based on an original family portrait.

She was appointed Lady of the Robe to the new queen, wife of the difficult George III, a position that allowed her to explain the perils of authorship to the throne: "The king went up to the table, and looked at a book of prints, from Claude Lorraine, which had been brought down for Miss Dewes; but Mrs Delany, by mistake, told him they were for me. He turned over a leaf or two, and then said:

'Pray, does Miss Burney draw too?'

The *too* was pronounced very civilly.

'I believe not, sir,' answered Mrs Delany; 'at least she does not tell.'

'Oh,' cried he laughing, 'that's nothing; she is not apt to tell; she never does tell, you know. Her father told me that himself. He told me the whole history of her *Evelina*. And I shall never forget his face when he spoke of his feelings at first taking up the book; he looked quite frightened, just as if he was doing it that moment. I never can forget his face while I live.'

Then coming up close to me, he said: 'But what! what! how was it?'

'Sir,' cried I, not well understanding him.

'How came you—how happened it—what—what?'

'I—I only wrote, sir, for my own amusement—only in some odd idle hours.'

'But your publishing—your printing—how was that?'

'That was only, sir—only because'——

I hesitated most abominably, not knowing how to tell him a long story, and growing terribly confused at these questions; besides, to say the truth, his own, 'what! what?' so reminded me of those vile Probationary Odes, that, in the midst of all my flutter, I was really hardly able to keep my countenance.

The *what!* was then repeated, with so earnest a look, that, forced to say something, I stammeringly answered: 'I thought, sir, it would look very well in print.'

I do really flatter myself this is the silliest speech I ever made. I am quite provoked with myself for it; but a fear of laughing made me eager to utter anything, and by no means conscious, till I had spoken, of what I was saying.

Thrale's Brewery, Southwark.

Thrale's Brewery
Southwark

He laughed very heartily himself—well he might—and walked away to enjoy it, crying out: 'Very fair indeed; that's being very fair and honest.'

Then returning to me again, he said: 'But your father—how came you not to shew him what you wrote?'

'I was too much ashamed of it, sir, seriously.'

Literal truth that, I am sure.

'And how did he find it out?'

'I don't know myself, sir. He never would tell me.'

Literal truth again, my dear father, as you can testify.

'But how did you get it printed?'

'I sent it, sir, to a bookseller my father never employed, and that I never had seen myself, Mr Lowndes, in full hope that by that means he never would hear of it.'

'But how could you manage that?'

'By means of a brother, sir.'

'Oh, you confided in a brother, then?'

'Yes, sir—that is, for the publication.'

'What entertainment you must have had from hearing people's conjectures before you were known! Do you remember any of them?'

'Yes, sir, many.'

'And what?'

'I heard that Mr Baretti laid a wager it was written by a man; for no woman, he said, could have kept her own counsel.'

This diverted him extremely.

'But how was it,' he continued, 'you thought most likely for your father to discover you?'

'Sometimes, sir, I have supposed I must have dropt some of the manuscript; sometimes, that one of my sisters betrayed me.'

'Oh, your sister? what! not your brother?'

'No, sir, he could not, for'——

I was going on, but he laughed so much I could not be heard, exclaiming: 'Vastly well! I see you are of Mr Baretti's mind, and think your brother could keep your secret, and not your sister. Well, but,' cried he presently, 'how was it first known to you, you were betrayed?'

'By a letter, sir, from another sister. I was very ill, and in the country; and she wrote me word that my father had taken up a review, in which the book was mentioned, and had put his finger upon its name, and said: "Contrive to get that book for me.'

'And when he got it,' cried the king, 'he told me he was afraid of looking at it, and never can I forget his face when he mentioned his first opening it. But you have not kept your pen unemployed all this time?'

'Indeed I have, sir.'

'But why?'

'I—I believe I have exhausted myself, sir.'

He laughed aloud at this, and went and told it to Mrs Delany, civilly treating a plain fact as a mere *bon mot*.

Then returning to me again, he said more seriously: 'But you have not determined against writing any more?'

'N—o, sir.'

'You have made no vow—no real resolution of that sort?'

'No, sir.'

'You only wait for inclination?'

How admirably Mr Cambridge's speech might have come in here.

'No, sir.'

A very civil little bow spoke him pleased with this answer, and he went again to the middle of the room, where he chiefly stood, and, addressing us in general, talked upon the different motives of writing, concluding with: 'I believe there is no constraint to be put upon real genius; nothing but inclination can set it to work. Miss Burney, however, knows best.' And then hastily returning to me, he cried: 'What! what?'

'No, sir, I—I—believe not, certainly,' quoth I very awkwardly, for I seemed taking a violent compliment only as my due; but I knew not how to put him off as I would another person."

George III was more difficult to put off as he grew increasingly unbalanced and Fanny found that her life in the palace was to mean an almost prison-like existence: "I am like ice so cold, so cold." Finally pensioned, she met and married General d'Arblay, one of the exiles from France. Their long and happy marriage was carefully chronicled in her diaries, as well as her friendships with some of the remarkable French Blues.

But if, as someone said, Fanny was a sweet glass of sherry, her friend Germaine de Staël was a full case of vintage burgundy.

France had long tolerated the brilliant woman. She was not only tolerated at table, but in bed as well . . . true the great literary courtesans were often only a step above the Greek hetaerae, but Germaine de Staël was in a class by herself. She said as she was dying

Madame de Staël. From an engraving
designed by Gérard.

that she had but three loves: God, her father, and liberty, but her
memory must have failed her: one would have to keep a chronologi-
cal chart to keep all her lovers straight.

Germaine never expressed an interest in marrying God—in
view of her amorous conquests it's doubtful if God would have had
her—but she did admit quite ingenuously that she always regretted
that she had not met her father before her birth—the ensuing
marriage would have been, she thought, divinely happy. One wonders why. Certainly her parents, the Neckers were anything but.
Necker, financier, writer, and politician who aimed high and fell low
in statesmanship was relatively cold to his wife, a difficult woman
to say the least. But he was warmly appreciative of his daughter;
when he danced with her, he proclaimed to bystanders: "There, sir,
I shall show you how one dances with a girl when one is in love with
her."

It was lucky that she had even learned to dance because her
mother had made sure that her education was entirely directed
toward the development of the mind. It was no wonder that Germaine, having been raised in a bluestocking salon, should want to
run barelegged in greener fields. Love was what she sought; love was
what she would extoll in her novels: "Love, supreme power of the
heart, mysterious enthusiasm, combining poetry, heroism and religion."

"She was one of the first women" said Fanny Burney, "I have ever met with for abilities and extraordinary intellect." But Dr. Burney was careful to warn Fanny that her morals were "unpure." Germaine's marriage to de Staël bothered her little; she recognized, she said, "no law but that of love."

Her love was difficult, obsessive. One of her lovers, Benjamin Constant was to complain:

"I have never known a woman who was more continuously exacting without realizing it. . . . Everyone's entire existence, every hour, every minute, for years on end, must be at her disposition; or else there is an explosion like all thunderstorms and earthquakes put together."

She literally exploded into her age, erupted into the world of the French Revolution and the Napoleonic Wars; she was, quite frankly, the first woman of Europe. Literary critic, novelist, political analyst (she was the first to consider that politics might be a science) she felt literature had to become "a weapon in the service of man." But as all weapons become, her writings have become outmoded;

Mrs. Thrale. From an engraving by W. Daniell, after a painting by G. Dance.

while the writings of her contemporary across the water, Jane Austen
(whose work Germaine found "contemptible") have the beautiful
permanancy of art practiced for delicious, private amusement. Jane,
poor dear, was often bored; Germaine refused to accept boredom
and, like Margaret Fuller, had difficulty even accepting the universe.
The most extraordinary woman of her time, she has one of her
characters say:

"I soon noticed that the feelings I expressed were turned into
jests, and that my intelligence was silenced, as if it were improper
for a woman to have any. Thus I locked up in myself everything
I felt. I early acquired the art of dissembling, and I stifled my natural
sensibility; only one of my qualities escaped my endeavor to control
them all: pride. When I was caught in a lie, I never gave any excuse
or explanation; I kept silent. . . . I was and I still am convinced that
women, being the victims of all social institutions, are destined to
misery if they make the least concession to their feelings and if, in
any way whatever, they lose control of themselves."

"Loss of control" was a phrase that haunted the eighteenth-
century woman writer. Jane Austen's books were to be all control;
Germaine preferred to control the world.

But Fanny Burney thought her charm and wit worthy to rank
beside that other delightful bluestocking, Mrs. Thrale.

In her own day, Mrs. Thrale was known for her literary "noto-
riety," but within the next century they were saying that she was
known only for her "parasitical celebrity." And that, in a way, is how
we remember her today—the good Dr. Johnson's unwavering friend
and his dear Hettie. "Long may live my lovely Hettie, always young
and always pretty; always pretty, always young; live my lovely Hettie
long; always young and always pretty; long may live my lovely Hettie." Johnson took to her as he seemed to have taken to no other
woman. She protected him, guided him, listened to him, and he in
chance listened to her. It was a strange household.

Henry Thrale was a brewer, and, as they said, "a perfect gentleman." He was, on the other hand, a bore. It was a reasonably
attractive marriage, but life had been pretty dull at table (a brewer's
table was not the best place to find zesty conversation) until Johnson

George Cruikshank: "The Dandies Coat of Arms" (1819).

was to dine with them. From then on he was either a member of the family or at least an omnipresent guest. At the Thrales he was, say the historians, always a center of attraction, flattered and fondled in spite of his uncouthness and occasional rudeness. It was at the Thrales that Johnson first became attracted to little Burney. It was here that he could talk with Garrick, where one could meet Goldsmith, where even "Bozzy," James Boswell, was to occasionally listen to someone else—at a table where sat Reynolds and Burke and all the great bluestockings.

Johnson's friendship with his lovely Hettie lasted for twenty remarkable years, then the good Mr. Thrale died a respectable brewer's death (from overeating) leaving the very respectable Mrs. Thrale in the throes of grief. But her mourning was shortlived. Her romanticism had been held in check for too long and she made a wild Italian marriage. Mr. Piozzi was no one—simply the music master of her daughters. But Mrs. Thrale could see herself Mrs. Piozzi, and a Mrs. Piozzi wildly in love.

The shock to Johnson was considerable. "Madame," he wrote, "If I interpret your letter right, you are ignominiously married. If it is yet undone, let us once more talk together. If you have abandoned your children and your religion, God forgive your wickedness; if you have forfeited your fame and your country, may your folly do no further mischief. If the last act is yet to do, I who have loved you, esteemed you, reverenced you, and served you, I who long thought you the first of womankind, entreat that before your fate is irrevocable, I may once more see you. I was, I once was, Madam, most truly yours. Sam Johnson"

Dear Hettie wrote back a reasonable letter:

"Sir, I have this morning received from you so rough a letter in reply to one which is both tenderly and respectfully written that I am forced to desire the conclusion of a correspondence which I can bear to continue no longer. The birth of my second husband is not meaner than that of my first. His sentiments are not meaner than that of my first. His sentiments are not meaner. His profession is not meaner, and his superiority in what he professes is acknowledged by all mankind. It is want of fortune then that is ignominious; the character of the man I have chosen has no other claim to such

Dr. Johnson's Room in Pembroke College.

an epithet. The religion to which he has been always a zealous adherent will, I hope, teach him to forgive insults he has not deserved; mine will, I hope, enable me to bear them at once with dignity and patience. To hear that I have forfeited my fame is indeed the greatest insult I ever yet received. My fame is as unsullied as snow, or I should think it unworthy of him who must henceforth protect it.

"I write by coach, the more speedily and effectually to prevent your coming hither. Perhaps by my fame (and I hope it is so) you mean only that celebrity which is a consideration of a much lower kind. I care for that only as it may give pleasure to my husband and his friends.

"Farewell, dear Sir, and accept my best wishes. You have always commanded my esteem, and long enjoyed the fruits of a friendship never infringed by one harsh expression on my part during twenty years of familiar talk. Never did I oppose your will, or control your wish; nor can your unmerited severity itself lessen my regard; but till you have changed your opinion of Mr. Piozzi, let us converse no more. God bless you."

The "right" marriage for our literary ladies was always fraught with peril. Mary Shelley married genius and experienced exhaustion: Mrs. Thrale married beer and suffered boredom; but one charmer simply decided not to marry at all.

George Cruikshank: "His Most Gracious Majesty George the Fourth" (1821).

Bluestockings and Bon Wits

Enter Jane. She came into literature as quietly as she came into a room. Never truly a "Blue," she found them ridiculous; never a loud voice (even Napoleon could neither outshout nor outwit Germaine); never lionized, as was Fanny Burney, never a great "figure," as was Mrs. Thrale, Jane Austen was simply *there*, with the proper genius at the proper time in the proper place. A supreme artist she defies any classification and for that reason she is the most extraordinary—only Emily Brontë of all the writing women of the nineteenth century would be such a maverick.

The genius
Best described by herself: "the little bit (two inches wide) of ivory."

The time
Born December 16, 1775. She would be nursed on the ferment of the Revolutions (and ignore them all in her world); come to maturity in the scandalous world of the Regency. Indeed *Emma* was dedicated to the Regent, but still in the fashionable world of the dandy she could not amuse! "I hope" said a fashionable Blue, "you like nothing of Miss Austen's. They are full of commonplace people that you recognize at once."

The place
The county of Hampshire where she lived for her first twenty-six years. Hampshire had little "ton."

Ton was the word of those seasons. As a contemporary explained: "The society of *ton;* the dynasty of *ton;* the court of *ton;* the empire of *ton;* devotees of *ton;* the elite of *ton;* the polished ultras of *ton;* ultra-tonism; The *ton;* the world of fashion; the fashionable multitude; the *canaille* of the fashionable world; a société choisi; a société distingué; a select coterie; a race apart; young men de la premiere volée; a *haut* grade insociety; the more recherche amusements; the corps élite; The Elite." There's always a word for them— café society, "the beautiful people"—the descriptions are as transitory as the peoples.

Hampshire was just Hampshire, and Jane was just plain Jane . . . born into a family however, with a sense of humor as neat as bonnet strings—and as taut.

O, Those Extraordinary Women

Jane's life was uneventful. If there had been a love affair, as some suggest, it seems to have left little mark on her. Her reality was that little writing desk; her private excitement, the hiding of her manuscripts under the muslin on the table; her private victory, the fact that she chose to be a "monster"; our delicious reward, the pride of her books. Still the prejudice against "a lady novelist" would long continue.

4

HOLY HANNAHS
AND PIOUS PAPAS

Sweet Sensibility! Thou keen delight!
Thou hasty moral! Sudden sense of right!
Thou untaught goodness! Virtue's precious seed!

Hannah More, 1781

Delicacy is a very general and *comprehensive* quality. It extends to everywhere where woman is concerned. Conversation, books, pictures, attitude, gesture, pronunciation, should all come under its salutary restraints.

Rev. John Bennett, 1789

I perceive it is written by a WOMAN! ! !

Lord Byron, 1820

T HERE are only two bad things in life," said Mrs. Hannah More, "bile and sin."

Always a bluestocking, but never a bride, Mrs. Hannah More carried the title of Mrs. or Mistress, an expression of dignity given to all of the learned and literary women of the late eighteenth and early nineteenth centuries. Today, when there is a movement to abandon the "Mrs." for the ambiguous "Ms.," it appears a literary step backward. Those elegant mistresses of those years were very overwhelmingly women indeed. And, of course, extraordinary. None more so than Holy Hannah.

If we are to meet her properly, we must accompany that indefatigable gossiper, Thomas De Quincey. If there were blemishes, De Quincey would find them. Why not? He had so many of his own, was so greatly talked about that a little poison-pen portraiture seemed the least of his talents. "I knew Mrs. More tolerably well," he explained, as he began his article for *Tait's Edinburgh Magazine* in 1833. "But" he brooded, "could anybody know her tolerably well that was not one of her admirers. Only on adulation did she thrive."

Indeed, she fed on it. She burned with a religious zeal, a kind of literary Aimee Semple McPherson, gathering around her devotees, the high priestess of the bluestockings. She was a woman who knew her way to sanctity and its handmaiden, sensibility. Jane Austen would mock this state of mind in *Sense and Sensibility*, but Holy Hannah never so much as cracked a smile. *Sensibility* was *the* word. Women were particularly prone to it; in fact, encouraged to express it. It was the natural result of their chastity, their piety, their delicacy, their . . . well, their sensibility, naturally. If one did not weep properly over a sad book, one worried about one's sensibility; if one were genuinely enthusiastic about any undertaking, one worried about one's oversensibility. Actually, our favorite maid of sensi-

Overpopulation was already beginning to disturb the articulate women of the nineteenth century, none more so than the remarkable Harriet Martineau. Print from a drawing by George Cruikshank.

Hannah More. "What unfailing Sunday books her books did make! And with what child-like awe we looked upon her good, kind, old peaked face as it looked out from the frontispiece—with soberly frilled hair all about the forehead, and over this a muslin cap with huge ruffles hemming in the face, and above this circumambient ruffle and in the lee of the great puff of muslin—which gave place, I suppose, to the old lady's comb—a portentous bow, constructed of an awful quantity of ribbon and crowning that saintly, kindly, homely face of Hannah More." Donald G. Mitchell, 1895.

bility is buried in Dorchester Abbey with an epitaph that reads:

When nerves were too delicately spun to bear the Rude Shakes and Jostlings which we meet with in this transitory world, Nature gave way; She sank and died a martyr to EXCESSIVE SENSIBILITY.

Holy Hannah held hers in perfect check.

At the close of the French Revolution, there was a new emphasis on religion. Lady Shelley, Mary Shelley's daughter-in-law, explained: "The awakening of the laboring classes after the French Revolution made the upper classes tremble. The parson no longer hunted or shot five days in the week, cleaning his fowling piece on the sixth prior to the preparation of a drowsy sermon, delivered on the seventh day to a sleeping congregation."

Religion had grown sluggish. The vicars looked, as Charles Lamb said, like so many mince pies. On the horizon there were new movements! The Quakers quaked—a dervish movement that, thank God, would challenge poverty and slavery; the Shakers shook, and simplified furniture, if nothing else; the Jumpers jumped headlong into a new century—over their depth, they would be heard from rarely; the Methodists were on the road to methodical salvations; and Protestants all protested; non-Conformists conforming to the Victorian age would be heard from again.

Holy Hannahs and Pious Papas

John Locke. The seventeenth-century philosopher, whose series about educating girls—that they should have a healthy and rational upbringing—bore fruit by the early nineteenth century.

Holy Hannah stood pat with a pen rough against the page and a profit in her pocket. Religion paid. When she and the other do-gooders of the nineteenth century entered drawing rooms, they were lionized along with God.

In the early nineteenth century began that religious transition which would culminate in a new god, the Victorian Papa . . . a truly religious presence and, we must say, a highly creative one. Behind every woman writer was Papa's shadow—for good or bad. Often he was an ingrate, or a profligate; often he was benign. It did not matter, he was there. A capital presence. (Could it be that the twentieth-century father, tied to business conventions rather than convention will produce no Brontë sisters?)

Hannah's father was there. He allowed her to talk. A misfortune, thought De Quincey, because later she talked about everything. Even that which obviously she did not understand, as he explained:

"Often, indeed, I had occasion to remember that cynical remark of Swift—that, after all, as respects mere learning, the most accomplished woman is hardly on a level with a schoolboy. In quoting this saying, I have restricted it so as to offer no offence to the female sex intellectually considered. Swift probably meant to undervalue women generally. Now I am well aware that they have their peculiar province. But that province does not extend to *learning* technically so called."

De Quincey was not against "brilliant" women; neither, said Swift, was he. But Hannah was truly abrasive. (So was De Quincey's mother, a friend of Hannah's, which perhaps explains a lot.) For the shy, retiring Dorothy Wordsworth, De Quincey felt only admiration. But one did not discover Mrs. More as, after walking for miles through the Lake Country, one would discover Dorothy and her brother William living almost in isolation on scanty food and great poetry. No, the problem seemed to have been that Mrs. Hannah More was omnipresent. One could hardly avoid her. She clung to the salons in those days the way sin clung to the air.

London air was even more polluted then than it is now, but in those days—those days we look back upon with supposed nostalgia—there was a deeper pollution, sin, and it was for the women to eradicate it.

It was their job, as one of the old mayors used to say about Boston snow: God brought it and God could take it away. It was the same with sin. Eve brought it; her daughters could take it away, or at least cope with it.

Hannah coped, and led the way for a sorority of soul sisters.

Women writers would take up their pens for the next hundred and fifty years to show the path to the good life, and in the process reform heaven. Some would be good, very good indeed, others would be so sanctimonious that their tracts and books would remain dusty and forgotten on old bookshelves.

Holy Hannah, all by herself, managed to write, beginning in the late eighteenth century, nearly all of the nineteenth-century New Testament. There they stand on the shelves: *Thoughts on Importance of the Manners of the Great to General Society,* followed in 1791 by *An Estimate of the Religion of the Fashionable World,* then by *Strictures on the Modern System of Female Education, Hints Towards Forming the Character of a Young Princess, Practical Piety, or the Influence of the Religion of the Heart on the Conduct of Life, Christian Morals,* then *Essay on the Character and Writings of St. Paul, Moral Sketches of Prevailing Opinions and Manners,*

Holy Hannahs and Pious Papas

Foreign and Domestic with Reflections on Prayer.
They came fast and quick from her pen, bound in gloom, printed in bile. One early twentieth-century writer who had been brought up on such books in the nineteenth century found that the only thing he could do was gather all those volumes which his mother had left him and bury them in the garden. They did not flower into any Garden of Eden.

But our Hannah had not always been so religious. At one point she had been extremely worldly. Hannah was the youngest of five sisters. Her father was ultrarespectable, a schoolmaster in Glouces- tershire. It was difficult even in the late eighteenth and nineteenth centuries to keep five girls down, and Hannah for one was not only witty and gifted but, for the time, also extremely comely. She had written the usual number of poems by the time she was fifteen. This would appear to be a critical age; so many of these women writers used their adolescence to express themselves on paper. By the time she was seventeen she had finished a pastoral drama. Then there is a certain period of mystery. She had attracted the attention of a wealthy neighboring landlord, and it seemed that they would make an appropriate marriage. No one knows what happened, but in an unusual transaction, the lover became what appears to be patron rather than bridegroom. In any case, for the rest of her life, she received from him two hundred pounds each year. One of her nineteenth-century biographers maintained "I think so well of her as to wish she had put it in an envelope and returned it with her compliments—year after year—if need were." Well, she didn't.

Thomas De Quincey tells a different story, crediting her with the receipt of four hundred pounds:

"However, there certainly *was* some story of a delicate nature (in the belief of Mrs. More's best friends). And I have received the following as the true fact from a clergyman of great respectability, and a fervent friend of Mrs. H. More's: The morning was fixed for the marriage; Mrs. More's friends were all in attendance, and, after breakfasting together, had actually proceeded to the church where, by appointment, they were to meet the bridegroom. They actually waited above an hour in the porch, looking out for his arrival, and as yet with no suspicion of his dishonourable intentions. At length a single horseman was seen approaching; he advanced to the steps, dismounted, and presented to Miss More a letter, in which the gentleman pleaded simply, as a reason for receding from his engagements, that he could not bring his mind, at the hour of crisis, to so solemn and so irrevocable a contract. He offered, however, to make such reparation as could be made, in a pecuniary sense, to Miss More; but this intention, if he really had it at the time, would, no doubt, have died away as soon as the immediate difficulty was overcome. The friends of Miss More, aware of that, pressed him vigorously, and would grant no delay. The sequel was that, rather than stand a prosecution, he settled on Miss More a handsome provision—my informant believes, not less, but rather more, than £400 per annum for life."

She found herself in London, where she inundated herself in the theater and became almost infatuated with the acting of the great Garrick. She managed to meet him, became intimate with his wife, and accordingly broke into that select little circle of Dr. Johnson's friends, Dr. Johnson's Wits. He rolled up to her one day like a lumbering bear and said, "I have heard that you have engaged in a useful and honorable employment of teaching young ladies." At that point Hannah, not having the stuffy manners that she was to acquire later, told him in an eager and delightful way, about the excitement of teaching the young and about her life with her sisters. "What," he cried, "five women live happily together in the same house! Bless me, I never was in Bristol, but I will come and see you. I'll come. I love you, all five."

One of the sisters, who had looked upon this little exchange, thought that the good doctor might eventually marry Hannah. Why not? He referred to her throughout the evening and throughout the rest of the time that he knew her as "my love" and "my kitten."

We have no pictures of Mrs. Hannah More in those early days, but her dedication was certainly not that of a little kitten. Quite the contrary. She almost attacked life as would a wildcat. In those early days the religious sermons and tracts for which she would remain known throughout the nineteenth century were still in the back of her mind. She was full of a more worldly life, and started to write for the theater. Garrick himself was her sponsor and her plays en-

"When I see an eloquent writer insinuating to every body who comes across her that she is the victim of her husband's carelessness and cruelty, while he never spoke in his own defence: when I see her violating all good taste by her obtrusiveness in society, and oppressing every body about her by her epicurean selfishnesses every day, while raising in print an eloquent cry on behalf of the oppressed; I feel, to the bottom of my heart, that she is the worst enemy of the cause she professes to plead. The best friends of that cause are women who are morally as well as intellectually competent to the most serious business of life, and who must be clearly seen to speak from conviction of the truth, and not from personal unhappiness. The best friends of the cause are the happy wives and the busy, cheerful, satisfied single women, who have no injuries of their own to avenge, and no painful vacuity or mortification to relieve. The best advocates are yet to come,—in the persons of women who are obtaining access to real social business,—the female physicians and other professors in America, the women of business and the female artists of France; and the hospital administrators, the nurses, the educators and substantially successful authors of our own country. Often as I am appealed to to speak, or otherwise assist in the promotion of the cause of Woman, my answer is always the same:—that women, like men, can obtain whatever they show themselves fit for. Let them be educated,—let their powers be cultivated to the extent for which the means are already provided, and all that is wanted or ought to be desired will follow of course. Whatever a woman proves herself able to do, society will be thankful to see her do,—just as if she were a man." Harriet Martineau's *Autobiographical Memoir* Edited by Maria Weston Chapman

The Scholastic Hen and her Chickens. Mifs Thimblebee loquitur. "Turn your heads the other way my dears, for here are two horridly handsome Officers coming." Girls' schools were consistently caricatured throughout the nineteenth century. Print from a drawing by George Cruikshank.

chanted the audience. Later Hannah would turn her back on the theater just as she did on idle young women, loose conversation and playing cards. But until the death of Garrick she enjoyed her worldliness to capacity.

But now she would start with what she knew—education—education for women.

The dawn of the eighteenth century had introduced a period that would later be recreated in the novels of Jane Austen, Maria Edgeworth, Mrs. Gaskell and even George Eliot. It was a new age with a new spirit, which perhaps accounted in part for the fact that women would burst forth in a geyser of writing. It was an age that would introduce new educational theories and an age in which for the first time children were reared something like children rather than the minute devils of the previous century.

Calvinism had perpetrated the theory that all children were basically evil. Cruelty, of course, existed everywhere. Now parents were beginning to think of their children as flesh and blood, not young flesh and blood, but at least as duplicates of themselves. For the first time, the forms of address found in so many Victorian novels that were to have such an effect on the Victorian age, Mama and Papa, were used. Up until that time, Sir or Madam was the only way a child addressed a parent. No child sat down in a parent's presence, and the kindest touch a daughter received was only, perhaps, a cursory pat on the head when she knelt down to receive a blessing.

For a while in the early eighteenth century there was a reaction, and children were "almost superindulged" the social historians of the time maintained. They screamed, ate what they chose, and drank as did their parents to "the verge of intoxication." They lived completely inside the house. Sports were forbidden, their clothes were tight and their bodies were pressed into shape by strange devices that supposedly would either make them grow straight or

March—Tossing the Pancake. When the woman's place was in the home—and she had at least two cooks to help her. Print from a drawing by George Cruikshank.

keep them well. These devices were still occasionally used in the latter part of the nineteenth century—Edith Sitwell suffered from one to improve her posture, while other women writers have told us of the constricting harnesses that braced them to meet the world. But in the early nineteenth century, Mrs. Sherwood reminds us, the fashion was for girls "to wear iron collars around the neck with backboards strapped over the shoulders. To one of these I was subjected from my sixth to my thirteenth year. I generally did all my lessons standing in stocks with the same collar around my neck. It was put on in the morning and taken off late in the evening. And it was Latin I had to study. At the same time, I had the plainest possible food—dry bread and cold milk were my principal food, and I never sat on a chair in my mother's presence."

Families were large and expendable. The mother of John Wesley, the great theologian, and herself a remarkable woman, had nineteen children. She did not find this too outstanding seeing that her own mother had had twenty-four. But Susanna Wesley, who could find little love for them all, at least found it obligatory to do her duty and to "educate" them. None of the children, she said, were taught to read until they were five years old. A child was allowed one day to learn his letters and each of them in that time did know all the letters, "except Molly and Nancy, who were a day and a half before they knew them perfectly, for which I thought them very dull."

The memoirs and letters of the daughters of the large families of the eighteenth and early nineteenth centuries sound always the same. "I could not please my mother, do what I would," wrote Susan Sibbald. Only her governess loved her, and when Swift remarked upon the education of women, he complained that those very governesses were generally the worst who could be obtained for money.

In the early nineteenth century the girl-child needed only to write, to read, and then only in the better households. She must know some housekeeping, a little cooking and the distilling of the endless medications and essences and cosmetics that were needed in the home. One thing she was always permitted, indeed required to learn, was dancing. Dancing was the high art of the period; needlework was well behind.

Miss Edgeworth's House. "It seems no very easy task to write books for children" said Maria Edgeworth, whose pietistic novels flooded nineteenth-century nurseries.

Some voices had cried out. Addison and Steele, of the *Spectator* papers, for example, but it took a while for the desire for better education to be of any significance. Then women were educated because the men wanted them to be. As the young gallant, for example, began to visit the Continent he found women who had a tradition of discussing the arts, who knew how to paint, who knew something of current events. The British mothers, not allowing their sons to take up European "cultured whores," put on some pressure for education. A girl must know "something" if she were to get a husband; the ones with "accomplishments" were those who were getting married earlier. Of course, one could be *too* accomplished. There were women, for example, getting talked about, who knew too much Latin and Greek. Other young women might have a famous relative like Lady Mary Wortley Montagu who exploded into the social and public eye with more learning than necessary and less morals. She set a bad example for those who came after her, including her grandaughter, who, with the terrible vision of Lady Mary still disturbing the family, was allowed hardly any education at all.

Madame Recamier whose early nineteenth century political and literary salon was the most famous in Europe. Maria Edgeworth wrote in November 1802, "We saw beauty, wealth, fashion, luxury—in a word a crowd. She herself is a delicious woman, living in the midst of a group of adorers and flatters, in an atmosphere in which wealth and taste are combined and modern art made more beautiful by ancient art. The centre in which she moves is a strange medley of commercial men and poets, philosophers and parvenus of English, French, Portugese and Brazilian nationalities." From an engraving, *Century Magazine* 1891.

The women who had succeeded in self-education were reluctant to admit their abilities. They always underplayed it. "A woman's learning," said the remarkable Elizabeth Smith, who had nine languages under her belt, "is like the fine clothes of an upstart who is anxious to exhibit all the world the riches so unexpectedly acquired."

Instead, social niceties were played to the hilt. "Girls of ten and eleven years of age keep their select companies and treat them with as much solemnity and expense as their parents do with their own acquaintance. This prevails not only in the court but in the city. There is as much fuss made at some houses against such a Miss or that such a Miss comes to visit the daughter, as if a Duchess was expected. When the visit is returned, she must be dressed up to the height of the mode and some new thing or other is always wanted; not to mention Top-Knots, Gloves, Coach hire and other avoidable expenses." (*The English Child in the Eighteenth Century,* Rosamond Bayne-Powell.) This world would be satirized in the pages of Fanny Burney and Jane Austen, but in those novels you will find almost nothing of a girl's schooling, despite the fact that the authors were extraordinary, even as children.

Despite the fact that Hannah was a friend of Fanny Burney's, she was particularly against novels which were the vehicles of "vice and infidelity." A friend of innumerable women poets of the day, she was also against poetry.

"Poetry!" she exclaimed, "Oh! as to poetry, I forswore *that* and think everyone else should forswear it, together with pink ribbons."

Shakespeare was the exception—if he *were* read correctly—and through that precept she made the acquaintance of the extraordinary Bowdler family who will live forever at least in the pages of dictionaries:

Bowdlerize: to expurgate prudishly (from Thomas Bowdler who in 1818 published an expurgated edition of Shakespeare).

The dictionaries are wrong—or rather right and wrong. Thomas Bowdler *did* publish the edition, but the dirty work was done by his sister Harriet. And behind her shoulder stood *her* papa.

Hannah More's father had been more or less put down by his five rambunctious daughters, but other papas of the period were to be less challenged. True, Jane Austen's father had introduced novel reading into the household. It was from him she first acquired her taste for that wicked form of delight, but the Austens were a fairly emancipated household.

The extraordinary Bowdler household was far different. There the evening pattern was the same, Papa standing before the hearth reading the Bible, but with a sneaking preference for Shakespeare. The good British squire read superbly. His son was to say, "In the perfection of reading, few men were equal to my father, and such were his good tastes, his delicacy and his prompt discretion that his family listened with delight to *Lear, Hamlet* and *Othello* without

David Garrick, who encouraged Hannah More to write plays. Only after his death did she become a major tractarian.

knowing that those matchless tragedies contain words or expressions improper to be pronounced and without having any reason to suspect that any parts of the plays had been omitted by the circumspect and judicious readers." In other words the good squire censored his books as he went along. No Doll Tearsheet, for example, was ever exposed by *his* voice in that drawing room.

Mary Ann Lamb. "She tumbled," said her brother, "early, by accident or design, into a spacious closet of good old English reading. Had I twenty girls, they should be brought up exactly in this fashion. I know not whether their chance in wedlock might not be diminished by it; but I can answer for it that it makes (if the worst comes to the worst) most incomparable old maids."

Holy Hannahs and Pious Papas

Delicacy and sensibility were the guiding factors of a good reader and it soon occurred to the family, having been brought up on such expurgated materials, that they should give the benefit of their higher principles to the world. Squire Bowdler's children were determined to carry on his great work. Jane, the eldest, constantly making note of the fact in her letters that "continued watchfulness must restrain the freedom of conversation," lived painfully and died young. Her poems—and a pretty poor collection of them they are too—entitled *Poems and Essays by a Lady Lately Deceased 1786,* were not published until after her death. In that family, only a lady lately deceased would put her name on any book.

Her brother John had one of those delightful early nineteenth-century habits of giving advice where no advice was wanted. He had composed a form letter which he sent out to all his friends upon the occasion of any marriage of a daughter. At that point John was unmarried, but it did not bother him. He knew all the details of what made a woman a good wife and explained the exquisite need for sensibility and delicacy. "Above all," he said, "avoid everything which has the least tendancy to indelicacy or indecorum. Few women have any idea how men are disgusted by the slightest approach to these in any female. By attending to the nursery or sickbed women are apt to acquire a habit of conversing on such subjects in language in which men of some delicacy are shocked at." One wonders just exactly what the early nineteenth-century woman was saying to her child.

John published the usual pamphlets that seemed to spring from everybody's pen at that period and occasional poems which he entitled "Poems Divine and Moral." In his preface he preened himself like a pious peacock. "My object was not to produce a collection of elegant poetry, but to do good." His poetry was certainly not elegant and one could hardly believe it did any good, but it made John feel better. It was his sister Harriet, however, who was the best do-gooder of all. Harriet was a true bluestocking. In one of the innumerable diaries of the period, we catch more than a frightening glimpse of her. On Thursday, writes Sir Gilbert Elliott, "I dined at Mundy's with Mrs. Galley etc., and a Miss Bowdler. She is, I believe a Bluestocking, but with the color of that part of her dress it must be mere conjecture, as you will easily believe when I tell you that she said she never looked at the opera dancers but always kept her eyes shut the whole time. And when I asked her why, she said it was so indelicate she could not bear to look." It was Harriet who had the glorious idea that the entire family should work upon a cleaned-up Shakespeare. That wonderful version of the bloodless Bard that they had inherited from pious Papa should be given to the world so that the words of the master would sully no one.

It was a period of rapidly changing values. A decade or two before had been one of wild abandon, when language went free and easy; now, the old aristocratic women said, you couldn't even spit out the window without antagonizing a peer. The language of the old dowagers had been crusty and would have done justice to a Grenadier Guard, but now all was changing. There was an emerging lower class and they, by God, would be protected from the wit of the aristocracy, from the language of the rakes. *Family Shakespeare,* a nice wholesome approach to a glorious Elizabethan, was the result.

Harriet did most of the work. How she was able to look at some of those indelicate words in Shakespeare so that she might be able to cut them is difficult to understand, but perhaps with her infinite delicacy and superb sensibility she forced herself to a kind of pious voyeurism. Not only did she and her brother Thomas eliminate sex from Shakespeare, wherever possible they eliminated God. It was a time when it was extremely impolite to take God's name in vain. Harriet must have divided her time with a kind of sanctimonious schizophrenia between writing a fabulously successful book, entitled *Sermons on the Doctrines and Duties of Christianity* and her expurgation of Shakespeare. When the book finally appeared, however, it appeared with her brother's name on it. Certainly she would have nothing to do with putting her name on any such book, because even in its most expurgated form Shakespeare was remarkably wicked. Her brother saw no reason to give her credit when credit she did not want, so it was not until long after her death that she was discovered to have had such a remarkable literary past.

Women would often play a role throughout the nineteenth century expurgating or adapting the classics for children. It even fell

Charles Lamb. "Gentle," who lived all his life with his sister Mary in a "sort of double singleness."

to the lot of the delightful Mary Lamb. There was a great deal obviously that Mary felt should be expurgated from her own life. She was, as that wise Noel Perrin said, a literary Lizzie Borden. There is no better description. In a fit of frenzy she killed her mother and was to live with her own insanity on and off throughout the rest of her life—and with her brother, one of the most delightful of all writers, Charles Lamb.

Charles, of course, had his difficulties. The nineteenth-century father had his foibles; the nineteenth-century brother often had his shortcomings. Always better educated than his sister, he was prey to less sensibility and more to the alarming realities of life. For Thomas De Quincey it was laudanum and ladies of the street, all good hearted, said Tom, and less pretentious than the *new* ladies of learning; for others it would be the gambling tables; for Branwell Brontë it would be brandy; and for Charles Lamb it was any cup that cheered.

"Charles was drunk last night and drunk the night before," Mary Lamb wrote to her friend Sarah. It was at the Godwin's and Godwin, as a rule, was not too generous with his liquor.

And although Charles staggered home, full of gin and water and snuff at twelve, he spent the rest of the night with Henry Robinson who drank only cold water leaving Charles drinking his inevitable gin. At the Burney's (the Lambs always traveled in rather

103

Dove Cottage About 1805. Not only fathers but often brothers overwhelmed women writers. Dorothy Wordsworth and her brother William lived in Dove Cottage in "perfect happiness" during the period that William wrote some of his greatest poems. Dorothy nursed him, fed him, and played that role that has so often been woman's—the perfect muse.

fashionable circles, despite their own indigent circumstances), Mrs. Burney presented Charles first with rum, then with champagne, then two bottles of her best currant wine. Charles staggered home again, this time supported by Mary.

"Poor fellow," said Mary, "he was so easily tempted." It meant, of course, that they were often in need of funds. True, Charles had his position in East India House, but one often wondered for how long. Hadn't he regaled Mary with the conversation he had with his employer that very morning? When he was asked why he always came late, hadn't he answered: "But sir, I always leave early!"

Hadn't Charles written that superb piece on "Poor Relations" about which London was agog; the one that pointed out that there was nothing so poor as a spinster sister? No education unless, as Mary said, one fell into that superb closet of learning, a small library of good books on the shelf. Mary had read Mary Wollstonecraft Godwin's *Vindication of the Rights of Women* as early as 1792. She was particularly struck by the comment, "If women be not prepared by education to be the companion of man, she will stop the progress

Elizabeth Fry, the great Quaker reformer and writer. A wife, the mother of twelve children, she still found time for pioneer work in prison reform. In 1826 she infiltrated Newgate Prison: a warren for women and children (all children under seven accompanied their mothers to prison. No clothing was supplied; no bedding). The reforms she instigated at Newgate were followed by her international efforts. From an engraving after the painting by C. K. Leslie, R. A.

of knowledge, for truth must be common to all."

Hannah More had read the same comment and found it ridiculous. Knowledge might make women as difficult as men and then where would the world be?

Mary brooded about the fact that she was a poor relation and finally wrote a remarkably pioneering piece for the *British Lady's Magazine* on "Needlework." She was the first writer to consider woman's work in the home in terms of that new phrase, "political economy." Could not she said, woman's work in the home be paid for? Needlework, for example, was a household duty—as every writing woman in the nineteenth century was to know. "Would it not" said Mary, "prove an incalculable addition to general happiness and the domestic comfort of both sexes, if needlework were never practiced except for renumeration?" "Real business," she continued "and real leisure make up the portions of men's time whereas women in the home have little real leisure, which may be one reason some are so dull and unattractive to their husbands."

It is a question still unanswered today. Even Charles did not get the significance of the article. Mary made the supper and he continued his evenings of wit.

She tried again. Approached by the Godwins she decided to undertake with Charles, and for an attractive fee, *Tales of Shakespeare.*

O, Those Extraordinary Women

Mary and Charles Lamb's *Tales of Shakespeare*, still delightful today, was in no sense bowdlerized. Mary and Charles simply rewrote Shakespeare, in a delightful fashion, to be attractive to children. Once again Mary was given little credit. She chose, one could understand well enough, to rewrite the comedies, her brother the tragedies. But she wrote nearly a third more of the book than Charles.

Plays, as such, were a dangerous undertaking. There was more wickedness on the stage than was appearing currently in books and the bowdlerization that went on with written plays on the stage was only equaled by the fact that for once women were coming forward and writing copiously for the strolling players. But all of their writings were of high morality and if, like Hannah More, they abandoned the theater, they then devoted themselves to works of piety. Mrs. Barbauld, Mrs. Inchbald are only old theater announcements today. Everyone, of course, who could afford it went to the theater. The papas seemed to enjoy it most.

And then there was papa again. Maria Edgeworth's father, Richard Lovell Edgeworth, for instance, who prances in and out of literary history with a voice as booming as an actor. Those early nineteenth-century fathers were indeed actors. They cast themselves in the main role and set their players around them. Occasionally, very occasionally, they produced a star. Maria Edgeworth was one. Papa certainly had planned to do the same with his son, but Maria had come first. The son who came afterward was brought up by the laws of Rousseau and hadn't turned out quite too well. The boy from the beginning had been dressed in jackets and trousers that left arms and legs bare. He was allowed to run where he pleased. He was a noble savage, for indeed the boy was growing up in Ascendancy Ireland and that could be very savage indeed. In a few years the old commentators said, "Edgeworth found that the scheme had succeeded completely so far as related to the youth's health, strength and agility were concerned, but the state of his mind induced some perplexity. He had all the virtues that are found in the heart of the savage. He was quick to feel, generous, but he knew not what it was to obey. It was impossible to induce him to do anything that he did not please or prevent him from doing anything that he did please. Under the former head, learning even of the lowest description was never included. This child of nature grew up perfectly ungovernable and never could or would apply to anything. There remained no alternative but to allow him to follow his own inclination of going to sea." That's the last ever heard of him. Perhaps the son was simply delighted to sail away from the sound of his father's voice.

Not so Maria. She thrived on it. She began to scribble as a child with her father standing at her shoulder. It was a position that she preferred to take throughout the rest of her life. She never wrote far away from him. She had him read and reread everything she had written and when he died her pen stopped. Maria too was a do-gooder, but it was a difficult challenge for anybody who had grown up as she had in England until she was thirteen and then moved to one of those great houses (as they were called in Ireland) not to be a little racy. Naturally enough her first piece of writing, when she was very young, was written with her father. "It was the happy experience of this," she said, "and my consequent reliance on his ability, position and perfect truth that relieved me from the vacillation and anxiety to which I was so much subject that I am sure I should not have written or finished anything without his support. He inspired in my mind a degree of hope and confidence essential on the first instance to the full expression of the mental powers necessary to ensure perseverance in any occupation." (*Literary History of England 1790–1825*, Margaret Oliphant.)

Maria was remarkably persistent. *Castle Rackrent*, hardly a "do-gooding" book, is one of the most exciting of all novels of the Ascendancy, but after a few years her books became more "moral." More devout, she became pious, or at least proper. Her fame was such that Byron was to complain that Madame de Staël had been the lion of London one year, he the lion the next year and quiet Maria was the presently reigning queen. She never acted like one. A simple and retiring Irish woman, certainly more Irish than British, she loved Edgeworthtown, her home, Papa, and a little less, God. A trinity of belief that would rule many a woman writer from then on.

Facsimile of Page of Emily Brontë's Diary

5

THE MOOR WAS MIGHTIER THAN THE MEN
THE BROODING BRONTËS

We had a vague impression that authoresses are liable to be looked on with prejudice.

Charlotte Brontë

The mind knew but did not feel its existence. It was away. It had launched on a distant voyage—haply it was nearing the shores of some far and unknown Island under whose cliffs no bark had ever cast anchor. In other words a long tale was perhaps evolving itself in my mind.

Charlotte Brontë's schoolgirl diary

Literature cannot be the business of a woman's life and it ought not to be.

Robert Southey to Charlotte Brontë, 1837

WE had very early cherished the dream of one day becoming authors. This dream, never relinquished even when distance divided and absorbing tasks occupied us, now suddenly acquired strength and consistancy: it took the character of a resolve. We agreed to arrange a small selection of our poems, and, if possible, get them printed. Averse to personal publicity we veiled our names under those of Currer, Ellis and Acton Bell; the ambiguous choice being dictated by a sort of conscientious scruple at assuming Christian names, positively masculine, while we did not like to declare ourselves women, because—without at that time suspecting that our mode of writing and thinking was not what is called 'feminine'—we had a vague impression that authoresses are liable to be looked on with prejudice: we had noticed how critics sometimes used for their justisement the weapon of personality and for their reward a flattery which is not true praise."

For the young Brontës, the compulsion to write had been overwhelming from their youth. It is not difficult to see why: their own story was one of overwhelming power and tragedy and the best place to reconstruct it is through those vital extraordinary pages of their own contemporary, Elizabeth Gaskell, herself a novelist, who wrote one of the greatest psychological biographies of her period and one that still lives as vividly as its characters, *The Life of Charlotte Brontë.*

Although most of the area around Haworth parsonage has not changed, the parsonage itself has. Mrs. Gaskell's pages evoke the geography and the heavy, dark terror of the landscape that permeates the Brontë sisters' writings. We can almost see Mrs. Gaskell trudging up there on her visit to Charlotte, long after Anne, Branwell and Emily were dead, passing over tolerably level ground, looking at the distant hills, listening to the Beck, a small stream flowing

Haworth Parsonage and Graveyard. Nineteenth-century print.

through the meadows, alive not only to the countryside, but to the factories, too, built on the banks of the water.

She can smell the smoke from the new industries of Yorkshire as well as the rich loam of the soil of the valley. A country woman herself, she climbs the road towards Haworth, watching the vegetation become poorer, trees disappearing, bushes and shrubs turning into moorland. Even the land looks starved, with hungry-looking green oats.

Haworth itself one can see in the distance two miles before one arrives; it stands on the side of a steep hill with the dun and purple moors all around it. The hills seem wavelike, sinuous, crowned with the wild, bleak moor.

The hills and moors give almost two different impressions: "Grand, from the ideas of solitude and loneliness which they suggest or oppressive from the feeling which they give of being pent-up by some monotonous and illimitable barrier, according to the mood of mind in which the spectator may be." (*The Life of Charlotte Brontë,* Elizabeth Gaskell.)

111

The parsonage consisted of a gray stone house, two storeys high, its roof securely protected because of the winds that always blew in from the moor. It had four rooms on each floor, and small old-fashioned window panes that, when Charlotte was still alive, glittered like glass due to her impeccable housekeeping. Above the church is the graveyard "terribly full of upright tombstones." In her remarkable ability to wring the heart and to make a valid biography, Mrs. Gaskell then resorts to a painful device, the shattering record of tombstones:

HERE

LIE THE REMAINS OF

MARIA BRONTË, WIFE

OF THE

REV. P. BRONTE, A.B., MINISTER OF HAWORTH.

HER SOUL

DEPARTED TO THE SAVIOUR, SEPT. 15TH, 1821,

IN THE 39TH YEAR OF HER AGE.

"Be ye also ready: for in such an hour as ye think not the Son of Man cometh."—Matthew xxiv. 44.

ALSO HERE LIE THE REMAINS OF

MARIA BRONTË, DAUGHTER OF THE AFORESAID;

SHE DIED ON THE

6TH OF MAY, 1825, IN THE 12TH YEAR OF HER AGE,

AND OF

ELIZABETH BRONTË, HER SISTER,

WHO DIED JUNE 15TH, 1825, IN THE 11TH YEAR OF HER AGE

"Verily I say unto you, Except ye be converted, and become as little children, ye shall not enter into the kingdom of heaven."—Matthew xviii. 3.

HERE ALSO LIE THE REMAINS OF

PATRICK BRANWELL BRONTË,

WHO DIED SEPT. 24TH, 1848, AGED 30 YEARS.

AND OF

EMILY JANE BRONTË,

WHO DIED DEC. 19TH, 1848, AGED 29 YEARS,

SON AND DAUGHTER OF THE

REV. P. BRONTE, INCUMBENT

The Moor Was Mightier Than The Men

THIS STONE IS ALSO DEDICATED TO THE
MEMORY OF ANNE BRONTË,
YOUNGEST DAUGHTER OF THE REV. P. BRONTE, A.B.
SHE DIED, AGED 27 YEARS, MAY 28TH, 1849,
AND WAS BURIED AT THE OLD CHURCH, SCARBORO'.

One tablet is a little removed. "After the record of Anne's death, there is room for no other." But one more of that generation—the last of that nursery of six little motherless children—was yet to follow, before the survivor, the childless and widowed father, found his rest. On another tablet, below the first, the following record has been added to that mournful list:

ADJOINING LIE THE REMAINS OF
CHARLOTTE, WIFE
OF THE
REV. ARTHUR BELL NICHOLLS, A.B.,
AND DAUGHTER OF THE REV. P. BRONTE, A.B., INCUMBENT.
SHE DIED MARCH 31ST, 1855, IN THE 39TH
YEAR OF HER AGE.

The Brontës are all—except Anne—buried in the family vault in the parish church and today a simple brass plate in the flagstone floor of the church marks their final resting place.

These are the sparse statistics of a turbulent family of genius, of passion, of a remarkable dedication to the written word.

When their mother died the children found themselves bound to one another with a remarkable cord of dependence and fantasy. They would make their own world, if only on paper. Outside were the moors, ever compelling; inside, despite their bereavement, were two persons who were to nurture their genius. One, the lonely tyrannical father, the vicar of the parish church, the Reverend Patrick Brontë, "Dear Papa." Papa introduced to them his own fabulous stories and conversations; he indulged them with books and magazines, and regaled them with his bitter Irish black humor. The other creative presence was the exciting Yorkshire woman, the servant of all work, Tabby, who brought in stories from the outside, related the strange tales of the moor, but who was never above interrupting the girls at their literary endeavors to get them to peel the potatoes.

The girls peeled and wrote, starting almost as babes, scratching a minute script in tiny notebooks, establishing their own world, romantic, pictorial, infinitely convoluted. They evolved some literary characters originally based on some wooden soldiers that had been given Branwell Brontë as a boy. The children pretended that they each lived on a large island and, isolated as they were both in fact and in fantasy, they were indeed islands on the moor.

In time the girls were shipped away from the moor to go to school. We know that school—just a few scenes about it on the television screen can turn *Jane Eyre* into a horror story. But the truth seems to have been even worse than the cinematic horrors.

It was a good school for its day; even the indomitable Mrs. Hannah More was on its board. But, while Holy Hannah was a great one for examining the school curriculum, she ignored the kitchen which would produce an outbreak of typhoid; she ignored the dark, damp rooms that would encourage tuberculosis.

Cowan's Bridge School, immortalized by Charlotte Brontë in *Jane Eyre* as Lowood, was a group of small cottages, unsanitary, poorly lit, with narrow, tortuous passageways and odors that lingered throughout the building. The smells were rarely of good food; burnt oatmeal porridge for breakfast, oatcake for those who "required luncheon" (and it was better if they didn't), with perhaps a little boiled beef. At five o'clock bread and milk for the youngest, and just one piece of bread for the older children. Beef, when it was served, was tainted, milk was "bingy" (the old country word for something far worse than sour and curdled milk), and the meals culminated in a Saturday-night dinner which consisted of leftovers of all the rancid food from the week. The children starved, they were not in good health to begin with, and there was the further abuse of poor sleeping quarters, terrible discipline and the quick tempers of the teachers. The girls longed for the moors.

Maria and Elizabeth "sickened" and died. Hand in hand, Charlotte and Emily returned home, Emily just seven, turned for comfort to her baby sister, Anne; Charlotte, to her brother, Branwell. The two pairs would vie with each other in their childish writings.

The Brontë Sisters, Anne (left), Emily and Charlotte (right). Portrait by Branwell Brontë. Courtesy, National Portrait Gallery, London.

No one turned to Miss Branwell, the children's aunt, who plagued them with the sorry state of their souls, and also of their sheets. The girls sewed sheets until their fingers were sore; Branwell was exempt of course.

Perhaps they should try another school. Papa was ill; what would the girls do if he were to die? They must have a livelihood; they must have schooling. Emily was rarely able to take the structures of schooling: she panicked when away from the moor, from her secret world of fantasy, from writing. Charlotte was of sterner stuff. She was a model student allowing herself little recreation. She punished herself in the one way she could; she would not allow herself to write. None of the friends she made at school realized how deeply she required creative expression. Roe Head school was followed by schooling on the Continent where she fell in love with her "professor." But in the outside world no one encouraged her to write. Why should she? Women didn't.

Even the man she loved did not understand. She wrote to M. Heger:

There is nothing I fear so much as idleness, the want of occupation . . . the lethargy of the faculties. . . . I should not know this lethargy if I could write. Formerly I spent whole days and weeks and months in writing. . . . But that cannot be—it is not to be thought of. The career of letters is closed to me—only that of teaching is open. It does not offer the same attractions, never mind, I shall enter it.

She had written to Poet Laureate Robert Southey earlier. It had taken great nerve for a shy, retiring girl to approach such an august figure and she awaited his reply eagerly. When it came she was crestfallen:

The Clergy Daughters' School, Cowan Bridge, engraving of 1824 by O. Jewitt of Derby.

Haworth Church. From *Scribner's Monthly,* 1871.

> . . . I, who have made literature my profession and devoted my life to it . . . think myself, nevertheless, bound in duty to caution every young man who applies as an aspirant to me for encouragement and advice against taking so perilous a course. You will say that a woman has no need of such caution; there can be no peril in it for her. In a certain sense this is true; but there is a danger of which I would, with all kindness and all earnestness, warn you. The day dreams in which you habitually indulge are likely to induce a distempered state of mind and, in proportion as all the ordinary uses of the world seem to you flat and unprofitable, you will be unfitted for them without becoming fitted for anything else. Literature cannot be the business of a woman's life, and it ought not to be. The more she is engaged in her proper duties, the less leisure will she have for it, even as an accomplishment and a recreation. . . .

Proper duties! But what were they? She knew she had a gift. Perhaps she had a duty to that gift, too. No, she would put the thought away, and start a school with her sisters. The plan was a disaster.

Then suddenly she made a discovery. Emily, the wild one who was always to ignore proper duties, was writing still and magnificently. The creative floodgates were reopened.

O, *Those Extraordinary Women*

There is no simple answer as to what is creativity—certainly it seems to be a gift distributed almost indiscriminately. Every writer, man or woman, must cope with the depressions, emotional upheavals, lassitude (writing is very difficult, said Gertrude Stein, one must spend so much time doing nothing), the false elation and the letdown. Professionalism is the ability to sustain such emotions for a long period of time; genius, on the other hand, is as demonic as Emily Bronte's landscape. Thoroughly professional in her work, her *Wuthering Heights,* as the twentieth-century critics have realized, is a well-controlled novel, absolutely pioneering the romantic novel. But off paper, Emily, as Charlotte said, was simply wild.

With extraordinary professionalism for one so inexperienced, Charlotte now took the family literary affairs in hand. Branwell was forgotten; that brilliant boy, equally creative as his sisters, had burned himself out. There would be endless talk about being an artist—but instead he would roam the streets of London barely able to enter the doors of the art school that was to lead him to a final career. He never enrolled, the competition was too keen. The nineteenth-century father who was often a creative presence for a talented girl could be a lodestone to a talented boy.

"You ask about Branwell," Charlotte wrote to one of her favorite schoolmistresses, "he never thinks of seeking employment, and I begin to fear that he has rendered himself incapable of filling any respectable station in life; besides if money were at his disposal, he would use it only to his own injury; the faculty of self-government is, I fear almost destroyed in him. You ask if I do not think men are strange beings? I do, indeed. I have often thought so; and I think, too, that the mode of bringing them up is strange; they are not sufficiently guarded from temptation. Girls are protected as if they were something very frail or silly indeed, while boys are turned loose on the world as if they, of all beings in existence, were the wisest and least able to be led astray."

Charlotte had gone into the world, found and lost love, trained herself for hard work, expected little and, if she longed for more, expressed it only in her novels. One can feel in her letters that she even blamed herself for not protecting Branwell more. Was not that one of her "proper duties"? But she had so many of them now, worrying over Papa with his cataracts, worrying over the affairs of the household with money always in painfully short supply, worrying over the health of both Anne and Emily, who, despite their creative energy—almost fiercely burning energy fired by the tuberculosis that would claim them—seemed at times far too tired. There was hardly time to worry about Branwell, but he made his presence known, too often and too well. Pieces of copper found their way into his pocket; every pub became his pulpit. Papa slept with him now, after his last attempt to burn the curtains in his room. Poor Papa. Poor Branwell. But for Charlotte there was no time for self-pity. There were books to be written and published.

She learned all she could about type and bindings, advertising and promotion. The Brontës would have to pay, of course, for the publication of their poetry. They had no great list of subscribers, as did Fanny Burney or Hannah More. They were unknown Yorkshire girls with no connections; no knowledge of fashionable literary London (often it was the same because this was the heyday of the "society novel," treacly trash with only the flavor of gossip to make it platable).

Even obtaining writing paper was difficult. An old tradesman of the villlage remembered how the sisters in their old-fashioned clothes used to come to his old shop for half a ream of paper, all they could afford, and how often he obtained it for them, walking in the rain to the next village because he could not stand the look of disappointment in their faces.

Charlotte wasted many such sheets before she was able to find any publisher even vaguely interested in taking on the manuscript. She pursued the task as she had pursued most of her tasks with a hard-headed dedication. Her sister Anne gave her a little support; Emily gave her practically none. In fact Emily had to be persuaded to even *consider* any publication at all; she, for one, was already brooding about a far more obssessive reality—the creation of *Wuthering Heights*. Emily had turned her back, if only temporarily, on her own intense morbidity that had resulted in one of the poems which had so attracted Charlotte:

> . . . Let Grief distract the sufferer's breast,
> And Night obscure his way;

They hasten him to endless rest,
And everlasting day.
To Thee the world is like a tomb,
A desert's naked shore;
To us, in unimagined bloom
It brightens more and more.

And could we lift the veil and give
One brief glimpse to thine eye
Thou woulds't rejoice for those that live,
Because they live to die.

. . . Three Gods within this little frame
Are warring night and day.
Heaven could not hold them all, and yet
They all are held in me
And must be mine till I forget
My present entity.

O for the time when in my breast
Their struggles will be o'er;
O for the day when I shall rest,
And never suffer more!

Yet all three, Charlotte, Emily and Anne, found it exhilarating to go through all their old poetry, to select, discuss with each other, comment, collate, and dream—because it seemed only a dream—so that their voices could even be heard beyond the confines of the parsonage. As they reworked them, the pain of their early years, the family's almost delicate obsession with death, its rendezvous with immortality became a thing apart. Their affection, awe, and belief in the printed word was such, and of such long standing, that even Emily's reluctance to publish was overcome. Imagine a printed book! One that could be held in the hand.

Finally the opportunity came. Charlotte found a religious publisher (all three girls would later be attacked for the sensuality of their writing as well as their ambiguity to religion—Miss Branwell's sense of sin was enough to burden anyone's Christian ardor) and her letter was sent off:

The Moor Was Mightier Than The Men

GENTLEMEN,—Since you agree to undertake the publication of the work respecting which I applied to you, I should wish now to know, as soon as possible, the cost of paper and printing. I will then send the necessary remittance, together with the manuscript. I should like it to be printed in one octavo volume, of the same quality of paper and size of type as Moxon's last edition of Wordsworth. The poems will occupy, I should think, from 200 to 250 pages. They are not the production of a clergyman, nor are they exclusively of a religious character; but I presume these circumstances will be immaterial. It will, perhaps, be necessary that you should see the manuscript, in order to calculate accurately the expense of publication; in that case I will send it immediately. I should like, however, previously, to have some idea of the probable cost; and if, from what I have said, you can make a rough calculation on the subject, I should be greatly obliged to you.

She added:

"You will perceive that the poems are the work of three persons—relatives—their pieces are distinguished by their respective signatures." She gave instructions that in further correspondence all contact should be in care of Miss Brontë, Haworth Parsonage, who was acting as agent for Currer, Ellis and Acton Bell, each girl having chosen a nom de plume that began with her first initial. Currer Bell found her own poetry poor—within two years she would be the famous writer of *Jane Eyre* and would disown her early "rhymes"; with Anne's weaker efforts she was kind, but for Emily's poetry, she was a tigress. She knew her sister had a remarkable talent. Although Emily scorned her own work, Charlotte insisted, "I know no woman that ever lived that ever wrote such poetry before."

One can only think of what such family support would have meant to Emily Dickinson, writing away as a recluse in her own poetic kingdom across the sea.

The Brontës lead, said their nineteenth-century biographers, quiet lives—but this period of their lives was hardly quiet. Their excitement as the page proofs came in gave them their first taste of printer's ink—a reeling experience for any author—and allowed them temporarily to put aside their anxiety about Branwell who was becoming as inconsistent in his behavior as any Heathcliff or Rochester. He now roamed the village, dissolute and depressed,

still flourish bright as ever I am at present
writing a work on the First Wars - Anne has
been writing some articles on this and a book
by Henry Sophona - We intend sticking firm by
the rascals as long as they delight us which
I am glad to say they do at present - I should
have mentioned that last summer the school
scheme was revived in full vigour - we had pro-
spectuses printed, dispatched letters to all acquaintances
imparting our plans and did our little all - but
it was found no go - now I don't desire a school
at all and none of us have any great longing for
it we have cash enough for our present wants
with a prospect of accumulation - we are all in
decent health - only that papa has a complaint in
his eyes and with this one exception of B who
I hope will be better and do better, henceforth,
I am quite contented for myself - not as idle
as formerly, altogether as hearty and having learnt
to make the most of the present and hope for
the future with less fidgetness that I
cannot do all I wish - seldom or ever troubled
with nothing to do and merely desiring
that everybody could be as comfortable as my
self and as undesponding and then we should
have a very tolerable world of it -

By mistake I find we have opened the paper
on the 31st instead of the 30th yesterday
was much such a day as this but the morning was divine -

Tabby who was gone in our last paper
is come back and has lived with us - two
years and a half and is in good health - Martha
who also departed is here too - We have got
Flossy, got and lost Tiger - lost the Hawk Nero
which with the geese was given away and

is doubtless dead for when I come back
from Brussels I enquired on all hands and
could hear nothing of him — Tiger died
early last year — Keeper and Flossey are well
also the canary acquired 4 years since
we are now all at home and likely to
be there some time — Branwell went
to Liverpool on ~~Tuesday~~ Thursday to stay a week
Tabby has just been teasing me to turn
as formerly to "pilloputate" — Anne and I
should have picked the black currants
if it had been fine and sunshiny. I must
hurry off now to my turning and ironing
I have plenty of work on hands and
writing and am altogether full of business
with best wishes for the whole
House till 1848 July 30th and as
much longer as may be I conclude

E J Brontë

blind with both drink and drugs, a figure of fun to the children, an embarrassment to the girls. The recurring thought that they might try to have a school was wiped away forever. Branwell's presence would make such a "flourishing seminary" impossible. No, they must take the pittance Miss Branwell had left them; she had departed this earth for the Lord's company where she must have stitched *His* sheets in heavenly satisfaction. But their money had to go far.

They did not look for fame with their little volume of poetry; they did look for a modicum of financial success. They were not the first, nor would they be the last of poets, women or men, to find that truism: "poetry does not sell."

The excitement of print was there, however, it gave them all they needed to complete their dearest secrets—their novels. Charlotte's *The Professor,* Emily's *Wuthering Heights,* and Anne's *Agnes Grey.* Charlotte's novel found no publisher; Emily's and Anne's were accepted in 1847.

Always tolerant of Anne, Charlotte found her novel good, but she worried about the crudities in *Wuthering Heights.* Emily had written a book as wild as herself. It took Charlotte a long time—and then only after Emily's death—to begin to evaluate it, and even then there is a grudging, embarrassed quality about the preface she wrote for a new edition:

"I am bound to avow that she had scarcely more practical knowledge of the peasantry amongst whom she lived than a nun has of the country people who sometimes pass her convent gates. My sister's disposition was not naturally gregarious; circumstances favoured and fostered her tendency to seclusion; except to go to church or take a walk on the hills, she rarely crossed the threshold of home. Though her feeling for the people round was benevolent, intercourse with them she never sought; nor, with very few exceptions, ever experienced. And yet she knew them: knew their ways, their language, their family histories; she could hear of them with interest, and talk of them with detail, minute, graphic, and accurate; but *with* them, she rarely exchanged a word. Hence it ensued that what her mind had gathered of the real concerning them was too exclusively confined to those tragic and terrible traits of which, in listening to the secret annals of every rude vicinage, the memory

Patrick Branwell Brontë.

is sometimes compelled to receive the impress. Her imagination, which was a spirit more sombre than sunny, more powerful than sportive, found in such traits material whence it wrought creations like Heathcliff, like Earnshaw, like Catherine. Having formed these beings she did not know what she had done. If the auditor of her work, when read in manuscript, shuddered under the grinding influence of natures so relentless and implacable, of spirits so lost and fallen; if it was complained that the mere hearing of certain vivid and fearful scenes banished sleep by night, and disturbed mental peace by day, Ellis Bell would wonder what was meant, and suspect the complainant of affectation. Had she but lived, her mind would of itself have grown like a strong tree, loftier, straighter, widerspreading, and its matured fruits would have attained a mellower ripeness and sunnier bloom; but on that mind time and experience alone could work: to the influence of other intellects, it was not amendable."

She felt strongly, too, about Anne's new manuscript *The Tenant of Wildfell Hall*, filled with all that drink and degradation (written quietly by sweet Anne while Branwell was asleep dead drunk in Papa's room). But her own despair over the lack of publication of *The Professor* brought in her own words, "a chill in the heart."

Driven, she wrote *Jane Eyre*. Published, it delighted Papa: Mrs. Gaskell relates the following:

"Now, however, when the demand for the work had assured success to *Jane Eyre*, her sisters urged Charlotte to tell their father of its publication. She accordingly went into his study one afternoon after his early dinner, carrying with her a copy of the book, and one or two reviews, taking care to include a notice adverse to it.

She informed me that something like the following conversation took place between her and him. (I wrote down her words the day after I heard them; and I am pretty sure they are quite accurate.)

Papa, I've been writing a book.

Have you, my dear?

Yes, and I want you to read it.

I am afraid it will try my eyes too much.

But it is not in manuscript: it is printed.

My dear! you've never thought of the expense it will be! It will be almost sure to be a loss, for how can you get a book sold? No one knows you or your name.

But, papa, I don't think it will be a loss; no more will you, if you will just let me read you a review or two, and tell you more about it.

So she sat down and read some of the reviews to her father; and then, giving him the copy of *Jane Eyre* that she intended for him, she left him to read it. When he came in to tea, he said, Girls, do you know Charlotte has been writing a book, and it is much better than likely?"

Fame was in the wings, but so was death. Branwell died, then Emily and Anne. Her heart broke over the death of Branwell, for the "ruin of promise"; concerning Emily and Anne, whose promise she had seen fulfilled, she was eloquent:

"My sister Emily first declined. The details of her illness are deep-branded in my memory, but to dwell on them, either in thought or narrative, is not in my power. Never in all her life had she lingered over any task that lay before her, and she did not linger now. She sank rapidly. She made haste to leave us. Yet, while physically she perished, mentally she grew stronger than we had yet known her. Day by day, when I saw with what a front she met suffering, I looked on her with an anguish of wonder and love. I have seen nothing like it; but, indeed, I have never seen her parallel in anything. Stronger than a man, simpler than a child, her nature stood alone. The awful point was, that while full of ruth for others, on herself she had no pity; the spirit was inexorable to the flesh; from the trembling hand, the unnerved limbs, the faded eyes, the same service was exacted as they had rendered in health. To stand by and witness this, and not dare to remonstrate, was a pain no words can render.

"Two cruel months of hope and fear passed painfully by, and the day came at last when the terrors and pains of death were to be undergone by this treasure, which had grown dearer and dearer to our hearts as it wasted before our eyes. Towards the decline of that day, we had nothing of Emily but her mortal remains as consumption left them. She died December 19, 1848.

"We thought this enough: but we were utterly and presumptuously wrong. She was not buried ere Anne fell ill. She had not been committed to the grave a fortnight, before we received distinct intimation that it was necessary to prepare our minds to see the younger sister go after the elder. Accordingly, she followed in the same path with slower step and with a patience that equalled the other's fortitude. I have said that she was religious, and it was by leaning on those Christian doctrines in which she firmly believed that she found support through her most painful journey. I witnessed their efficacy in her latest hour and greatest trial, and must bear my testimony to the calm triumph with which they brought her through. She died May 28, 1849.

"What more shall I say about them? I cannot and need not say much more. In externals, they were two unobtrusive women; a perfectly secluded life gave them retiring manners and habits. In Emily's nature the extremes of vigour and simplicity seemed to meet. Under an unsophisticated culture, inartificial tastes, and an unpretending outside, lay a secret power and fire that might have inflamed the brain and kindled the veins of a hero; but she had no worldly wisdom; her powers were unadapted to the practical business of life: she would fail to defend her most manifest rights, to consult her most legitimate advantage. An interpreter ought always to have

Interior of Haworth Church. From *Scribner's Monthly,* 1871.

stood between her and the world. Her will was not very flexible, and it generally opposed her interest. Her temper was magnanimous, but warm and sudden; her spirit altogether unbending.

"Anne's character was milder and more subdued; she wanted the power, the fire, the originality of her sister, but was well endowed with quiet virtues of her own. Long-suffering, self-denying, reflective, and intelligent, a constitutional reserve and taciturnity placed and kept her in the shade, and covered her mind, and especially her feelings, with a sort of nun-like veil, which was rarely lifted. Neither Emily nor Anne was learned; they had no thought of filling their pitchers at the well-spring of other minds; they always wrote from the impulse of nature, the dictates of intuition, and from such stores of observation as their limited experience had enabled them to amass. I may sum up all by saying, that for strangers they were nothing, for superficial observers less than nothing; but for those who had known them all their lives in the intimacy of close relationship, they were genuinely good and truly great.

"This notice has been written because I felt it a sacred duty to wipe the dust off their gravestones, and leave their dear names free from soil."

Charlotte at thirty-three, her father at seventy-two went on together, clinging to each other like the ivy in the graveyard. She continued to write; she met and was lionized by the great, and with one great streak of personal independence she married. Papa never thought her well enough to marry—and once again she proved him right—it was a short-lived marriage. Nevertheless, her last words were to her husband: "I am not going to die, am I? He will not separate us, we have been so happy."

Charlotte's life often has been well and copiously documented. She was the successful woman writer; Emily was the other side of the coin, the solitary writer, disdaining all but her own talent and sometimes disdaining even that. When, however, one conjures up that extraordinary group, writing on the same table, one longs for more than a glimpse of Emily whose life has no documentation, whose book has even been declared a product of Branwell's imagination.

To find the outline of her story, one must really return to that great nineteenth-century biographer, Mrs. Gaskell, so unlike the wild Emily. She has given us, says May Sinclair, "a vivid and ineffaceable idea of Emily: Emily who was tall and strong and unconquerable; Emily who loved animals, and loved the moors; Emily and Keeper, that marvelous dog; Emily kneading bread with her book propped before her; Emily who was Ellis Bell, listening contemptuously to the reviews of *Wuthering Heights;* Emily stitching at the long seam with dying fingers; and Emily dead, carried down the long, flagged path with Keeper following in the mourners train.

"And, all through, an invisible, intangible presence, something mysterious, but omnipotently alive; something that excited these three sisters; something that atoned that not only consoled for suffering for solitude and bereavement, but that drew its strength from these things; something that moved in this book like the soul of it; something that they called genius. It eliminates the inessential and preserves the proportions; above all, it preserves the figure of Emily Brontë, solitary and unique.

"Anyhow, I have never been able to get away from it." Nor have we.

6

I ACCEPT THE UNIVERSE MARGARET FULLER AND THE PEABODY GIRLS

I accept the Universe:

Margaret Fuller

By God, she'd better!

Thomas Carlyle

Such a predetermination to *eat* this big universe as her oyster or egg, and to be absolute empress of all height and glory in it that her heart could conceive I have not before seen in any human soul

Thomas Carlyle, referring to Margaret Fuller

Another sign of the times is Female Authorship. These have been great, and are constantly increasing. Women have taken possession of so many provinces for which men had pronounced them unfit, that though these still declare there are some inaccessible to them, it is difficult to say just *where* they must stop

Margaret Fuller, 1845

W as this thy welcome home, a howling hurricane, a pitiless sea, a wreck on a sandbar, beach pirates and not one friend? Did that last scene of agony seem a fitting close for a life of storms where even the nearest help seemed to be always too far away, or just too late to help!"

Even taking into account William E. Channing's nineteenth-century polemics, his words were a fitting epilogue for Margaret Fuller's life. Within her there was always the tempest that she could not quiet; without there was always some storm she thought she could quell. Torn and twisted as the jetsam on the Fire Island beach where her own letters came ashore at the time of her death, she knew what it was to be awash in life.

Storms on the south shore of Long Island are not uncommon. The Fire Island side of the barrier beach had had hundreds of ships founder off shore, but most of them in the nineteenth century made only local news. The baymen and their wives would pick up whatever cargo had been swept ashore; their children would be dressed in rare calicoes from the East, their meager pantries would be enriched by foreign teas. It was not unusual to awaken in the middle of the night and go rushing to the beach with almost a certain wild joy to watch the waters devastate a ship. The stories made the newspapers, generally only local gazettes—such wrecks were not of national news.

But that storm which had arisen so sharply in July, 1850, was a storm that made headlines. The barque, *Elizabeth*, had gone down offshore at what is now Point o' Woods. Even then it took two days for the news to reach the *New York Tribune* for which Margaret Fuller had been the European correspondent. It took even more time for Henry Thoreau to make the pilgrimage from New England to find if there could be any trace of Margaret or her papers, that extraordinary manuscript on which she was working, the story of the

The Emerson living room. It was here that Ralph Waldo Emerson first heard Margaret Fuller's conversation.

Italian Revolution that she felt was her life's work.

No trace was found of Margaret, no trace of her handsome, young husband; only the body of her young son, in whom, for the first time, she had found some one individual wholly satisfying. All Thoreau could find was one button, obviously from Margaret's cloak, which he picked up from the sand and pocketed. A day or so before, a farmer's wife had found a trunk of letters; they were all to Margaret and the names of the signers stood out sharply, despite the staining of the salt water. They were her friends, these were their letters— Ralph Waldo Emerson, Henry Thoreau, William E. Channing, Horace Greeley—the leading names of the nineteenth-century intelligentsia, addressing a woman whom some said had simply been the greatest of her day. Certainly she was the most talked about and the one, quite honestly, who had done the most talking.

She was not easy to know and it was sometimes difficult to remain her friend. Emerson, when he heard of her death, wrote down rapidly some of his memories about her:

Women writers of the nineteenth century were often caricatured. This print shows one of the industrious ladies at work.

"She was then twenty-six years old. She had a face and frame that would indicate fulness and tenacity of life. She was rather under the middle height; her complexion was fair, with strong fair hair. She was then, as always, carefully and becomingly dressed, and of ladylike self-possession. For the rest, her appearance had nothing

A caricature of Henry David Thoreau, a close friend of Margaret Fuller's. Sketch by D. Ricketson.

prepossessing. Her extreme plainness,—a trick of incessantly opening and shutting her eyelids,—the nasal tone of her voice,—all
repelled; and I said to myself, we shall never get far. It is to be said,
that Margaret made a disagreeable first impression on most persons,
including those who became afterwards her best friends, to such an
extreme that they did not wish to be in the same room with her.
This was partly the effect of her manners, which expressed an over-
weening sense of power, and slight esteem of others, and partly the
prejudice of her fame. She had a dangerous reputation for satire,
in addition to her great scholarship. The men thought she carried
too many guns, and the women did not like one who despised them.
I believe I fancied her too much interested in personal history; and
her talk was a comedy in which dramatic justice was done to everybody's foibles. I remember that she made me laugh more than I
liked."

But despite the arrogance, despite the shrillness, she collected
friends and wore them, as Emerson said, "Like a necklace of dia-
monds about her neck." She was also an indefatigable visitor. Emerson said that every home was open to her, that she was welcomed
everywhere, but those were words put down by a man still in grief
for a personal friend. The truth was that Margaret felt she *deserved*
a welcome anywhere and could be remarkably obtuse when her
welcome wore out.

It was Margaret, for example, who proposed to accompany the
Hawthornes on their honeymoon and then to move in with them
immediately when they took up residence at the Manse in Concord.
Sophia, Hawthorne's wife, simply called her Queen Margaret, and
Nathaniel himself was forced to write to Margaret, "Had it been
proposed to Adam and Eve to receive an angel into their Paradise's
borders, I doubt whether they could have been altogether pleased
to consent." For once Margaret seemed to get the message.

Hawthorne always found her vaguely difficult. When she visited Brook Farm where he had lived before he married, he commented on Margaret Fuller's private cow, "Miss Fuller's cow hooks
the other cows and has made herself ruler of the herd and behaves
in a very tyrannical manner."

So, she was not loved by all, but almost all respected her. Who
could not respect her, Emerson explained, when she not only looked

upon herself not only as an artist but also as a work of art and, to be truthful, often saw others under the same guise. But a work of art, as a rule, has little opportunity to respond directly to the observer. The persons that Margaret chose to expend her energies upon—and they were considerable, both energies and persons— were not always too keen to be fashioned almost Pygmalion-like by Margaret. She saw herself, said Emerson, a living statue, standing on a polished pedestal . . . perhaps translated from transcendentalism, one might say simply she was an overpowering woman trodding on many toes.

Intensely intellectual, with an intellectuality that today we might find downright tiresome, she also had what Emerson called her nocturnal side. She could quite frankly be unbalanced about a number of things. "I'm a worse self-tormenter than Rousseau," she admitted and, "all my riches are fuel to the fire." She hoarded private superstition, a whole collection of the most primitive lore, the secret meaning of gems, ciphers, talismen, omens, coincidences and birthdays. She wrote to friends in the language of flowers and was sure enough of her own demons. She was none too sure, however, of her "demon's" sex, sometimes feeling herself feminine and other times feeling quite male, and wore a garnet which only she was able to discover was a male one. Of course with all of this she had to be a figure of fun and there were many who laughed at her behind her back and many who scoffed at her eternal self-analysis. "I've known some happy hours, but they all lead to sorrow and not only the cups of wine but of milk seem drugged with poison for me. It does not seem to be my fault, this destiny, I do not collect these things, they come. I'm a poor magnet with power to be wounded by the bodies I attract." In retrospect those words seem honest enough, but we cannot share her thought that she did not court trouble because she did appear to go out courting life too vehemently, her intellect confusing her emotions, her emotions confusing her intellect, to the extent that she always seemed just one step ahead of disaster.

Margaret Fuller was born on May 23, 1810, in Cambridgeport, Massachusetts, a short way from Boston which saw itself as almost the center of the world but which was, in fact, a town of just forty thousand inhabitants. The United States had but ten million persons, and Margaret seems to have been born with a desire to know all of them. At least she knew all of Boston.

Margaret was the eldest of eight children and her father, disgruntled that she was not a boy, began to rear her, at least intellectually, as one. By the time she was six she read Latin with more ease than English, then she moved on to German, French, Italian, Greek, and went off to school to learn what else the world had to offer.

She was unhappy, she had fearful nightmares and walked in her sleep and had the usual nineteenth-century obsession. "My earliest memory," she said, "was of death." Such obsessions, the specialists of the day said, were easily cured. A milk diet would get rid of the melancholy and the sleepwalking at the same time. Whether it was the milk or not, she then took up a form of activity that first delighted her schoolmates, and afterwards confused them. She quite fancied herself a whirling dervish and would dance around and around all night, agitating herself rather than quieting down, and ending up once more sleepwalking. Fortunately she walked fairly directly in her sleep, and those that encountered her found it was one of the rare times she was ever quiet.

She soon had a circle about her. As difficult as she was she could talk the stars out of the sky and even her schoolmates would sit in awe at her most juvenile pronouncement. By the time she was twenty-two she knew herself well. "Conversation's my natural element," she said. "I need to be called and never think alone without imagining some companion, whether this be nature or the force of circumstance, I know not. It is my habit and bespeaks a second rate Mind." She was only partly right, and she very rarely even self-confessed to "a second rate Mind." And if she had any doubt about MIND (she put it in capitals, as she did with all her aspirations), SELF CULTURE, in all caps, for example, or in all caps, VERY EARLY I KNEW THAT THE ONLY OBJECT IN LIFE WAS TO GROW.

One thing that grew fulsome was her prose. "How is it that I seem to be this Margaret Fuller?" she wrote to herself. "What

Marchese Giovanni Angelo Ossoli, Margaret Fuller's husband.

does it mean? What shall I do about it? I remember all the times and ways in which the same thought returned. I saw how long it must be before the soul can learn to act under these limitations of time and space of human nature, but I saw also that it must DO IT."

MARGARET WAS GOING TO GROW, MUST GROW, WOULD GROW; JUST HOW WAS A WOMAN OF THE NINETEENTH CENTURY GOING TO DO IT?

Suddenly, what to do became no idle musing. Her father was seized with cholera and in a matter of days was dead. Money instantly became a problem. In addition she became the head of the family. "As it is" she said, "I am very ignorant of the management and value of property and the practical details. I always hated the din of such affairs, and hope to find a life long refuge from them in the serene world of literature and the arts." She was to learn that literature and the arts were by no means serene, but the grubbing for money was even more difficult. "I long for a guide," she said, and with that indefatigable energy of hers, managed to find one. It was, of course, Ralph Waldo Emerson.

Her first visit to him was not appreciated; he quite frankly admitted he could barely put up with all of the intellectual activity. In addition, that tic in the eye bothered him. For a transcendental philosopher he had difficulty overlooking some of the physical draw-

Giuseppe Mazzini, Margaret Fuller's intimate friend and founder of the revolutionary organization, "Young Italy," assumed the dominant role in the triumvirate formed after the proclamation of the Republic of Rome in 1849. An engraving after the painting by Ashurst. Museo Centrale del Risorgimento, Rome.

backs of even such a wild transcendental spirit as Margaret. But he had not seen the last of her. There was that overwhelming need for SELF CULTURE and obviously Emerson was the one she needed. She wrote in her journal of her need for a friend who would "comprehend me wholly, mentally and morally and enable me better to comprehend myself." It was a frightening task for anyone. Emerson dodged it, but not for long. After a couple of weeks of her pursuit he had to admit that it was always a great refreshment to see a very intelligent person. "It is like being set in a large place, you stretch yourself and dilate to your utmost size."

Not only he, but his very living room began to expand and for the first time Margaret brooded less about writing a fabulous life of Goethe and drowning in the German philosophy of the period and turned to talkers as great as she: Emerson for one, Elizabeth Peabody for another, Amos Bronson Alcott for a third. The third suddenly took precedence. Alcott had a school. Why shouldn't she work there? She worked there. "I think her," said Alcott, "the most brilliant talker of the day."

But the school waxed thin, like many of Alcott's ideas, and she moved on to another school in Providence. She was an iconoclastic teacher, bringing in adult voices from the outside so that her students might feel as she did, a citizen of the world. But the monotony bored her. "Every year I live I dislike routine more and more" she

Ralph Waldo Emerson.

said, "though I see that society rests on that and other falsehoods. The more I screw myself down to hours, the more I become expert at giving out thought and life in regulated rations. The more I weary of this world and long to move upon the wing without props and sedan chairs."

Then she paid a fatal visit to the Transcendental Club. In a rare move for the nineteenth century it had opened its ranks to women. They included the Emerson women, Sarah Ripley, Elizabeth Hoar and Margaret. That word *transcendental* confused them as much as it has confused the historians that have examined it afterwards. Even Margaret admitted, "As to transcendentalism and the nonsense that is talked by so many about it, I do not know what is meant. For myself I should say that if it is meant that I have an active mind, frequently busy with large topics, I hope it is so. If it is meant that I am honored by the friendship of such men as Mr. Emerson, Mr. Ripley, or Mr. Alcott, I hope it is so. But if it is meant that I cherish any opinions which interfere with domestic duties, cheerful courage and judgement on the practical affairs of life, I shall challenge any or all in the little world which knows me to prove any such deficiency from any acts of mine since I came to woman's estate." In other words, she was thinking, but also working hard. And she longed to be more finished, to be polished, to be cultured.

I Accept the Universe

Egged on by the transcendentalists, Boston discovered culture in a big way. New England was old enough, Margaret pointed out, and had leisure enough to look inward. They went to eternal lectures, wrote endless letters, talked and talked. When Emerson complained once that he had lost a night's sleep, Margaret chided him, "Lost a night's rest, as if an intellectual person ever had a night's rest." And even if they did, they must have talked to themselves in their sleep, because life seemed one long endless conversation. If not with each other, with the shades of the great, Shakespeare, Goethe, Coleridge, and for the few, with God. Margaret never numbered the latter as a supreme friend. She wanted more articulate responses to her own extraordinary gift of gab. Then suddenly she found an outlet. One could talk *and make money.*

She introduced what today might be called a rap session, an encounter group with the women of Boston. Madame de Staël had given her the idea, but her own vehemence made it possible for the "Conversations" to last for five years. The first course was thirteen meetings of two hours each. The conversations began at noon and in those early hours of the afternoon, Margaret was able to cover

State Street, Boston, during Margaret Fuller's time.

with certain glory practically the history of the world. If she did not talk herself, she got others to talk and indeed they were an extraordinary group of women: the famous three Peabody sisters, Mrs. Joseph Bancroft, Mrs. Josiah Quincy, Lydia Child, the brilliant abolitionist, Theodore Parker's wife, and daughters of the intellectual center of Boston. It is easy to make fun of some of the elaborate topics that she chose. But basically she had one concern, human liberation. Indirectly her conversations became seeds that laid the groundwork for the growth of women's colleges, women study clubs, women's efforts to expand the horizons of their own minds.

Conversations were not enough and she took over an editorship of a new journal, *The Dial.*

"I wish," she said, "that we might court some of the good fanatics and publish chapters on every heading in the whole Art of Living."

She was an "impertinent editor," even asking Emerson for revisions of his contributions. Her salary was miniscule, her work, fatiguing. She resigned and in almost a holiday spirit paid a visit to that Utopian colony, Brook Farm.

She immediately began to give some of her famous "Conversations." She changed her topics, however, because she frankly found that there was entirely too much spontaneity at Brook Farm and not enough reflection. After spending their days in the fields the men and women were also a little less intellectually oriented. Many yawned and there was a good smell of cow dung rather than culture all around.

It amused Margaret to discover that she was, quite frankly, a conservative and that the farm itself was not what she wanted. Indeed she had loathed the family farm as a girl and could never understand why anybody would find enough satisfactions in earth and trees when there was the glory of great talk in the cities. Or in even a new section of the country.

Go West, young woman—and she did. With fifty dollars she toured the country. She was a careful observer of everything from Indian life to the stern faces of Oregon pioneers. She speculated on what the new American should be. "No thin idealist, no coarse realist, but a man whose eye reads the heavens while his feet step·

firmly on the ground. A man to whom this world is no mere spectacle or fleeting shadow, but a solemn game to be played with good heed. A man who hives from the past, yet knows that its honey can but moderately avail him. When there is such a man for America the thought which urges her on will be expressed."

As for the woman America needed, Margaret presently made no comment. Obviously it was herself. Her comments on the trip West resulted in a book, and, what was more important, an offer of a job. She would be the first woman member of the fourth estate. She would not simply be writing random articles for a newspaper, she would be a member, and a hardworking one, of the working press. Besides, she would invade New York.

Horace Greeley of the New York *Tribune* was an exceptional man. Not only did he hire Margaret as an editor of a daily newspaper, but he also gave her free rein, and she accepted it so completely that she fell in love.

His name was James Nathan and he had, said Margaret, a "lower nature." To her own shock she responded to it, only to have Nathan renege.

But she managed for a while to hold onto him. He maintained that he had to go abroad; she maintained that he should stay. "Perhaps I am as you say too sensitive." She obviously was. But conditions did not improve and Nathan went to Europe. He promised to write, he promised to return. He wrote briefly. As the letters decreased she became more and more certain that she had exhausted the possibilities of New York. She moved out of the Greeley household, where she had been a permanent guest, into Greenwich Village. She had grown to know all the literati, not only to know them but to review them in the pages of her newspaper. She had also written and published a pioneer book, *Woman in the Nineteenth Century.*

It was the most seminal book of its time; the first to argue in the United States that women had the right, indeed the duty, to develop all their talents . . . and she felt the same for men. She examined women in history, women in the home and out of it, women in the professions, to the extent that Horace Greeley was to tease her incessantly about women as sea captains. "Why not?"

said Margaret. She demanded women look into themselves and men too. "You see the men, how they are willing to sell shamelessly the happiness of countless generations of fellow-creatures, the honor of their country, and their immortal souls for a money market and political power. . . . Tell these men that you will not accept the glittering baubles, spacious dwellings, and plentiful service they mean to offer you through these means. Tell them that the heart of Woman demands nobleness and honor in man, and that if they have not purity, have not mercy, they are no longer fathers, lovers, husbands, sons of yours."

In the meantime, she brooded about Nathan. Why didn't he write?

She was able to convince Greeley that she would make a good foreign correspondent and as such she became the first woman correspondent in the United States. It was a trip that she said would give her genius wings. She was not able to shore up her relationship with Nathan, but crossing the water did something for her. Her reputation preceded her. She was always welcomed with warmth, even if with some trepidation.

In London she paid a visit to Cheyne Walk in Chelsea, that famous home, for all its grubbiness, of the Carlyles. For once she did not move in with Thomas and Jane. In the first place she had no invitation, but that had not necessarily deterred her at other times, and Jane, despite her caustic tongue, could be agreeable enough to a guest. But Thomas, so concerned with his high principles and his poor stomach, would not consent to such an overnight guest. It did not matter: Margaret would at least go and spend an evening with them. And the first time, she said, she was utterly delighted, Thomas being full of wit and pathos without being over-bearing or oppressive. She had to admit, grudgingly, that he could talk. She, who had heard great talkers before, admitted to being carried away with his rich "discourse." He seemed to sing each sentence, making it large and full until it was like the stanza of a narrative ballad. When she grew a little edgy he didn't notice, but he was at least sensitive enough to let somebody else talk upon occasion and, as she said, she got an opportunity "to free her lungs" and change her position once in a while. "I left them that night

Sketch of George Sand, by Alfred de Musset, 1833.

intending to go out very often to their house," she said, but in all truth she did not go too frequently. No one could stand *that* kind of beautiful Scottish gab, rolling over one like a fog, until one was inundated in discourses of men of power, fanatics, tales of the Scottish peasantry, poetry, the French Revolution and Shakespeare.

Thomas Carlyle.

Elizabeth Palmer Peabody in 1887.

Shakespeare, Carlyle maintained, didn't have enough good sense to see that he should have written in prose instead of all those ridiculous attempts at drama. In subsequent visits Margaret felt that his eyes roved around, looking for all the world "like eyes of a bird of prey and a beak that kept going on and on."

"The worst of Carlyle," she wrote, "was that you cannot interrupt him. I understand the habit and power of haranguing had bequeathed very much upon him so that you were a perfect prisoner when he once got hold of you. To interupt him is a physical impossibility. If you get a chance to remonstrate for a moment, he raises his voice and bears you down. True, he does you no injustice and with his admirable penetration sees the disclaimer in your mind so that you are not morally delinquent. But it is very pleasant to be unable to utter it."

At their table she met a flippant sort of man, writing the history of philosophy and working on a life of Goethe, whom Margaret, of course, felt was her own literary province. She little knew that this was *the* Mr. Lewes with whom a woman even more magnificent in intellect, George Eliot, would live in the beautiful state of Victorian abandonment until his death. Margaret paid the proper calls in England to the aged Wordsworth, to Mary and William Howitt, the children's writers of the period, to Joanna Baillie.

Her most important encounter was one evening with her friends, the Springs, the American couple who had accompanied her

In contrast to Margaret Fuller, who was a public personality, Emily Dickinson was the most private of poets. At her death in 1886 she left a request that all of her poetry be burned. It was only when her sister discovered her horde of genius, great bundles of poems tied with ribbons, that her creativity was fully recognized, and publication inevitable. By permission of the Trustees of Amherst College.

to Europe. It was in their apartment that she met Carlyle again. Carlyle at this point had dignified her by reading her book. "It was," he said, "greatly superior to all I knew before, in fact the undeniable utterances of a true heroic mind. Altogether unique, so far as I know among the Writing Women of this generation. Rare enough, too, God knows among the Writing Men."

But the Carlyles she already knew. It was Giuseppe Mazzini who really impressed her—who sat there with a kind of dignity flowing from him, the man who planned to free Italy from a monstrous oppression. This was the man described by Margaret as "the most beautious person I have seen." More importantly she found a cause. None of her other ventures had quite been causes. Despite her feelings that women should play a more active role in life, that they should seek their own identity, she was not really obsessed with the idea of her own womanhood. Nor had she felt that she had ever been neglected by men. Indeed, she felt that many, including her father, had been obsessed with her.

All the men to whom she had been attracted were Emerson-like, remarkably dispassionate. They spoke of philosophy instead of passion, and often blather instead of bed. Now she was suddenly thrown in with a group of passionate men—Europeans who seemed to feel differently about life itself, who were not content to talk, but who also *felt.*

She crossed to Paris and met the Polish poet Mickiewicz, a

147

revolutionary in exile who became one of her dearest friends. "I find in him the man I had long wished to see, with the intellect and passion in due proportion for a full and healthy being, with a soul constantly inspiring. . . . How much time had I wasted on others which I might have given to this real and important relation." She began to plan with him whatever they might do in a small way to free Italy. She also met the remarkable woman writer, George Sand.

"At last, however, she [George Sand] came; and I went to see her at her house, Place d'Orleans. I found it a handsome modern residence. She had not answered my letter, written about a week before, and I felt a little anxious lest she should not receive me; for she is too much the mark of impertinent curiosity, as well as too busy, to be easily accessible to strangers. I am by no means timid, but I have suffered, for the first time in France, some of the torments of *mauvaise honte*, enough to see what they must be to many.

"It is the custom to go and call on those to whom you bring letters, and push yourself upon their notice; thus you must go quite ignorant whether they are disposed to be cordial. My name is always murdered by the foreign servants who announce me. I speak very bad French; only lately have I had sufficient command of it to infuse some of my natural spirit in my discourse. This has been a great trial to me, who am eloquent and free in my own tongue, to be forced to feel my thoughts struggling in vain for utterance.

"The servant who admitted me was in the picturesque costume of a peasant, and, as Madame Sand afterward told me, her god-daughter, whom she had brought from her province. She announced me as *Madame Salere,* and returned into the ante-room to tell me, *Madame says she does not know you.* I began to think I was doomed to a rebuff, among the crowd who deserve it. However, to make assurance sure, I said, Ask if she has not received a letter from me. As I spoke, Madame S. opened the door, and stood looking at me an instant. Our eyes met. I never shall forget her look at that moment. The doorway made a frame for her figure; she is large, but well-formed. She was dressed in a robe of dark violet silk, with a black mantle on her shoulders, her beautiful hair dressed with the greatest taste, her whole appearance and attitude, in its simple and ladylike dignity, presenting an almost ludicrous contrast to the vulgar caricature idea of George Sand. Her face is a very little like the portraits, but much finer; the upper part of the forehead and eyes are beautiful, the lower, strong and masculine, expressive of a hardy temperament and strong passions, but not in the least coarse; the complexion olive, and the air of the whole head Spanish, (as, indeed, she was born at Madrid, and is only on one side of French blood.) All these details I saw at a glance; but what fixed my attention was the expression of *goodness*, nobleness, and power, that pervaded the whole,—the truly human heart and nature that shone in the eyes. As our eyes met, she said, *C'est vous*, and held out her hand. I took it, and went into her little study; we sat down a moment, then I said, *Il me fait de bien de vous voir*, and I am sure I said it with my whole heart, for it made me very happy to see such a woman, so large and so developed a character, and everything that *is* good in it so *really* good. I loved, shall always love her.

"She looked away, and said, *Ah! vous m'avez écrit une lettre charmante*. This was all the preliminary of our talk, which then went on as if we had always known one another. . . .

"Her way of talking is just like her writing,—lively, picturesque, with an undertone of deep feeling, and the same skill in striking the nail on the head every now and then with a blow.

"We did not talk at all of personal or private matters. I saw, as one sees in her writings, the want of an independent, interior life, but I did not feel it as a fault, there is so much in her of her kind. I heartily enjoyed the sense of so rich, so prolific, so ardent a genius. I liked the woman in her, too, very much; I never liked a woman better. . . .

"I forgot to mention, that, while talking, she *does* smoke all the time her little cigarette. This is now a common practice among ladies abroad, but I believe originated with her. . . ."

Margaret Fuller could feel her life changing as she settled in Italy. She wrote back to William Channing, "Art is not important to me now," but she did not keep everybody fully advised as to the growing importance, not only of her feeling for the freeing of Italy, but also for a young nobleman quite down at the heels and penniless, quite uneducated—everything she thought she did not desire in a man. She fell madly in love with him. A friend of hers later said,

"Her heart, which few knew, was as great as her mind which all knew."

Her life, turbulent always, moved on to its final tragedy. Those days with her young nobleman, Ossoli, were a "sphere of destiny." Her young lover, later her husband, fought under the command of Garibaldi. Margaret had a child and a wild hope for happiness. But the republic tumbled and with it her dreams. They booked passage on the barque, *Elizabeth.* . . .

Even after her death, Boston was slow to forget some of Margaret's more aggressive statements. "Who would be a goodie when they could be a genius?" she had once declared. Boston had sniffed. They did very well, the New England do-gooders . . . it was almost the highest role an American woman could play.

Wasn't it possible to be both a goodie and a genius? Witness Elizabeth Peabody, dear Lizzie, omnipresent everywhere, moving into drawing rooms, in rather fusty, old-fashioned clothes, but with a voluminous heart underneath the voluminous bosom of pleats and brooches.

You always met Lizzie coming and going. She had a finger in every pie and a half-baked friend in every room. Why, look what Lizzie managed to do with that extraordinary Bronson Alcott! Always interested in education, Lizzie at one point had set up her own school. Then she met the remarkable Mr. Bronson Alcott. They had met, appropriately enough, at Alcott's wedding. All three Peabody girls were there, that remarkable trio of New England virtue: Mary, who was to marry Horace Mann; Sophia, who was to marry Nathaniel Hawthorne; and Elizabeth, who was to marry herself to the idea of education. All three marriages were remarkable. But that wedding, too, had been memorable. For the first time they heard Bronson Alcott speak. His first words were, of course, directed to old Colonel May's daughter, his bride. And when she had said yes to him, little did she know what she was taking on. Not yet was there a gleam in the eye for the Louisa May Alcott who would continue a line of extraordinary little women.

Alcott was a great speaker and capable of remarkably obtuse

Margaret Fuller, From the painting by Chappel, Courtesy, Harvard University Library, Cambridge, Massachusetts.

remarks. He offered his "sayings." "Every soul," he would mutter, "feels at times her own possibility of becoming a God. She cannot rest in the human. She aspires after the Godlike. This instinctive tendency is an authentic augery of its own fulfillment." Elizabeth Peabody couldn't help but agree. She was always aspiring after something and sometimes, with her energy, her enthusiasms hardly seemed human. In New England God easily could have been a woman. As a matter of fact, the remarkable Mary Baker Eddy would imply that very shortly. But even Alcott must have seen Him as some great schoolmaster in the sky, educating all to life eternal, the struggle of the soul, immutable impeccability of the conscience.

For his part Mr. Alcott found Miss Peabody a singularly sensible lady. "She has a mind of a superior order and its range of thought and the philosophical discrimination of its character, I have seldom if ever found a female mind to equal it." Her notions of character, the niceties of analysis, her accurate knowledge of the human mind are remarkable, original and just. Her views of morals are very elevated."

The Peabodys were extraordinarily hospitable, particularly because Mrs. Peabody, herself a driving ambitious woman, had at that time three unmarried girls on her hands. One of them obviously would never marry. She was far too frail, wraithlike, one of those dreaming nineteenth-century New England women who fluttered from bed to couch, with nobody ever quite sure what ailed them.

Then, one day came a tall, exquisitely handsome young man, Nathaniel Hawthorne by name, whom Sophia looked upon and found not wanting. Sophia managed to make a remarkable recovery and a marriage of unusual satisfaction. Sophia herself was capable of flights of fancy, then called private philosophies. She said, "Sometimes it seems to me as if my life were a pathway of peculiar beauty—an indefinable atmosphere of music, a mingling of birds voices floating around glimpses of endless visions which is heard of the distant falling of fountains and the sighing of the leaves. This is always my life, if left to itself."

Lizzie, for her part, heard the birds singing, but she attacked life more as though it were a giant bird of prey, one that she could peck away at until somehow or other she had gotten it under submis-

Margaret Fuller.

sion. The way you would do that certainly was by education. She was particularly interested in Alcott's school, established in September, 1834, with, as Elizabeth said, a lovely set of children. Elizabeth had done everything she could to help Bronson start the school. She was the one who actually wrote the letters to get the parents to submit their children to the hands of what many considered, despite the fact that the great Dr. Channing himself endorsed it, a peculiar venture. This school would be a school that exemplified the principles and methods of moral culture. There were very young children, but they were subjected to a great deal of self-analysis. "Which of you," said Mr. Alcott pointing to the children in the room, "have gone inward and viewed yourself?" None, noted Lizzie, but she and Bronson would do all they could to so educate them. As a matter of fact, Bronson and Lizzie used extraordinary means to develop insight into a child's own mind. In many ways they were remarkably successful. It was a startling example of the most contemporary kind of education. Although Lizzie could not sponsor all his ideas, she found his mind exciting and soon moved into a furnished room at the Alcott home. Unlike some of our other extraordinary women who made such a move, Miss Lizzie was not bothered by any troubles of the flesh. She was a good talker, even upon occasion a gentle nurse, often fondling the Alcott baby, who was called Beth after her

153

name Elizabeth, and would be so portrayed in the book *Little Women.*

The school foundered because Bronson interjected a note of sex education. A child *did* come from a mother's body explained Alcott. He confused the issue by saying the mother gave her body to God who worked on it in a "mysterious way." It was no mystery to Boston that Bronson was a damn fool.

His school failed, but no one could defeat Elizabeth Peabody.

She returned home to Salem. She continued her usual active social life, paying a call on Park Benjamin who had bought the *New England Magazine* and merged with it the *American Monthly.* They discovered a rather remarkable man, a Mr. Hawthorne, who had written some rather remarkable stories. Hawthorne, thought Lizzie, Wasn't that the name of the boy of a family who had once lived behind them in Salem?

She would find out herself. Old Mrs. Hawthorne was a recluse. There were a couple of girls at home, but one rarely saw even the young Nathaniel on the streets of Salem. Lizzie couldn't quite figure it out. Certainly one should be seen and heard. She went to the house of her old neighbors and without further ado first found it was true that Hawthorne had written the stories.

"Well," said Lizzie to Nathaniel's sister, "if your brother can write like that, he has no right to be idle."

"My brother is never idle," was the reply. And indeed, he was not. He was at that very time spending those years in his attic room, writing copiously.

It did not appear to him that he needed an agent, in fact, the very concept of a literary agent was new. But our Lizzie knew what to do. From then on, she did all she could to make him better known. True, Emerson didn't like what he wrote at all, and Hawthorne wasn't to like what Emerson wrote. Perhaps Nathaniel should take up journalism . . . but no, he didn't want to do that. Well, he must then meet more people, including her sister.

Eventually some of Hawthorne's books would appear under her own imprint, because Lizzie, one of the finest teachers, was also one of the finest publishers. She was the first woman publisher in Boston and the colophon E. P. Peabody became well known. Her book shop on West Street sold everything from books to the simple elixir made up by her brother.

She was extraordinary, Elizabeth Peabody, but also kind. Louisa May Alcott, Bronson's daughter, would always remember her for both qualities. Long after Margaret Fuller in Boston was forgotten—her ways had been just too strange—Lizzie Peabody was somebody.

Original illustration from Louisa May Alcott's *Little Men*.

7

THE PENS THAT ROCKED THE CRADLE
AND THE WORLD
LOUISA MAY ALCOTT, HARRIET
BEECHER STOWE

> To see a lady of such taste,
> So slatternly is shocking:
> Your pen and poetry lay by
> And learn to darn your stockings.
> *Nineteenth-Century Popular Rhyme*

> Very poorly. Feel quite used up.
> Dont care much for myself, as
> rest is heavenly even with pain;
> but the family seem so panic
> stricken and helpless when I break
> down, that I try to keep the mill going.
> *Louisa May Alcott's Diary*

America is wholly given over to a d—d mob of scribbling women . . . no chance of success while the public taste is occupied with their trash—and should be ashamed of myself if I did succeed.
Nathaniel Hawthorne

I, the author of *Uncle Tom's Cabin?* No, indeed! The Lord himself wrote it, and I was but the humblest instrument in His wise hand. To Him alone be all the praise.
Harriet Beecher Stowe

I F, to Elizabeth Peabody, Nathaniel Hawthorne would always be the boy behind the back fence, to the Hawthornes—once they moved to Concord—Louisa May Alcott would be the girl next door.

At the outbreak of the Civil War, Sophia Hawthorne said, "Louisa goes into the very mouth of the war," as the indomitable Louisa took off to nurse the wounded in Washington hospitals. Louisa had always gone into the mouth of life with all the dedication of Jonah going into the body of the whale and, like Jonah, she started to suffer early but, unlike him, managed to maintain a sense of humor. God knows she had to have one, because the Alcott household was always fraught with great thinking, poor eating, too many girls, and parlous Papa, Bronson Alcott by name.

Great thinkers do not generally make great farmers. Perhaps the competition with nature is just a little too strong, but in any case, the perfect farm, the dream farm, was always a fantasy of Bronson Alcott's, and by the time Louisa was ten years old he had acquired a group of enthusiasts with the same dreams and potentiality for disaster. They located a farm near Concord which they named Fruitlands. The name was about the last productive harvest the farm realized and, as Louisa was to say in later years, the whole venture was one of transcendental wild oats.

At ten, young Louisa began keeping a diary. It started with fortitude. "I arose at five and had my bath. I love the cold water!" She had to—there was no other water available. "Father asked us what was God's noblest work. Anna said men, but I said babies. Men are often bad. Babies never are. . . . We had bread and fruit for dinner." That was a good day. At least Fruitlands occasionally harvested some fruit. Whatever went on in the farm did not miss Louisa's sharp eye. The supposed harmony and contentment that should exist seemed to evade her. Still ten years old, she noted, "In

Louisa May Alcott. A photograph taken about 1862.

the evening we danced and sung, and I read a story about contentment. I wish I was rich, I wish I was good and we were all a happy
family this day." Obviously, none of the wishes was true or would
come true for a considerable space of time, but if Louisa proved
determined enough there was hope. The happy family might be
impossible with Bronson at the helm, but perhaps a pen led a way
to riches. As for goodness, well, she would try.

On Friday, November 2, that same year, she noted that she
and her sister did all the work in the kitchen, and in the evening
one of the philosophical farmers asked her, "What is man?" The
children answered, "A human being, an animal with a mind, a
creature, a body a soul and a mind. After a long talk, we went to
bed very tired." As an adult Louisa added her own annotation to
the comment of her ten-year-old self; "No wonder we were tired,"
she wrote, "after doing the work and worrying our little wits about
such lessons."

Often she wrote down some of the foibles of the farm. They
ate, for example, vegetarian wafers, an unusually dull concoction for
a child, further sanctified by the fact that each wafer, rather like
a Chinese fortune cookie of today, was inscribed with an appropriate
motto. One read, "Vegetable diet and sweet repose, animal food
and nightmare." Another argued, "Pluck your body from the or-
chard, do not snatch it from the shamble." Another suggested,
"Without flesh diet, there would be no blood-shedding war." A

159

Concord, Massachusetts, when Louisa May Alcott was a girl.

particularly hard cracker announced cryptically: "Apollo eats no flesh and has no beard. His voice is melancholy as melody itself."

In December she wrote, "I did my lessons, and walked in the afternoon. The farm is obviously not going well. I was very unhappy, and we all cried. Anna and I cried in bed, and I prayed God to keep us all together." To which the older Louisa May annotated, "Little Lou began early to feel the family cares and peculiar trials."

In her diary she recorded a sample of her lessons with Mr. Lane, one of the philosophical farmers who directed her education:

"What virtues do you wish more of?" asks Mr. L.
I answer:—

Patience,	Love,	Silence,
Obedience,	Generosity,	Perseverance,
Industry,	Respect,	Self-denial.

"What vices less of?"

Idleness,	Wilfulness,	Vanity,
Impatience,	Impudence,	Pride,
Selfishness,	Activity	Love of cats.

MR. L.   L.
SOCRATES.   ALCIBIADES.

160

How can you get what you need? By trying.

How do you try? By resolution and perseverance.

How gain love? By gentleness.

What is gentleness? Kindness, patience, and care for other people's feelings.

Who has it? Father and Anna.

Who means to have it? Louisa, if she can.

[She never got it.—L. M. A.]

Write a sentence about anything. "I hope it will rain; the garden needs it."

What are the elements of *hope?* Expectation, desire, faith.

What are the elements in *wish?* Desire.

What is the difference between faith and hope? "Faith can believe without seeing; hope is not sure, but tries to have faith when it desires."

No. 3.

What are the most valuable kinds of self-denial? Appetite, temper.

How is self-denial of temper known? If I control my temper, I am respectful and gentle, and every one sees it.

What is the result of this self-denial? Every one loves me, and I am happy.

Why use self-denial? For the good of myself and others.

How shall we learn this self-denial? By resolving, and then trying *hard*.

What then do you mean to do? To resolve and try.

[Here the record of these lessons ends, and poor little Alcibiades went to work and tried till fifty, but without any very great success, in spite of all the help Socrates and Plato gave her.]

The diary complains, "And more people coming to live with us. I wish we could be together and no one else." But then she began to find an outlet, "I was dismal, and then went for a walk and made a poem."

When she was thirteen the family moved into the village of Concord. For once there is a happy entry in her diary. "Hillside, March 1846, I have at last got the little room I wanted so long, and am very happy about it. It does me good to be alone, and mother has made it very pretty and neat for me. My work basket and desk are by the window, and my closet is full of dried herbs that smell

Illustration from Mrs. Burnett's Little Lord Fauntleroy.

very nice. The door that opens into the garden will be very pretty
in summer, and I can run off to the woods when I like.

I have made a plan for my life, as I am in my teens and no
more a child. I am old for my age and don't care much for girls'
things. People think I am wild and queer, but Mother understands
and helps me. I've not told anyone about my plan, but I am going
to be good. I made so many resolutions and written sad notes and
cried over my sins, and it doesn't seem to do any good. Now I am

going to work really, for I feel a true desire to improve and be a help and comfort—not a care or sorrow to my dear mother."

Hillside was the home that later became Wayside, the home of Hawthorne. Its purchase was made possible, not by any efforts on Bronson's part, but by the fact that old Colonel May, the father of Mrs. Alcott, had died leaving a small legacy. Ralph Waldo Emerson, who often helped the Alcotts in the penurious problems, gave them an additional five hundred dollars toward the purchase. It was this home that meant so much to Louisa; Hillside would be the scene of *Little Women*, and that time of her life, the happiest.

They had a house over their heads, but the little money that Alcott managed to bring in would hardly feed a family of six. In 1848 once again they had to move—this time to Boston. Mrs. Alcott was offered a social-work job, while Mr. Alcott did the thing he could do best—talk. He began his "Conversations" in Elizabeth Peabody's shop. He would lecture on anything—diet, for example, and the great advantage of vegetarianism. It was one of his idiosyncracies most disliked by Louisa. A close friend was to say later that when she had first met Louisa her father was declaiming that a vegetable diet would produce unruffled sweetness in temper and disposition. Louisa said softly, "I don't know about that. I've never eaten any meat, and I'm awfully cross and irritable very often."

She tried to sew for a living. By 1853 she had started the inevitable school which was the outlet for every bright New England woman who desired to attempt a living, but by the time she was twenty-two, Louisa decided that teaching was not her forte. She had been scribbling little stories and selling them with a certain success, and by Christmas, 1854, she had succeeded in publishing a book, receiving for it the grand sum of thirty-two dollars. It moved her to write immediately to her mother.

Dear Mother, Into your Christmas stocking, I put my "first born" knowing that you will accept it with all its faults (for Grandmothers are always kind) and look upon it merely as an earnest of what I may yet do; for with so much to cheer me on, I hope to pass in time from fairies and fables to men and realities.

Whatever beauty or poetry is to be found in my little book is owing to your interest in and encouragement of all my efforts from the first to the last. And if ever I do anything to be proud of, my greatest happiness will be that I can thank you for that. This I may do for all the good that there is in me. And I shall be content to write if it gives you pleasure.

Jo is fussing about,
My lamp is going out
To dear Mother, with many kind
wishes for a Happy New Year and
Merry Christmas, I am,
Your ever loving daughter,
Louy

The Pens That Rocked the Cradle and the World

It is true that that first little book was just about what she said—fairies and fancies. They were easier to cope with than the terrible realities; the family more than ever needed whatever money she could contribute. When she didn't write, she sewed, and when she didn't sew, she taught. Finally she wrote to her father, "I am very well and very happy. Things go smoothly, and I think I shall come outright and prove that although an Alcott I can support myself." It was a dig quite lost on father, "I like the independent life," she said, "and although not an easy one, it is a free one, and I enjoy it. . . . I will make a battering ram of my head and make a wave through this rough and tumble world." In her diary she noted: "Read Charlotte Brontë's life, a very interesting one but a sad one, so full of talent and after working long, just as success, love and happiness comes, she dies. I wonder if I shall ever be famous enough for people to care to read my story and struggles."

She continued to write admitted "pot boilers," but at least she was learning. "Life is my college," she said. "May I graduate well and earn some honors."

Finally, in 1860, she headed her diary, "The year of good luck." Alcott was working as a superintendent of schools and had regained some of his authority. "He is," said Louisa, "stirring up the schools like a mild pudding stick." She stirred up something within herself and wrote her first actual book, *Moods*. The shorter pieces that she turned out with ease sold better. Some did not sell. They were anti-slavery, and as she said bitterly, "the dear South must not be offended." She attempted another school, again it was disastrous. Besides, the outside world was troubling her. The war was now at its height, and she went South to the Union hospital at Georgetown. She worked hard but she found within the hospital an intensity of human emotion, or perhaps she simply allowed herself, for the first time, to look at her own compassion.

She came down with a terrible fever and returned home, sickly it's true, but with a manuscript—*Hospital Sketches*, for which she received two hundred dollars. She was thirty years old. Still she had not quite found herself.

It was not until May, 1868, that she makes a notation: Mr. N. wants a girl story, and I begin *Little Women*. So I plod away though

I don't enjoy this sort of thing: our queer plays and experiences may prove interesting, though I doubt it." To which the elder Louisa May Alcott annotated the words, "Good joke." Being the most businesslike of the Alcotts, she kept her copyright, even though the publishers offered to buy it outright.

At thirty-six she had come into her own, and would be a success. She was able then to pay all the family bills, to travel to Europe, enjoying a little freedom from the endless work which she had laid out for herself. She began to be extremely well known. "Dear Mommy," she wrote in 1872, "I had a very transcendental day yesterday, and at night my head was swelling visibly with the ideas cast into it. The club was a funny mixture of rabbis and weedy old ladies—the "oversoul" and oysters. Papa and B. flew clean out of sight like a pair of platonic balloons, and we tried to follow but we couldn't. In the p.m. went to R.W.E.'s reading—all of the literary birds were out in full feather. This humble worm was treated with distinguished condescension."

Her family life was deteriorating distressingly. Her mother was increasingly ill, her favorite sister Beth had died, her brother-in-law had died, and all she could write now was, "When I had the youth, I had no money, now I have the money I have no time, and when I get the time, if I ever do, I have no health to enjoy life. I suppose this is the discipline I need, but it is rather hard to love the things I do and see them go by because duty chains me to my galley. If I come into port at last with all sails set, that will be reward perhaps. Life always was a puzzle to me, and gets more mysterious as I go on. I shall find it out by and by and see that it is all right if I can only keep brave and patient to the end."

Even in her middle age she was still urging herself on like a small child. Woman's suffrage now took a great deal of her time. All the while the books kept pouring out, written under adverse circumstances, written often when she was exhausted or depressed: yet all of them, curiously enough, having a light, delicate touch. She felt herself genuinely harnessed, and yet she could write with the sweet distinction of *Under the Lilacs*. She was a celebrity, but unhappy.

The Pens That Rocked the Cradle and the World

She was attacked by vertigo and rheumatism. She lost another of her sisters, then her father. When she died shortly after, she was a well-known woman, but a sad one.

Yet for her time she was a symbol—a symbol of the writing woman trying her best under enormous difficulties. "I never had a study," she wrote. "My pen and paper would do and my old Atlas on my knee is all I want. . . . I carry a dozen plots in my head and think them over when I am in the mood . . . sometimes I keep one for years and suddenly find it already to write, often lie awake and plan whole chapters word for word, then merely scribble them down as if copying. I used to sit fourteen hours a day at one time, eating little and unable to stir until a certain amount was done." Near the end, she was free with advice to young writers. "Dear sir," she wrote to a young boy in a piece from the old *St. Nicholas* magazine, "I never copy or polish, so I have no old manuscripts to send you, and if I had it would be of little use, for one's personal method is no rule for another. Each must work his own way, and the only drill needed is to keep writing and profit by criticism. Mind grammar, spelling and punctuation. Use short words and express as briefly as you can your meaning. Young people use too many adjectives and try 'to write fine.' The strongest simplest words are best, and no foreign ones, if it can be helped."

As she had arranged everything throughout her life, she arranged her own funeral.

The bare bones of a life, a resumé, a summary, a story. No writer's personal history seems of much moment, and the women writers in particular seemed more often than not (to quote Louisa and Margaret Fuller's friend Thoreau) to have led lives of quiet desperation. Unlike Thoreau, however, there was barely the respite of a Walden Pond. They lived awash in daily affairs . . . work, headaches, a pittance for that story, a pence for another. Behind the scenes often was a family, as demanding as any put upon any man—not only must money be supplied, but also emotional support. But Hawthorne, Emerson, Longfellow—the man of genius, or even talent, was overwhelmed with favor in this period. Hawthorne had his Sophia making for him the proper dressing gown lined with a

Bronson Alcott.

colored silk that would match the ink, a tower room of his own where he would brood about what he would no longer write; Emerson, his Livia, catering to each transcendental whim—the whims were worse than the transcendental wild oats; Carlyle, his Jane, catering to dyspepsia and depression, trying vainly to get a word in edgewise (but when she did they were sharper than a penknife); Longfellow, indulged and venerated; even Thoreau, the neighborhood eccentric, coddled as a slightly demented cousin the other side of the coin of genius.

Louisa? No genius of course. Talent? Yes. Neurotic? Of course. When the twentieth century came there was no better way to describe the hard-working woman writer. She worked. She was brought up on work; the pioneer American woman, shouldering a gun against invaders, planting corn, making a log cabin livable, made work a woman's job. Woman's place was in the home, to be sure—there she worked and there she wrote. On the kitchen table, in a hayloft, by a sickbed (even Jean Kerr in the twentieth century, making light of her own need for a room of her own, sought out the family car and wrote in the street).

Naturally, Louisa was filled with hostility. In the nineteenth century that was a vulgar word. Instead she got headaches (glasses were poor), other aches and pains and experienced a low level, like the persistent fever of discontent. Louisa was unmarried; the talented old maid. It's easy to blame her hypochondria on her spinster

Mr. Alcott's Home.

state. Why? The married women writers had even more to cope with—often there was not only a useless papa but a useless husband as well . . . to be catered to. Was the work a chore or a refuge? Was it not the one place temporarily that they could be free? Needlework, blessed needlework, had always been the woman's refuge—she could stitch, tear out, rip, scissor, piece together: now she could discover a new field, using almost the same technique, stitching, ripping, piecing together.

Louisa started sewing for a living and ended up writing. A book certainly was more lasting than a sampler, and one could cram in a lot more.

Look at *Little Women,* a beautiful story of a joyous family life by a woman who didn't like girls. Why should she? She had supported her sisters, emotionally and financially, a good part of her life. But she was a girl with a beloved, the incredible Marmee—no woman was so good, so sweet, so demanding, although Marmee did not demand love: that came as her natural due. Marmee was the original Jewish mother, by virtue of the Bostonian old Testament, where you not only honored your mother and father but supported them with gentility as well. And Papa, dear Papa. In *Little Women,* Papa is away at war. A graceful literary device. We all know that Louisa's papa was out talking to the world, and the world, even if it listened, wasn't paying for the privilege.

Someone had to pay up. It was Louisa. Her journals were filled

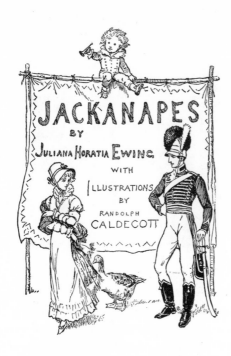

Women were becoming active editors of magazines for children. Juliana Horatia Ewing had started working for such magazines, even as a child, because her mother published the famous *Aunt Judy's Magazine for Children* in Britain. A prolific writer, *Jackanapes* was her most famous book.

with the high points of her life: if she made twenty dollars, she sent fifteen dollars home: if she had a best seller, she paid off the family mortgage. The only sigh of relief that occurs in her pages is the final languishing of family debts.

And yet, how they greeted *Little Women!* That happy home, those joyous girls, sweet death, merry misery . . . and what a great new market had arrived for the lady writer—the world of children's books—or particularly, that little world that was peculiarly her own, the world of girls' books.

Writing for girls was bound to make money. There were so many of them, they were so repressed, they had time on their hands and dreams instead of marbles in their pockets—why not cash in?

The publishers thought so. And a very good word must be said for them because publishers do not, in fact, divide the world into men and women. Writers seem to be a sex completely unto themselves—to be treated halfway between children and cans of soup. Their emotions are childlike, unpredictable—their wares are, as has been stated regularly, like soup—but different kinds. All soup can be merchandised under one label, but publishing a book is like

separately marketing each can. Louisa was the first to can sentiment
—it carries a gourmet label—but it's sentiment all the same.

Soup needs a factory—at least to make it pay. The Brontës kept
their genius simmering on the back of the stove; even if only for
their own satisfaction. But times changed. Publishers became factories. Louisa had written her adult book, *Moods,* and it had failed.
"Some feel it isn't moral," she wrote, "because it speaks freely of
marriage." She atoned by trying to write a book on work, but she
had enough of that. Her life then consisted of debts, dishpans and
despondency. Her own words. She was thirty-one, unmarried. So she
wrote a piece on women. "Happy Women" she called it. Who were
they? That "glorious phalanx of old maids," Theodore Parker called
them, who worked themselves to the bone in his society for the
world.

And then she hit the jackpot with a book for girls. She hadn't
wanted it that way. She had thought of a book for boys, but the
publishers . . . well, the publishers thought a book for girls would
sell better.

She took their advice. She already had a manuscript entitled,
understandably enough because of her own story, "The Pathetic
Family." Why not revise it? "I want to realize my dream of supporting the family and being perfectly independent." Heavenly hope!
Then she thought of the title, *Little Women*—heavenly title. She
was on her way.

And so was every other woman, thought Nathaniel Hawthorne;
"America is now wholly given over to a d—d mob of scribbling
women, and I should have no choice of success while the public taste
is occupied with their trash—and should be ashamed of myself if
I did succeed."

He was right, a great deal was trash . . . and a great deal was
written by women. They turned out, for example, endless books of
etiquette—America needed *refinement* and the early nineteenth-
century woman who had been required to express sensibility now
was absolutely obliged to be refined. Not only that, it became her
role to "refine" man. The "great revolution" in book publishing in
America made her job easier. Etiquette books cajoled, argued, de-

manded a propriety of conduct. The man's place was at business, his concern was making money; the woman's place was at home, and it was her place to make it cultured.

The men thundered from the pulpit. The Reverend Lyman Beecher, for example, with the connivance of a Protestant God and the vessel of a wife, produced six minister sons and three "scribbling" daughters—all concerned with culture and reform. His wife, understandably enough, bought him an etiquette book—he needed it. In East Hampton, on Long Island, when Beecher held the pulpit there, "thundering to his parishioners" ("a regular caution," they said), he had a fierce love of eeling in the local bay. When he came upon a particularly rich harvest of fish and eel, he'd remove his trousers, knot the legs together, deposit the fish and eel therein, and walk home through the village, "a sight to see."

Perhaps in reaction his daughters were exceptionally refined: they also suffered from "nerves." A nervous condition was almost adamant for the ladies of the time, and the women "scribblers" seemed to have had more than their share of headaches, nausea, fainting spells, lassitude, and the eternal vapors. (Louisa May Alcott had been particularly prone to vapors—as had been her married sisters, who never put pen to paper—in part the vapors served as a kind of birth control, holding a husband at bay.)

Lyman's daughter, Catherine, recognized early that it was not etiquette the country needed so much as a good look at the health of the women of the United States, where one found a "terrible decay." Why not find new remedies for these constant complaints: the old water cures, sulphur cures, chemical baths, and rhubarb treatments had failed. Why not try "Light, Air, Sleep, Food and Clothing?" It was an innovative suggestion, and her books were milestones.

Her sister, Harriet, took her advice, even to the extent of a long separation from her husband, himself a particularly "nervous" type, prone to piles, nervous passions and pusilanimity. When she left him to take a "health cure," writing back to him to "soak" his feet to keep himself calm, she suddenly found her mysterious paralysis of the left side had subsided. Reconciled with him, she found him a job, and herself a measure of liberation. She wrote *Uncle Tom's*

Harriet Beecher Stowe. From a daguerreotype by Southworth and Hawes.

Cabin. A true reformer she *was* concerned with the problem of slavery, but in her eyes that influential book stemmed from the breakdown of family life as witnessed by her own marriage. The greatest selling book of the nineteenth century—by man or woman—*Uncle Tom's Cabin* was in part a retreat from Calvin Stowe.

While Nathaniel Hawthorne, wrapped in his velvet writing robe and indulged in his tower study (just as he had been indulged for the seventeen years he had lived under the eaves in blissful solitude, waited on hand and foot by his mother and sisters), complained of scribbling women, it might be interesting to take a look at Harriet and the "scribbler's" average working conditions. She writes to her sister of settling in Brunswick where Calvin would teach:

"From the time that I left Cincinnati with my children to come forth to a country that I knew not of almost to the present time, it has seemed as if I could scarcely breathe, I was so pressed with care. My head dizzy with the whirl of railroads and steamboats; then ten days' sojourn in Boston, and a constant toil and hurry in buying my furniture and equipments; and then landing in Brunswick in the midst of a drizzly, inexorable northeast storm, and beginning the work of getting in order a deserted, dreary, damp old house. All day long running from one thing to another, as, for example, thus:—

Mrs. Stowe, how shall I make this lounge, and what shall I cover the back with first?

Mrs. Stowe. With the coarse cotton in the closet.

Woman. Mrs. Stowe, there isn't any more soap to clean the windows.

Mrs. Stowe. Where shall I get soap?

Here, H., run up to the store and get two bars.

There is a man below wants to see Mrs. Stowe about the cistern. Before you go down, Mrs. Stowe, just show me how to cover this round end of the lounge.

There's a man up from the depot, and he says that a box has come for Mrs. Stowe, and it's coming up to the house; will you come down and see about it?

Mrs. Stowe, don't go till you have shown the man how to nail that carpet in the corner. He's nailed it all crooked; what shall he do? The black thread is all used up, and what shall I do about putting gimp on the back of that sofa? Mrs. Stowe, there is a man come with a lot of pails and tinware from Furbish; will you settle the bill now?

Mrs. Stowe, here is a letter just come from Boston inclosing that bill of lading; the man wants to know what he shall do with the goods. If you will tell me what to say, I will answer the letter for you.

Mrs. Stowe, the meat-man is at the door. Hadn't we better get a little beefsteak, or something, for dinner?

Shall Hatty go to Boardman's for some more black thread?

Mrs. Stowe, this cushion is an inch too wide for the frame. What shall we do now?

Mrs. Stowe, where are the screws of the black walnut bedstead?

Here's a man has brought in these bills for freight. Will you settle them now?

Mrs. Stowe, I don't understand using this great needle. I can't make it go through the cushion; it sticks in the cotton.

"Then comes a letter from my husband, saying he is sick abed, and all but dead; don't ever expect to see his family again; wants to know how I shall manage, in case I am left a widow; knows we shall get in debt and never get out; wonders at my courage; thinks

Original illustration from Uncle Tom's Cabin.

I am very sanguine; warns me to be prudent, as there won't be much to live on in case of his death, etc., etc., etc. I read the letter and poke it into the stove, and proceed. . . . had divers communings with Deacon Dunning of the Baptist church. Also during this time good Mrs. Mitchell and myself made two sofas, or lounges, a barrel chair, divers bedspreads, pillow cases, pillows, bolsters, mattresses; we painted rooms; we revarnished furniture; we—what *didn't* we do?

"Then came on Mr. Stowe; and then came the eighth of July and my little Charley. I was really glad for an excuse to lie in bed, for I was full tired, I can assure you. Well, I was what folks call very comfortable for two weeks when my nurse had to leave me. . . .

"During this time I have employed my leisure hours in making up my engagements with newspaper editors. I have written more than anybody, or I myself, would have thought. I have taught an hour a day in our school, and I have read two hours every evening to the children. The children study English history in school, and I am reading Scott's historical novels in their order. To-night I finish the Abbot; shall begin Kenilworth next week; yet I am constantly pursued and haunted by the idea that I don't do anything. Since I began this note I have been called off at least a dozen times; once for the fish-man to buy a codfish; once to see a man who had brought me some barrels of apples; once to see a bookman; then to Mrs. Upham, to see about a drawing I promised to make for her; then to nurse the baby; then into the kitchen to make a chowder for dinner; and now I am at it again, for nothing but deadly determination enables me ever to write; it is rowing against wind and tide."

Harriet Beecher Stowe's only holiday had been two weeks in bed after the birth of her son Charley; Aunt Harriet's cabin might have been graced with finer curtains, but it was slave quarters none the less.

Children, however, were often a comfort. With few exceptions writing women were inordinately fond of children—and dogs—and witness Beatrix Potter's rabbits, moles, mice, ducks and drakes! One feels Beatrix might have been happier if a child were a barnyard animal.

If the writing woman had no children, she had another role; she could write about them *and* make money. So began the golden age of children's literature. Books and magazines rolled from the presses. Every home had a library of sorts; every household had a reading child. The woman writer had become a literary pacifier.

8

THE QUEEN WAS IN THE PARLOR
AND OTHER VICTORIAN PRIVATE LIVES

The Queen is most anxious to enlist everyone who can speak or write to join in checking this mad wicked folly of Women's Rights, with all its attendant horrors, on which her poor, feeble sex is bent, forgetting every sense of womanly feeling and propriety.

Letter of Queen Victoria to Mrs. Theodore Martin

The pursuits of art and literature are not so unfortunate for women in that they do not involve any unfeminine tendancy. At worst they rob a woman of domestic life, and rob domestic life of a woman—two of the worst robbings to be sure that can be effected either by selfish violence, or misdirected views of good.

Scribners Monthly, 1871

What can our daughters want more than they have now," they would ask. They have a good home and every comfort and the society of their parents' friends; perhaps a carriage to drive in and horses to ride. What more can they possibly desire. To such parents I would only reply: *Your daughter wants herself.*

Alys W. Pearsall Smith, 1894

Women are intelligent; they are not creative.

A. Orr, 1876

THE year was 1837. Princess Alexandrina Victoria had gone to bed one night and awakened early the next morning Queen Victoria.

Her age, as Margaret Fuller said, by the mere fact that it bore a woman's name, had to have some effect on the position of women. Rights was a word yet to be heard; no one had them. There were no unions of any kind, labor was yet to have a voice; for that matter, in the countryside, very few could read and write. In the cities the populations doubled. London was filled with hawkers and ballad-mongers selling their wares, and the Grub Street writers who wrote such "scurrilous libels" in daily poems went to jail for their wit.

The few ladies who suffered literature found that the keepsake books sufficed. They appeared from the presses with astonishing regularity: *The Forget Me Not, The Book of Beauty, Flowers of Loveliness.* You could look at the pictures and forget them. As new ones arrived they were shelved, their pages stuck together with old locks of hair, four-leaf clovers, a sprig of heather. Often compiled by women, they were written for women; filled with painfully weak verse, they would often, however, give some concrete advice.

"There is something unfeminine in independence," wrote Mrs. John Sandford. "It is contrary to Nature and therefore it offends. A really sensible woman feels her dependence, she does what she can, but she is conscious of inferiority and therefore grateful for support. In everything that women attempt they should show their consciousness of dependence. They should remember that by them influence is to be obtained, not by assumption, but by a delicate appeal to affection or principle. Women in this respect are some-thing like children—the more they show their need of support, the more engaging they are."

A Victorian woman writer, from a print by J. W. Orr.

"My wife is a woman of mind."

"Nonsense," said Mary Russell Mitford. After all, she was the only "best seller" woman writer of the year with her charming picture of country life, and she had been supporting Papa for years. She had preened herself that year, not so much for the book's success, as for the pride she took in the silver medal won at the horticultural show for her entry—garden parsley. Her next greatest delight was a new pen pal.

"Dearest Miss Mitford, when you are out in your garden, do you *sit* a great deal? Now at night—during those watching writing nights—against which there is no use remonstrating—do you sit them all? If you do—indeed it is very bad for you. And it would be so wise if you could learn to be a *lollard* like me, and establish yourself on the sofa instead of on a chair, and study the art, not a very difficult one, of writing in a recumbent position. I can write as well or as badly when I lie down, as at a desk. I used once to suffer from a feebleness in the spine; and even now it is exceedingly fatiguing to me to sit bolt upright without the mediation of the back of a chair, for any length of time. But with *your* tendency I am quite sure that a recumbent—not merely a leaning position—would be essentially useful to you. Would lessen both the actual fatigue, and the evils consequent upon sedentary habits."

Miss Mitford, to whom Elizabeth Barrett wrote this letter, was indeed inclined to sit far too long at her desk writing innumerable articles, letters, and, a few lasting, enchanting books. She supported herself and her father (the dear, dear Doctor Mitford, Elizabeth called him), who was not only an outrageous gambler, but also the last of the quacks.

Dr. Mitford had received his training from the remarkable Dr. Graham who had established the Temple of Health, the adventuresome "new sciences of magnetism and electricity" (both highly appealing to many of the literary ladies of the day). For all the physical complaints of the time Dr. Graham (no relation to the Dr. Graham of health-bread fame) offered cures for "the whole art of enjoying health and vigor of body and mind, and of preserving and exalting personal beauty and loveliness; or in other words, of living with health, honor and happiness in this world, for at least a hundred years."

One of the best ways to live a hundred years was to take mud baths; he and his officiating junior priest, Dr. Mitford, publicly sank into the mud up to their necks to show its effectiveness, but they gained less attention than another devotee of natural cures—an extraordinary lass indeed who had given up a job as a nursemaid, to become Vestina, the Goddess of Health, for our two mountebanks. She attracted one of the largest audiences in London, being of surpassing beauty, and managing despite the mud, to keep intact a fabulous hair-do, elaborately dressed with feathers, powder, ropes of pearls and flowers. Later she would be far better known as Lady Hamilton, wife of Sir William Hamilton and friend of Lord Nelson. Before she gave up her larks in the mud, however, she was advertised in the press as "Vestina, the rosy Goddess of Health, presides at the evening lecture, assisting at the display of the celestial meteors, and of that sacred vital fire oven which she watches, and whose application in the cure of diseases she daily has the honor of directing."

The "vital fires" died down fast. Graham died bankrupt, Vestina moved on to the aristocracy, and Dr. Mitford moved on to squander three fortunes before he discovered he had a "vital fire" in his own parlor, a petite, plain paragon of a daughter, Mary Mitford, who could write nearly as fast as Papa could pocket the profits.

The "Bloomers" in Hyde Park, or an extraordinary Exhibition for 1852.

The Victorian paterfamilias was often remarkable, drinking a little too much, gambling a little too much, talking a little too much, oftentimes denying his daughters the affection of their friends, particularly their literary friends. The good Dr. Mitford, for example, found no one in the world of letters worthy of his daughter with the possible exception of Elizabeth Barrett, and it was Elizabeth's father that kept her Elizabeth Barrett for far too long. Because if Dr. Mitford was irascible and a spendthrift, Mr. Barrett, as the world has long since discovered, was a tyrant and a misanthrope.

It was a strange combination, these two literary ladies of Victorian England. Mary Russell Mitford was, in the terms of her society, almost overactive. She was always dashing about with remarkably good temper. She described herself as a good-humored old maid and a very likeable person. She was fifty years old with no undue respect for herself, despite the fact that in her day she managed to conjure up as much enthusiasm as had Madame de

Staël. Indeed a friend had actually told her—and as she related the comment to her father—that "No one had been received recently with such a mixture of respect and enthusiasm as I have been—not even Madame de Staël." It must have given the sweet Miss Mitford a momentary delight to be coupled with the wicked Germaine. Of course it was the conversation of Madame de Staël's that was so memorable, so Miss Mitford hoped. Certainly that lady's private life with all that business of having gentlemen jump in and out of her carriage to pursue her to bed was nothing that Miss Mitford would emulate. Germaine in the latter years had grown unattractive, but wasn't it the truth, Miss Mitford said, not discounting herself, that all literary ladies were ugly? "I never met one in my life" she wrote, "that might not have served for a scarecrow to keep the birds from the cherries."

Then she changed her mind. She met one so gentle, so pretty, even at thirty a sweet, immature flower. She met the world's most famous invalid, Elizabeth Barrett. They were so remarkably different. One fifty years old, famous, outgoing; one thirty, thirsty for life, and utterly dependent.

Miss Mitford resentfully felt that she was chained to her desk, a galley slave to the oar. Miss Barrett, who sneaked in the writing of a little poetry or even the reading of a book out of the careful watch of Papa's eye, rejoiced in her dark and pallid life. There was no color, she said, only the color in her poetry; the rest of her, "nothing but a root fit for the ground and the dark."

Well, that must have been a challenge to Miss Mitford indeed. Could she not make any living thing grow? Was she not a creature of the open air, was she not the famous author of *Our Village?* Could she not do for poetry what she had done for parsley?

She was a pioneer, the forerunner of the woman writer today who does almost a monthly magazine article filled with birdsong and the making of jam and the foibles of neighbors. But Mary Mitford went deeper, she was the first to try to delineate country scenery and country manners with a hearty love of her subject. She was the first to look upon village life as "copy" and her own village as the ideal one; not with the genius of the Brontës or of George Eliot who would use their countryside as a canvas of private passions, but just with the delicate touch of a woman who was confined too long at her desk, and who balanced it with fresh air and the sunshine of nature. She wrote with immediacy about the first primrose or violet or the cowslip ball or a hard summer or nutting. She could write as simply as Dorothy Wordsworth at times, and there were certainly those who preferred her to Dorothy's brother, the muckamuck of the north who, once his early drive and creative spirit were extinguished, grew pompous about his own countryside.

Victorian England took to its heart her delightful book, *Our Village.* They bought it because of their own nostalgia. The industrial revolution was beginning to destroy the landscape and even the most staunch Victorian would pretend to himself that, reading the pages of such books as Miss Mitford's, he too was a flower child, walking in an ideal rural atmosphere, past tidy, square, red cottages, well-stocked gardens, fat, noisy children, "the very essence of vulgarity and plenty," Miss Mitty would add.

Girls in white frocks melted into the background of a profusion of white stocks, delicate maidens and strong men stood before whitewashed inns with gentle landlords—an ideal community. But Miss Mitford had a nice touch; she was jealous. There were those whose gardens grew when hers did not and then she would say about a neighbor, "It is very magnanimous of me not to hate her for she beats me in my own way, chrysanthemums and dahlias and the like. Her plants are longer lived, mine have a sad trick of dying, perhaps because I love them, not wisely but too well and kill them with overkindness."

So she picked up a new flower, already rooted in poetry, Elizabeth Barrett, and proceeded to "kill" her with overkindness. Elizabeth Barrett was overjoyed, better to be killed with overkindness than to be shattered by neglect. At least the neglect of the thinking part of herself; the rest was, if anything, overindulged. The inadequate medical help of the day further confused her, digitalis for her pulse because it was too weak, then laudanum because her pulse was too strong. She had headaches and bilious fevers, she coughed blood, was constipated and, all in all, was the suffering poet. She might go out tomorrow if Papa would let her, she might go downstairs if Papa would let her, she might write a letter if Papa would let her. She might, God forbid, write a poem, if Papa turned aside his eye. Occasionally she quoted an old rustic friend of her father's who said, "Why sir, I enjoys very bad health, indeed." Her fantastic interest in her ill health was shot through with enjoyment. She had to watch out for the prevalent east wind that always brought an attack. She had to suffer the passive fatigue of being carried down the stairs— that always brought on an attack. She had to suffer Papa's patience and love for her that always brought on an attack.

Miss Mitford was patient; her flower would bloom, she would be introduced by publication slowly to the literary world. She should be encouraged to write and eat properly and to sit in the garden, perhaps even on a straight-backed chair. She must have a dog, and one of the famous Flush's ancestors was sent by Miss Mitford from her farm at Three Miles Cross. Elizabeth enjoyed acting the child to the older Miss Mitford. "There never was an emptier-headed body than I am," she would say with delight in one letter, but the

As It Ought To Be or the ladies trying a contemptible scoundrel for a "Breach of Promise."

adult part of her wanted more of the outside world, even books. "What can I do bound hand and foot in this wilderness in the way of book ferreting, with a physician who groans in the spirit when he sees within my reach any book larger and graver looking than the last new octavo neatly bound. Luckily my Plato looks as good as a novel on the outside, but you tempted me with Bishop Andrews and the Bishop is in folio and I was in an obstinate fit and I did read and was scolded. And all for the love of you."

The letters of mutual adulation continued for a long while, then suddenly there was a new note in Elizabeth's to Mary Mitford:

"I have read the *Bells and Pomegranates!* 'Pippa passes' . . . comprehension, I was going to say! Think of me living in my glass house and throwing pebbles out of the windows!! But really 'Pippa passes,' I must say, Mr. Browning's ordinary measure of mystery. Now laugh at me. Laugh, as you please. I like, I do like the 'heart of a mystery' when it beats moderate time. I like a twilight of

mysticism—when the sun and the moon both shine together. Yes—
and I like 'Pippa' too. . . . After all, Browning is a true poet—and
there are not many such poets."

Miss Mitford for her part gave a critical sniff. They were not
always in agreement on the poets and the novelists about whom they
corresponded, but they were usually not in complete disagreement.
Now such a disagreement sprang up. Miss Mitford had met Robert
Browning long before Elizabeth ever met him and had found him
intolerable. As a matter of fact she had met him the day before she
became acquainted with Elizabeth and in a later letter to a friend,
she made very clear what she thought of him: "I saw Mr. Browning
once and remember thinking how exactly he resembled a girl dressed
in boy's clothes, and, as to his poetry, I have just your opinion of
it. It is one heap of obscurity, confusion and weakness. Do you know
him personally, did you ever see him? I met him once, as I told you
when he had long ringlets and no neck cloth and when he seemed

"The Rights of Women" or the Effects of Female Enfranchisment.

to me about the height and size of a boy twelve years old—Femmelette—is a word made for him." Then in after years she commented, "A strange sort of person to carry a woman such as Elizabeth Barrett off her feet."

Elizabeth Barrett was, according to Miss Mitford, "the most remarkable woman probably that ever lived." With a certain amount of ambiguity she had written to Elizabeth, "My love and ambition for you often seems to be more like that of a mother for a son or a father for a daughter (the two fondest of natural emotions) than the common bonds of even close friendship between two women of different ages and similar pursuits. I sit and think of you and of the poems that you will write and of that strange brief rainbow crown called fame until a vision is before me as vividly as ever a mother's heart hailed the eloquence of a patriot son. Do you understand this and do you pardon it? It is a strange feeling, but one of undescribable pleasure, my pride and hopes seem almost merged in

you." Now what was this talk of Browning, sniffed Miss Mitford. After all, marriage itself was one of the most foolish things under the sun. "Women of genius," in particular she noticed, "make great mistakes in choosing husbands."

At fifty Miss Mitford was much happier just supporting Papa. There was, after all, the possibility in those days that a woman who made money from her pen would not only have to support Papa, but a husband as well, and certainly that would be foolish.

Miss Barrett was a true romantic. Was not marriage every woman's chief concern? Was not a happy marriage the happiest state? Miss Mitford used to say tut, tut to the "romantic child." On that she was right; Elizabeth was utterly romantic. But fortunately, when the next attack came it came not from the east wind, but from Browning and instead of taking to her couch Elizabeth rose from it like one resurrected.

The rest of the story is as well known as the drama and film world could make it. The elopement from Wimpole Street, the escape to Italy, the ideal marriage. Before she was, as Miss Mitford and Elizabeth's father would have it, "almost abducted," Miss Barrett's tone was changing. Where once she had urged Miss Mitford to get out of her chair and write in bed (the most unlikely of possibilities; it's rather like seeing Queen Victoria stretched out as Madame Recamier), now she argued, "You made a mistake in fancying before that I never change my position from a reclining one, also was a mistake that you said that I like to shut my windows and live in the dark."

All these were changed now and in one of her final letters from Wimpole Street she wrote to Miss Mitford regarding Browning: "He overcame me at last, whether it was that an unusual alikeness of mind (the high and low may be alike in the general features) a singular closeness of sympathy on a thousand subjects drew him fast to me, or whether it was love simple, which after all is love proper, an unreasonable instinct, accident "falling" as the idiom says, the truth became obvious that he would be happier with me than apart from me. And I . . . why I am as any other woman in the world with a heart belonging to her. He is best, noblest, if you knew him *you* should be the praiser."

One can still hear Miss Mitford sniff as she put down that note. To look back upon Miss Mitford today we can delight at some of the stretches of *Our Village*, but for the rest she is almost a shadow on the literary landscape. But Elizabeth, that great, that noblest of women writers, as so many called her, has suffered perhaps a fate more difficult. She knew an embarrassment of riches in her own time and as such is a little figure of fun today. And yet, she too was a pioneer because she used her pen, as they said in the nineteenth century, with "a general philanthropic impulse in an effort to alleviate the distress of factory operators of overworked children and of all men and women into whose souls the iron of an indifferent and cruel civilization had too deeply entered."

The lady writer, then, of Mrs. Browning's type was the noble one, and not only noble but, as Browning himself described her, also the perfect wife. There she sat with her "great brow propped by the spirit small hand," writing away with a great passion—misunder-

Harriet Martineau wrote about her experience at the coronation of Victoria in 1837.

stood, but with frequently a far greater understanding of the depth of her age than we would suspect. "This alive throbbing age that brawls, cheats, maddens, calculates and aspires," she said.

Yes, she was good, but not as good as the Victorian critics would have her. Yet the always somewhat negative attitude towards women's ability to write was never better used for effect than Peter Bayne in his contemporary summing up of Elizabeth Browning:

" 'I am, of course, not acquainted,' I remarked when, many years ago, I first had occasion to print my estimate of Mrs. Browning, 'with the works of all great female writers, perhaps not even of many. But as you look towards the brow of a towering mountain, rising far over the clouds, and crowned with ancient snow, you may have an assurance, even though it rises from a plain, or, if amid lower hills, though you have not actually taken the elevation of each, that in height it is peerless. In the poems of Mrs. Browning are qualities which admit of their being compared with those of the greatest men; touches which *only* the mightiest give. These may not come often enough, or they may be too often associated with the spasm of woman's vehemence, to permit her a seat beside those mightiest. With the few sovereigns of literature, the Homers, Shakespeares, Miltons, she will not rank. But in full recollection of Scott's vivacity, and bright, cheerful glow; of Byron's fervid passion and magnificent description; of Wordsworth's majesty; of Shelley's million-coloured

191

Florence Nightingale comforts a wounded soldier during the Crimean War. Lithograph by J. A. Vinter after Henry Barraud, 1855.

fancy; of Coleridge's occasional flights right into the sun-glare; of Bailey's tropic exuberance, and of Tennyson's golden calm; I yet hold her worthy of being mentioned with any poet of this century. She has the breadth and versatility of a man; no sameliness, no one idea, no type character; our single Shakespearean woman. In this I am agreed with by the author of *The Raven*, a critic of great acuteness and originality. 'Woman, sister,' says Thomas De Quincey, 'there are some things which you do not execute as well as your brother, man; no, nor ever will. Pardon me, if I doubt whether you will ever produce a great poet from your choirs, or a Mozart, or a Phidias, or a Michael Angelo, or a great scholar; by which last is meant, not one who depends simply on an infinite memory, but also on an infinite and electrical power of combination, bringing together from the four winds, like the angel of the resurrection, what else were dust from dead men's bones, into the unity of breathing life. If you *can* create yourselves into any of these great creators, why have you not?' Mrs. Browning has exalted her sex; this passage *was* true.

"There is, perhaps, more of enthusiasm than of discrimination in these young-mannish sentences. Mrs. Browning I still hold to be, in the full sense of the term, a great poet, but I now see that De Quincey might have maintained the negative on that question with more weighty reasoning than I then surmised; and when I so confidently pronounced Mrs. Browning the greatest of women, fame was but beginning to whisper the name of George Eliot. I would now content myself with saying that, in fervour, melodiousness, and splendour of poetic genius, Mrs. Browning stands, to the best of my knowledge, first among women; that, in tunefulness, the distinctive quality of the poet, George Eliot is greatly her inferior; but that, in knowledge of life, insight into character, comprehensiveness and penetration of thought and the plastic energy by which the literary artist moulds his figures, she was not the equal of George Eliot."

And so, too, George Eliot. Perhaps the most revealing glance is as she strides along Westminster Bridge to be constantly accosted by autograph hunters. The woman writer is now news, a popular figure, her name a household word. Yet George Eliot's real name was Mary Ann Evans—for women of true genius were still hiding their identities under a masculine pseudonym—books still sold better that way. Besides, Mary Ann Evans had more to hide in that Victorian age; she had given up God and was living in sin. Who would have predicted such a future? The first truly modern novelist, an agnostic, and a woman living with someone else's man?

She had been a deeply religious little country girl; her religion had been further entrenched by eight years at a school where she

Charles Dickens.

had become a raging Calvinist. Her "finishing school" was three years at an evangelical school taught by daughters of a Baptist minister. Germaine de Staël had said she loved God, Papa and Liberty. The young Mary Ann loved God, Papa and Duty.

For ten years she dealt with all three. Her mother died when she was eighteen and for ten bitter years she was Papa's housekeeper. Ten years, ten awful years of boredom and tedium, of looking in the mirror and just seeing the face that even she could not respond to—how could others?

Yet they did. There was always in Mary Ann Evans' life somebody who would sense her great need for expression, that need for experience, that passionate desire to live more fully than other persons. First there were her friends, the Brays, who introduced her to a circle in Coventry. Bray was madly evangelical, a more exciting outlook than Calvinism. From there it was a step perhaps, but a hard and difficult one, to agnosticism. Too much religion leads to none at all and Mary Ann Evans was to be without one of the great rocks on which Victorian life so easily chained itself. Her books show almost a pagan delight in the world around her, they also show that she was satisfied with lesser gods than the Calvinists had set up.

As a matter of fact she went out of her way to find lesser gods, and her personal life in those early years before she went to live with George Henry Lewes as his wife was filled with minor episodes of ill-concealed devotion to some great man.

First there was Dr. Brabant, "a learned man" as he was known in those days. His name now means nothing to us, but his method of writing was an eternal Penelope's web, "always writing and rewriting, correcting and destroying." He was one of those great figures, or so it would appear to this young girl, who was going to accomplish something, and yet never accomplished anything. He was already sixty-three years old when she, a young woman, fell to her knees before him, eager to devote her life to his service as she had once devoted her life to God. It was an unfortunate encounter. He had a wife who, alas, was blind but not stupid, and a vigilant sister-in-law, who knew that such devotion would be "abortive." So Mary Ann Evans left the house a sadder woman than she had entered it.

Then there was Chapman, the bon vivant, sometimes a seducer, the publisher of her first book, her translation of Strauss's *Jesus*. Looking for another god, she found one curiously enough in John Chapman, living like some Zeus, not on Mt. Olympus but in a rather squalid house in London, and not only with his wife, a strange Hera, indeed, but also with his mistress, Elizabeth Hilley. Young Mary Ann Evans, with, as Henry James said, her "horsey features," gamboled into this idyllic situation with all the grace of a bewildered Pegasus.

In January, 1851, Mary Ann found herself boarding in this curious menage, looking, as too many literary women have, for the joy of sharing her great mind. Chapman's mind was not great, but that did not matter because Mary Ann had the enormous satisfaction of projecting upon many of the men she knew her own intellectual desires. With Chapman she went a step further. More than a roué, he was undoubtedly able to arouse the girl. She admitted that she feared her father's death because she did not know what feelings this would let loose, what repressions might break down. For three months this strange Victorian encounter went on, the long-suffering wife, Susanna, the vivacious and hostile mistress, Elizabeth, the painfully infatuated Mary Ann, and "the callous dog," Chapman. After three months he wrote in his diary, *"M* departed today. I accompanied her to the railway. She was very sad and hence made me feel very sad too. She pressed me for some information of the state of my feelings. I told her that I felt great affection for her, but that I loved *E* and *S* also, though each in a different way. At this avowal she burst into tears. I tried to comfort her and reminded her of the dear friends she was returning to, but the train whirled her away very very sad."

She was whirled away to her friends the Brays again, but at least Chapman had done several things for her. He hadn't taken her to bed, but at least he had taken her to the *Westminster Review*, where she learned the daily chores of editing and getting a magazine to press. In reality he started her on her professional career, a career in which so many women in the nineteenth century combined both their writing and their knowledge of publishing at the same time.

Chapman also introduced her to two men who were to have extraordinary effects on her life, the great philosopher Herbert Spen-

Robert Browning. From an oil painting by Gordigiani.

cer, and the man whose mistress she would be until his death, George Henry Lewes. If she sought a god, she did not necessarily find an Adonis in Spencer. He was without doubt one of the great eccentrics of his age. He was an inveterate hypochondriac, stopping in the middle of any conversation to take his own pulse. If his pulse became overstimulated by conversation that he overheard, he would simply put plugs in his ears and be quiet for the rest of the day. The earplugs "were formed of a band, almost semicircular in shape with a little velvet covered knob at either end which was pressed by the spring in the band of the flaps over the hole of each ear." They protected him from lots of conversations he did not care to hear, and he was known for saying "musn't talk now" as he retreated into his own private brown study. However, in reality in his own house, it wasn't a brown study, it was purple.

He had a particular passion, his early lady biographers explained, for "impure" purple, and it was their delight that somewhere along the line, he had fallen in love with a lady with an impure purple aura. It wouldn't be surprising—certainly he was not one to attract the great beauties of the day, but he did have that godlike quality that attracted Mary Ann.

One could picture him driving in the streets of London in his victoria, crying wildly, "Stop, stop!" The traffic was wicked in the London of those days, but it would have halted. Mr. Spencer would have stopped for a good reason—to take his pulse.

196

Elizabeth Barrett Browning. From an oil painting by Gordigiani.

Like all unattractive men, he was attracted to beautiful women. He was known to remove himself from a luncheon the minute an unattractive woman sat down, and he maintained that "beauty is but skin deep" was absurd praise; it is a skin-deep saying because "the beauty of features is generally accompanied by the beauty of nature." He must have brought out some beauty in Mary Ann because it was rumored they would marry. He made long, detailed lists of the advantages and disadvantages of marriage and obviously the nays outweighed the ayes by far. Still they went to the theater together, and to the opera. He found her mentally "the most admirable woman he ever knew" but love was quite far from his mind. He was simply too involved with his own pulse.

Many years later Beatrice Webb wrote in *My Apprenticeship,* "Poor Herbert Spencer on reading the proof of his *Autobiography,* I often think of that life given up to feeling his pulse and analysing his sensations with no near friend to be all in all to him. . . . Strange that he should never have felt the sacrifice he was making. "I was never in love," he answered when I asked the question straight."

And Mary Ann Evans wrote pathetically on April 27, 1852, "We have agreed that we are not in love with each other."

But it was through Spencer that Miss Evans met Lewes, a man with whom Spencer found his ear plugs a necessity. Lewes was a philosopher, a vivacious man, a great talker, interested in all the questions of the day. Some meanly said, a jack-of-all-trades and a

Edward Moulton Barret. From a painting by H. W. Pickersgill, R. A.

master of none. He was free as the wind. For the first time we get a comment on Mary Ann Evans' appearance that is touched by love: "Striking by its power when in repose, her face was remarkably transfigured by a smile." With Lewes, one thinks, she must have smiled a great deal.

Lewes' father had been a famous comedian. He himself was a great raconteur and a superb mimic. He'd actually been in theatrical companies of Dickens and had appeared once or twice professionally in Manchester in Shakespearian plays. For the first time he had played a Shylock that had never been seen in England, with a new conception in which the Shylock was represented as a champion and an avenger of a persecuted race. The stage could not hold him. He became a drama critic, an excellent one, but that job, too, could not hold him. He must turn to a biographical history of philosophy and, in his spare time, work on the life of Goethe. He was one of the first popularizers of knowledge, a true gentleman of letters.

Mary Ann met Lewes in 1851. He was beyond doubt a minor literary god; Mary Ann could quite safely believe that she might join his pantheon. He was so amusing, and she needed amusement. She had little else, just dedication and high resolve and an almost extraordinarily dull devotion to the more tedious books of literature. This fellow was something else again; the Carlyles, Jane and Thomas, who were apt to be a little bitter about many London celebrities, liked him enormously. "He is the most amusing little fellow in the whole world—if you only look over his unparalleled impudence which is not impudence at all, but man of genius, bonhomie. He is the best mimic in the world and full of famous stories. Neither spleen nor envy nor bad thing in him, so that you receive him with open arms in spite of his immense ugliness."

He was ugly. There again they had something to share, Lewes and Miss Evans—two ugly people, making a valiant attempt to grasp a beautiful life. He was married, of course, although his marriage had foundered. Jane Carlyle described the breakup: "Perfect little lovebirds cuddling on the same perch had blown to pieces in the spring winds and the little female lovebird had hopped off taking a somewhat critical view of her shaggy little mate." Shaggy Lewes combined his dress, as the contemporary comments say, between morning and evening clothes with the less pleasing aspect of both.

Ugly, it didn't matter; shaggy, it didn't matter. Mary Ann loved him and that was enough . . . besides he encouraged her to write. Only after their "marriage" did those sturdy novels come from her pen: novels that pointed their way to a new shape. "She stands," said Lord David Cecil, "at the gateway between the old and the new, a massive caryatid, heavy of countenance, uneasy of attitude, but nobly monumental, profoundly impressive."

Another portrait: Margaret Oliphant. Even in the Victorian age she looked like someone's maidenly aunt. The face is soft, the mouth slightly pursed, the gray hair prematurely giving her an older look, the white ruffled cap on her head, the starched white stand-up collar, the black brooch, the two crosses, the slightly puffed sleeves. All carefully modeled in soft black pencil, Mrs. Oliphant, called Maggie by her friends . . . an almost forgotten voice today, but in the nineteenth century omnipresent on every publishing list, the indefatigable worker, the pride of letters. We can total her books from the bibliographies; they come to more than one hundred and fifty-two published works and of them more than a fair proportion are in three volumes. How did she do it?

She was a Scot. Hard work comes as naturally to a Scot as a

Elizabeth Barrett Browning.

gift for words, and certainly in the history of Scottish literature women writers seem to have had a vigorous desire to put their thoughts on paper. The men wrote too, but they had other fields of expression: in the pulpits, in the law courts, in the medical schools, in public life. But Mrs. Oliphant did not write to "express" herself; she wrote to keep her home together. She wrote, as did a legion of Victorian women, because it was a way to make money. If in the

A contemporary pencil drawing of George Eliot, born Mary Ann Evans, who became one of the greatest novelists of the nineteenth century.

course of their working lives they were occasionally visited by genius, they rejoiced. Some of their work might live; a great deal of it, they knew, would not. Mrs. Oliphant had the sharp sense of reality that comes to most Scots, hard pressed. And that she was a woman made that reality even more significant. There had been her dear husband, a gentle artist, who died young, and her boys to raise, then her brother's boys to raise. One could not be idle. One could rarely, if ever, be alone.

Mrs. Oliphant admitted that she was timid about one thing. She did not care to have anyone sitting at the table while she worked. That did not mean that she could not write and share in the conversations that went on around her. As she said, she never once had a separate room, or had been able "to hedge herself off." Her study was a little second drawing room where life went on and only once did she complain rather wistfully, "I don't think I ever had two hours undisturbed (except at night when everybody was in bed) during my whole literary life."

"Miss Austen," she commented once, "I believe wrote in the same way and very much for the same reason: but at her period the natural flow of life took another form. The family was half ashamed to have it known that she was not just a young lady like the others doing her embroidery." Her own family, she added proudly, "was quite pleased to magnify me and to be proud of my work, but always with a hidden sense that it was an admirable joke and no idea that any special facilities or attirement was necessary." Once, she admitted, almost in a fit of temper she withdrew at a relative's house and took her paper and inkstand out of the drawing room very conscious of her own ill temper, and feeling extraordinarily guilty about it. It was the one and only time.

She never became a literary lion. True, she knew everybody, and some of the most enchanting literary ancedotes of the nineteenth century were preserved by her. But she was painfully shy and at literary gatherings always stood in a corner, "never venturing to make an approach." If some gentleman went out of his way to single her out and appeared to like her she would feel it worth recording. "He liked me, I think, and complimented me by saying he did not like literary ladies—a sort of thing people are rather disposed to say to me."

A caricature of Mary Russell Mitford.

The most liberated of women professionally, she was first of all a mother and one who was to suffer, in the usual pattern of the nineteenth century, the loss of one child after another. Recording her long, full life she said, "When I look back on my life among the happy moments which I can recollect is one which is so curiously common and homely. It was the moment after dinner when I used to run upstairs to see that all was well in the nursery and then to turn into my room on my way down again to wash my hands as I had a way of doing before I took up my evening work which was generally needlework, something to make for the children." After that there was another kind of work, her writing, which often went on until well into two o'clock in the morning.

Because she has left us with some of the most remarkable supernatural short stories that have ever been written, stories as fresh with terror and dark horror as any written today, her name still lives for us. Her many novels, however, are long forgotten. She expected that they would be: "I was reading," she wrote, "of Charlotte Brontë the other day and could not help comparing myself with the picture more or less as I read. I don't suppose my powers are equal to hers. My work to myself looks perfectly pale and colorless beside hers, but yet I've had far more experience and, I think, a fuller conception

202

of life. I have learned to take perhaps more a man's view of mortal affairs—to feel that the love between men and women, the marrying and the giving in marriage occupy in fact so small a portion of either existence or thought. When I die I know what people will say of me, they will give me credit for courage (which I almost think is not courage but insensibility) and for honesty and honorable dealing. They will say I did my duty with a kind of steadiness not knowing how I have rebelled and groaned under the rod. Scarcely anybody who cares to speculate further will know what to say of my working power and my own conception of it; for, except one or two, even my friends will scarcely believe how little possessed I am with any thought of it at all; how little credit I feel due to me, how accidental most things have been, and how entirely a matter of daily labor, congenial work, sometimes now and then the expression of my own heart, almost always the work most pleasant to me this has been. I wonder if God were to try me with the loss of this gift, such as it is, whether I should feel it much? If I could live otherwise I do not think I could. If I could move about the house and serve my children with my own hand, I know I should be happier. But this is vain talking. Only I know very well that for years past neither praise nor blame has quickened my pulse ten beats that I am aware of. This sensibility saves me some pain, but it also must also lose me a great deal of pleasure."

The few autobiographical chapters that she wrote about herself she wrote primarily for her children but, as every professional writer does, she wondered at the same time if she were writing for other eyes. Was she making pennyworth's of herself when she put her own memories on paper? She thought not, it was for the eyes of her dear sons and daughters. The autobiography that she chose to leave us is almost unbearable because the children that she loved so much had long since died, before her work was completed.

Even the least self-conscious of writers wonders about others in the profession. Although Mrs. Oliphant published, published, published, and though she knew she was an adequate craftsman with an occasional flash of genius, she could not but wonder about the other literary lights, particularly that fabulous literary lady, George Eliot, whose working habits were so far different, whose genius was

Doctor Mitford. From a painting by John Lucas, 1839.

so corrosive and whose personality was almost the direct opposite. She had recognized almost instantly on publication of *Adam Bede* that George Eliot was a woman. Such recognition was possible, she said, because "George Eliot is feeble in her men." Although in the twentieth century a woman is able to know a man in more dimensions than was ever possible before, the nineteenth century rarely allowed more than a side glance. Mrs. Oliphant, for example,

Mrs. Oliphant. From a drawing made in 1895 by Janet Mary Oliphant.

thought she handled wicked women rather well, but that she gave a softness to her men. The men were, after all, shadowy figures. It is in "only members of our own sex that we can fully bring out the bad and good." She singled out how much of a fantasy a man was to the nineteenth-century woman novelists; a shortcoming that also applied, she thought, to the women painters of that period. "The same want of anatomical knowledge and precision must, I imagine, preclude a woman's ever being a great painter." In an age when even marriage was conducted with a kind of fig-leaf morality, she knew what she was talking about.

Her friendships were endless. There was, for one, that remarkable Jane Carlyle, whose gossip about George Eliot was to the point. "Mrs. Lewes has mistaken her role, that nature intended her to be properest woman and that her present equivocal position is the most extraordinary blunder and contradiction possible." Our Jane was accurate as always. A mistress George Eliot might be, but there was never anyone more "properest."

Mrs. Oliphant's friendship with Mrs. Carlyle, the indomitable Jane, began when the latter was over sixty. She reawakened in Mrs. Oliphant all the nostalgia for her own Scottish childhood, particularly the area of East Lothian where Maggie's mother had come from. Jane needed nobody to urge her on to great conversation: she had that power of narration that comes to many Scottish women, the flashes, as Mrs. Oliphant said, of keen, witty sarcasm, occasionally even a little sharpness, that made her a delight to be with. Mrs. Oliphant could get anyone to talk—a friend told her that she had the gift in such a fashion that it was almost like the art of rolling a hoop. Give it a touch and her willing victim rolled on and on.

"But I was not," said Mrs. Oliphant, "a student of human nature." Her observations seemed to come from within herself. But, like any professional, she knew when she was writing well. "I always took pleasure in a little bit of fine writing (afterwards called in the family language a "trot"), which, to do myself justice, was the only time when I got moved by my subject, and began to feel my heart beat, and perhaps a little water in my eyes. . . . I've always had my sing-song, guided by no sort of law but by my ear which was in its way fastidious to the cadence and measure that pleased me: but it

Reading at the tea table.

is bewildering to me in my perfectly artless art, if I may use the word at all, to hear of the elaborate way of forming and enhancing style and all the studies for that end."

No, she could not understand George Eliot, nor all those others that went deep, deep for some great emotion. It was only in the short stories, the supernatural stories of the seen and unseen, those stories that came to her so rarely, that her true genius was shown. She could write about anything, and did, from travel books to a history of a great publishing company to a three-volume and still pertinent and important literary history of England. She could do all those things at the drop of a hat or, rather, the drop of a little white cap. But a ghost story? Oh no, that would not come that easily: she must not be pressed, it had to come quite out of the blue.

She moved to Windsor and there made the acquaintance of, or rather was summoned to the side of, another literary lady. The dear queen had overcome her objections to "writing women" long enough to do an opus itself. It would start a literary ball rolling that was to have no end as ladies of the court and widows of the great gave their personal stories to the world. The queen's foray into literature was entitled *Leaves from the Journal of Our Life in the Highlands.* It was bound, naturally, in tartan because Victoria was

Yachting for Ladies—Mayfair in the Mediterranean.

at the height of her Scottish period, which called for her rooms decorated in plaid, her servants all in Royal Stuart kilts, and, after the death of Albert, her one good right arm, John Brown, the Scottish ghillie, who drank a quart of malt whisky a day and, some said, gave more than an arm to the queen at night: a rumor, of course, that Mrs. Oliphant would not ever admit, let alone discuss. No, the queen and she discussed Scotland, and occasionally those mad women who were writing about being given the franchise.

However, all these ladies, from Elizabeth Barrett to Mrs. Oliphant, although interested in the welfare of children, never once thought of suffrage for women. The nineteenth century was drawing to an end. There were, said Mrs. Oliphant "confusing opinions" appearing in such magazines as *The Nineteenth Century*.

For example, A. Orr argued. "Women are intelligent; they are not creative. Whether in their home or beyond it, their successes can only be achieved through the contact with other minds; the impulse to mental action must always come to them from without, or at least the form in which the impulse will be clothed. That man possess the productiveness which is called genius and that women do not, is the one immutable distinction that is bound up with the intellectual idea of sex." Moreover, if one "improved women" it would only mean that they would be inferior men.

George J. Romanes, for his part, maintained that the female brain was short five ounces and it would take many centuries of heredity before there was a chance of any kind of equality.

Charles Whibley stated bluntly: "The lady novelist is not a lasting danger: she dies of her own popularity and is forgotten: but if the women who clamour for degrees are not foiled in their design. . . . " Well, civilization would fall.

Voices rose in protest. Voices that would be heard frequently in the approaching twentieth century: Beatrice Webb, for one, the famous Fabian and the wife and collaborator of Sydney. Beatrice had no feelings of inadequacy: she quite thought *her* brain outweighed any contenders. Never shy, she admitted, "If I ever felt inclined to be timid as I was going into a room full of people, I would say to myself, 'You're the cleverest member of one of the cleverest families in the cleverest class of the cleverest nation in the world, why should you be frightened?' "

Her household rang with the voices of the great—and the soon-to-be great. One young man, Bertrand Russell, met a charming American family, Philadelphia Quakers, with a flippantly delightful son, Logan, and two remarkable daughters. One married Bernard Berenson and the other, Alys, became the first wife of Russell. It was Alys Pearsall Smith who offered a beautiful rejoinder to the attacks on the "encroaching rights of women" in *The Nineteenth Century* magazine.

"They must arrange the flowers, help with the housekeeping, pay the family calls, entertain the family visitors, always be at hand, well-dressed, cheerful, and smiling, like household angels, as they are often called, without any personal preferences or pursuits, ready to meet every call, and to contribute to everyone's pleasure but their own. All this, it is true, is a part, and a very essential part, of the duty belonging to an unmarried daughter at home; but it is only a part. The tyranny of it comes in when it is considered to be all. It is the fact that she must always be 'on tap,' if we may use the expression, that makes life so hard and dull in its effects. Under such circumstances the girl can never sit down to read or write without

Christina Rossetti. Engraved by Walter
& Turner, after a chalk drawing by D.
G. Rossetti, made in 1866.

fear of being disturbed; she can never undertake any definite work
or pursuit, lest it might interfere with some of these unceasing
claims. She never, in fact, has an hour that she can call absolutely
her own, free from the danger of interruption. There is always
something wanted by somebody, and a girl of average conscientious-
ness would feel very selfish should she refuse to meet these unceasing

A fashionable beauty of 1837. By A. E.
Chalon, R. A.

claims, even though most of them may be very unimportant, and although she herself may have on hand at that moment some important work of her own. Her brother, who is reading at home in his vacation, is never to be disturbed; but that, of course, is because he is reading for his examinations, and expects to do some thing afterwards. But are the girls, who are not going in for examinations, and who never expect to do any great things, not to be allowed some definite time for study and self-improvement, or for some outside philanthropic work? . . .

"The suffering endured by many a young woman under these circumstances has never yet been told. Possessing no money in her own right, and obliged to beg, too often from an unwilling father, for all she gets, a girl of character, as she grows into maturity, and lives on as a woman in her father's house, suffers from a sense of bitter humiliation that no one who has not experienced it can understand. Many young women under these circumstances would gladly engage in any honourable labour, however menial, that would enable them to be independent and to own themselves. But this, of course, 'is not to be thought of for a moment'. Could the parents of these daughters, who have never thought of them as independent beings, but only as appendages to themselves, created for the purpose of ministering to their pleasures, and waiting upon their fancies—could they for one single moment get a glimpse into the hearts of their quiet, uncomplaining daughters, they would be astonished and perhaps horrified. 'What can our daughters want more than they have now?' they would ask. 'They have a good home and every comfort, and the society of their parents' friends; perhaps a carriage to drive in and horses to ride. What more can they possibly desire?' To such parents I would reply: Your daughter wants herself. She belongs to you now, and can only walk in your paths, and enjoy your pleasures, and live your life. She wants to belong to herself. She has paths of her own she longs to walk in, and purposes of her own she is eager to carry out. She is an independent being, created by God for the development of her own talents, and for the use of her own time. Her capacities were not given to her parents, but to herself; her life is not their possession, but her own; and to herself God looks for an account of it. Put yourselves in her place, and ask yourselves how

Child "hurriers" at work in a mine.

Girl dragging coal tubs.

Hewing coal in 1842.
(Woodcuts from the official report of the Commission on Mines and Manufacturers.)

you would like to have no independence, but be obliged always to live someone else's life, and carry out only someone else's purposes. You have had aims and purposes in your lives, and have been free, perhaps, to carry them out. Can you dare, as mere human beings like themselves, to lay hands upon the mature lives of your daughters and say, 'It shall be as we please, not as they please'? If they yield to your demands it can only be at the expense of a grievous waste of energies and capabilities that were meant by God to accomplish, through their instrumentality, some personal and instrumental work for Him. But this is an aspect of the question that very few adequately realize. There is no sadder sight in the world than that of a wasted life. And when this waste is the result of carelessness or selfishness on the part of the strong towards the weak, it becomes no less a tragedy even although it is done under the name of parental love. Such tragedies are no fiction, but the very common occurrence of everyday life around us. How wanton is the waste continually going on in the lives of thousands of women, whose powers, by a long course of trivialities and mental starvation, deteriorate year after year, until they themselves and all their friends suffer incalculable loss."

It was no wonder that some extraordinary women simply picked up and left home. A Bedouin tent was often far more comfortable than the Victorian parlor.

9

FOOTLOOSE AND FANCY CAMELS

I wish I could manage to travel on the approved lines, but the fates are against me.

Gertrude Bell, 1899

The dish is really excellent, even when made with boa constrictor, hippo or crocodile. It makes the former most palatable; but of course it does not remove the musky taste of crocodile; nothing I know will.

Mary Kingsley, 1894

There is a great moment, when you see, however distant, the goal of your wandering. The thing which has been living in your imagination suddenly becomes a part of the tangible world. It matters not how many ranges, rivers or parching dusty ways may lie between you: it is yours now forever.

Freya Stark, 1952

W EARING Paris frocks and applying Mayfair manners, Gertrude Bell quite literally put Arabia on the map. At least the British map, and in doing so not only supplied the British with invaluable intelligence, but was instrumental in creating a king. The latter accomplishment was one that she found fatiguing—"I would not do it again."

It had started simply enough when she was thirty-one. She had gone to Jerusalem for the first time and had decided to learn Arabic. Trained as an archaeologist, with a private income that permitted travel, and a supportive and loving family at home, there seemed to be no reason that this beautiful, witty and attractive woman would play out her role in anything except a formal English garden with perhaps a few forays into the archaeology of country churches and the geneaology of country families.

Extraordinary British and American women have found their destinies, however, in strange places. They have learned to speak the most obscure dialects in convoluted languages and have walked upright and alone in strange places. Although the woman writer has not always been comfortable even within British culture, the woman traveler has been accepted because she is that glory of glories to the British, an eccentric. A nation of armchair travelers, Britain has always delighted in the occasional rakish, delightfully informative, beautifully written letters, journals and books that have come out of the desert from such extraordinary women as Lady Hester Stanhope, Lady Mary Wortley Montagu and Gertrude Bell. Gossipy, sometimes frivolous, the letters all have the enchanting quality purveyed by a foot-loose aunt traipsing the world with aristocratic disdain and a camellike haughtiness. The poor find it hard to travel; the rich, certainly of the last century and the century before, found the very squalor of the places they traveled to and the fatigue of

An Arab Encampment.

travel just their cup of tea. English might have been the mother
tongue, but the idiosyncracies of other languages, the more difficult
the better, seemed to attract them.

It was not easy, as Gertrude pointed out. Arabic has sounds
quite unfamiliar to the European throat. Many of the syllables
mimic the sound of the camel cries. The aspirated *H* particularly
disturbed Gertrude. She could not, she felt, go through the rest of
her life carrying on a conversation with her finger down her throat,
the only way she could get the proper accent. But with a remarkable
dedication she became extraordinarily proficient. She learned from
everyone, beggar boys on the streets, maids, camel drivers, cooks and
Bedouin escorts. Some of the most cutthroat Bedouins she simply
approached as perfect dears. Danger was not in her vocabulary:
hostility was never to be expected. She rode blissfully into the twentieth century with a glorious innocence. She traveled to spots where,

Frances Trollope was one of those nine-teenth-century writers who met adversity with a firm pen. Her husband was successful only at failure, having gone bankrupt as a lawyer, a farmer and finally a shopkeeper. Her most famous book was her critique of the United States, *Domestic Manners of the Americans,* published in 1832.

it had been carefully explained to her, she would never get permission to enter. It never bothered her: she never felt the need to ask permission at all.

What made her like this? She had been left motherless when very young, had a tremendously devoted father and, early enough, a stepmother who returned her own affection. Brilliant at school, she was still not able to earn a degree because degrees were not allowed women. But she felt no particular problem so far as her identity was concerned. She was Gertrude Bell and that was quite enough.

The desire for travel built up. She had been around the world several times but Greece and the desert lands attracted her most. Every country she looked at she looked at in a new way: "Often one sets out on a journey, one travels on all the roads according to the latest map. One reaches all the places of which the history books speak. Duly one rises early and turns one's face toward new countries, carefully one looks and laboriously one tries to understand and for all one's trouble, one might as well have stayed behind and read a few big archaeology books. But I would have you know that's not the way I have done it this time. I said to myself I will go and see the Greece of Asia. The seas and hills are all full of legends and the valleys are scattered over with the ruins of the rich Greek cities. Here is a page of history that one sees with the eye that enters into the mind so no book can relate it."

Lady Florence Caroline Dixie. (A spy cartoon from *Vanity Fair.*) Florence Dixie was a great Victorian personality. She was a war correspondent during the Boer War, and returned to Britain to become a famous feminist.

At first she traveled with her brother, Hugo, in a proper post-Victorian fashion. It was not Gertrude, however, that their friends worried about—it was Hugo. A friend, later to become the Bishop of St. Albans, recalled a typical "Gertrude" conversation: "In her delightfully blunt and provocative way, she turned on me suddenly and said in a very defiant voice, 'I suppose you don't approve of this plan of Hugo going round the world with me?' 'Why shouldn't I?' I said. 'Well you may be pretty sure he won't come back a Christian.'"

But she preferred to be a solitary traveler and soon abandoned Hugo.

Gertrude had been in love once but, romantically enough, her lover had died. Now she fell in love again, not just with Greece, but once and for all with the desert. The old Arabs would say to her: "By the head of your father, how can you leave the Garden of the World and come out into this wilderness?" Perhaps it did need an explanation. She never gave one. It is evident in what she wrote that everything about desert life attracted her: the camels ("the most charming of animals"), a bit of frost on the sand, the terrible lack of water, the mirages, and mad winds.

Tunis Market, Cairo. (After a drawing by Amelia B. Edwards. From an engraving by G. Pearson.) Amelia Blandford Edwards was one of those multitalented Victorian women who could draw as well as write. Her travels to Egypt encouraged her to study hieroglyphics and her monumental book, *A Thousand Miles Up the Nile*, was the standard work on Egypt for many years.

"We got off at four this morning and made a twelve hour stage. It was freezing a little when we started, it took us two hours to climb up out of the Wady Hauran. I was talking to Muhiyyed Din when the sheik came up and said, 'Oh lady, speech before dawn is not good.' He was afraid of raising some hidden foe, reckless courage is not his characteristic. We have camped into a low bank selecting carefully the east side of it so that our campfires can be seen only by the friendly Delein to the east of us. We are nowhere tonight, just out in the open wilderness which has come to feel homelike. Four of the sheik merchants left us yesterday, hearing that the sheiks with whom they deal were camped near at hand. Each man deals every year with the same sheik. If you could see the western sky with the evening star burning in it, you would give thanks—as I do." And finally they crossed the difficult Syrian desert and she wrote home to her father: "As you see we have crossed the Syrian desert as easily as if it had been the Sultan's High Road and we have made many friends and seen the ruins we went out to see. Over and above all I have conceived a new theory about the medieval roads through the deserts which I will prove some day by another journey and all that remains is the hope that this letter which is a true history of all will not be lost in the post."

After that journey the desert was irrevocably in her blood. "Marching through the Nefud is like marching through the labyrinth. You are forever winding around deep sand pits, sometimes half a mile long with banks so steep that you cannot descend. They are mostly shaped like horseshoes and you wander along until you come to the end and then you drop down into low ground only to climb up anew. How one bears it, I don't know." Just as she treated the muleteers with the high hand of an older sister, she treated the reigning sheiks of the desert with the graciousness of a charming niece. They were simply avuncular characters in robes and family tents. They fed her, entertained her, instructed her, and in time grew to be her devoted friends.

When Gertrude had completed her desert trip, she did not know she was making history. She had made the first recorded journey of the desert and it was to lead a much more spectacular figure into strange byways. Gertrude Bell's name has become greatly overshadowed by the name of T. E. Lawrence, but she accumulated the information that made possible the Arabian campaigns of Lawrence during 1917 and 1918. She had mapped wells, knew every tribe, knew the Arab mind like no one else, and was to become the major interpreter of central Arabia and its most important political intelligence operator during World War I.

As a girl Gertrude had been befriended by a remarkable and very difficult Orientalist, David George Hogarth, who was keeper of the Ashmolean Museum at Oxford. Hogarth has been described by one of his friends as a cynical and highly educated baboon. True, he was bearded and had long almost simian arms, but he was a remarkable man and a dedicated imperialist. He spoke French, German, Italian, Greek, Turkish and Arabic, had been a director of the British school at Athens and was well fitted to become the head of an extraordinary espionage group. But espionage of the old school, the school of Kipling's *Kim,* when espionage was "the great gaming board of life" needed more concrete stakes. Hogarth gathered around him a remarkable group of archaeologists and scholars who knew the inside of the countries they explored as they knew their

Mary Kingsley, aged thirty-four. A superb pioneer traveler, Mary Kingsley, deserted middle-class British life to travel to West Africa. Her famous book, *Travels in West Africa,* had strong political impact.

Lady Mary Wortley Montagu.

own skins. Lawrence was to become one of his favorites and an agent for him. Gertrude Bell was to become a friend, but she had a far richer mind than Lawrence, an affinity for the desert which was never that of an Arabian poseur. She was a woman who simply loved the country and knew it with a dedication that was unbelievable for that time. Lawrence almost showed a dislike of the Arabs, despite his ability to disguise himself as one of them. Hogarth didn't give a damn about them, except the way they affected the imperialistic demands of Britain. But Gertrude loved them and her letters reveal that when the cry of independence arose her aspirations for them were quite different from the imperialistic power play in which she became involved and which put Faisal on the throne. When she received the order of Commander of the British Empire in 1917 she thanked her friends for their congratulations, but said, "I don't really care a button about these things." What she really needed was eight pairs of white stockings.

One never gets the impression, however, that Gertrude Bell had run away. Obviously the gardens of England and its horizons for women were too limiting to her—her place of achievement had to be somewhere else. That the desert called her was clear enough, but she, like Mary Kingsley, might have been a great explorer of the west coast of Africa, or she might simply have become one of those indefatigable women travelers of the Victorian age who knew mountains, lakes, rivers, oceans, and strange, indiscreet sections on the map as well as they knew their own estates.

Utterly liberated, she was totally disinterested in the idea of woman's suffrage. Free as the desert, she could not identify with the women who could not skylark around the world as the spirit moved them. She was one of the first "intellectual" women of the twentieth century who would consider suffrage "mad, mad, mad." With enough brains and enough money, who needed the vote? Particularly when one could help create kings in faraway places.

Gertrude Bell was in the tradition of Lady Hester Stanhope who a century earlier had created her own kingdom. Lady Hester had everything, society admitted, particularly position. She was the niece of William Pitt and had been his hostess for some years. Her beauty was known in many countries, as well as her wealth, rank and wit. Once again there was a story of a love affair—some young English general killed in Spain. But if Lady Hester had set her mind on a young English general only to lose him, *she* would have found another. No, there seemed to be something else driving her from the shores of England into a peripatetic life of distinct eccentricity. She was a wow in Constantinople and then pulled up stakes to embark for Syria, moving like some Arabian potentate with extraordinary coffers of jewels and presents for those she might encounter.

Her ship struck upon a rock near the island of Rhodes and a great part of her fortune was lost. A beautiful lady Robinson Crusoe, she barely escaped drowning. By clinging to some of the ship's jetsam she reached a small deserted island where, for twenty-four hours without food and chilled to the bone, her plight seemed hopeless. But when a ship founders there is hope, for there usually will be spoilers looking for treasures. She was rescued. Never daunted, she found her way back to England, collected another fortune, selling parts of her estate, and once again set out on her own eccentric voyage. This time she landed on the coast of Syria and prepared herself for a journey into the desert, learning Arabic as easily as she had learned her mother tongue.

Her gift for organization was extraordinary. She raised a large caravan worthy of a sheik, loaded the camels with rich presents for the Arabs, and began her journey. She visited Jerusalem, Damascus, Aleppo, Homs, Baalbek and Palmyra. Palmyra and Baalbek in those days were not easy spots to visit: one needed "a patent" from the Arabs for protection. Lady Hester had no difficulty; the niece of William Pitt was as much at home in the desert as she was in her drawing room and, if possible, commanded even more attention. As she made her way to the ruins, some forty or fifty thousand wandering tribal Arabs gathered around her, charmed by her beauty, astounded by her gracious arrogance, worshipful of the magnificence of her entourage. She was proclaimed Queen of Palmyra. Upon the payment of one thousand piasters she bought the "security of the desert"—a protection not easy to come by in those days. When Alphonse De Lamartine visited her in 1832 the treaty was still in effect. She made friends and enemies as she moved, but the friends seem to have been far more powerful than the enemies. One, the

Pasha of Acre, ceded to her an old convent in the country of the Druzes, legendary site of travel and one that has drawn even such contemporary women travelers as Freya Stark.

Lady Hester was in every sense an eighteenth-century monarchist. But her architectural designs were closer to the Middle Ages and she built herself a medieval wall around the collection of houses that surrounded the old convent which became her home. Behind the wall was an elaborate garden designed by Lady Hester herself, based on the elaborate horticultural horrors that the Turks had evolved with the rich patterns of flowers and fruits, arabesque sculpture and paintings—and water flowing everywhere. She was not lonely, she had quantities of European and Arabic dragomans, slaves and an enormous suite of attending women. And, of course, her friends, the most important sheiks of the deserts of Syria and Mesopotamia.

Hers was a material magnificence that could not last forever. She had sold off only parts of her land in England, but the estate that remained was no longer as productive as it had once been. She suffered losses, disposing of a slave here and there. Her once lavish gifts to the Arabs grew scanty and her friendships of the desert grew a bit sandy. Eventually her great entourage fell apart. But she did not leave. There Alphonse de Lamartine found her, a woman completely out of touch with Europe, with no books, journals or letters and few friendships, but enjoying her own glorious solitude. Her name was known throughout the East, her story was "the astonishment of Europe." But she had turned her back upon all English travelers, and particularly any members of her own family. It was said that she was possessed by exalted religious ideas, that she had become a mystic and that she was especially in tune with "the ravings of astrology." It was at this time that Alphonse de Lamartine, in the hope of winning her protection while traveling in the desert, attempted to see her. He thought it highly unlikely; she was seeing no one, but in any case he sent her a letter.

Lady Hester's desert delirium preceded Gertrude's by well more than a century, and was far more manic. Curiously enough, she answered him and allowed him an audience. He found it fantastic, as he went through the savage hills bitten by the relics of

Isabella Bishop was the first woman to become a fellow of the Royal Geographical Society. She wrote extensively. Wherever she went she carried all her luggage "in four small boxes, twenty inches long, twelve wide and twelve high."

earthquakes, that Lady Hester would have secreted herself in this country. Going up mountains and down, he finally found a deep, broad valley and a "confused and strange aggregation"—ten or twelve little houses—Lady Hester's home. De Lamartine would not be seen until the appropriate hour, four o'clock in the afternoon. He and his friends were taken to narrow cells without furniture and prepared almost ritually for the introduction.

Lady Hester was then fifty years old. de Lamartine had to admit the freshness of color and the grace of youth were gone but that she was still beautiful. She wore not a Mayfair hat but the white turban that she had affected, and on her forehead a little fillet of purple wool which then fell on each side of her head to her shoulders. In addition she was bundled up in yellow cashmere and a great Turkish robe of white silk with long, hanging sleeves, opened slightly at the neck to show another robe of stiff and flowered Persian silk,

224

fastened by a clasp of beautiful pearls. Her feet were encased in yellow boots embroidered in silk and the whole outfit was spectacular to say the least.

Her words of greeting to de Lamartine were "You've come a long way to see a hermit." She admitted she had investigated their mutual stars and had discovered that they were compatible. She could also tell from the sound of his footsteps that he was a friend. She did not care to know anything about him, but "knew what he was before God." She launched into a long dissertation. "Do not take me for a fool as the world often calls me, but I cannot resist the inclination to speak to you with an open heart. There is a science, lost, at present in your Europe, a science which was born in the East where it has never perished and where it yet survives. I possess it. I read it in the stars. We're all children of one of those celestial fires which preside at our birth and whose fortunate or malignant influence is written in our eyes, on our foreheads, in our features, in the lines of our hand and the form of our foot and our gesture and in our gait."

She offered then to predict de Lamartine's future. He was unwilling but, at least in his re-creation of the meeting, he did sit still long enough for her to be able to say that he was indeed a remarkable man in every fashion, that his stars were extraordinary, that he had the intellect and the power of expression, that he was a poet.

Alphonse de Lamartine accepted this humbly. "See my lady, what glory is! I have composed some verses in my life which have made my name be reechoed a million of times in the literary circles of Europe, but this echo was too weak to traverse the sea and mountains and here I am quite new man, a man completely unknown with a name never pronounced."

She was able to tell that he was a remarkable man by her own simple test. "Look at your foot" she said. "See the instep is very high and between your heel and toe when your foot is on the ground, there is sufficient elevation to let water pass without wetting you. It is the Arab's foot, it is the foot of the East. You are a son of these climates."

Arab's foot or not, she was not going to eat with de Lamartine;

she never ate with anyone. She dismissed him from her presence and then, when she was ready, summoned him again. This time he found her smoking an Eastern pipe. It seemed to him now that she had become an enchantress, a Circe of the desert, but he also brooded upon the fact that she might be quite mad. He decided not. "Madness which displays itself in the eyes is never to be mistaken." She had her own reasons for appearing insane. No, instead, it was imagination; some extraordinary quality of imagination that had intimidated even the Arabs around her. De Lamartine seemed to have passed whatever tests were necessary and she allowed him finally to enter her sanctuary, her garden. Then they went to the stable where she showed him two magnificent Arabian mares. Lady Hester explained to him that one, the finer of the two was the mare that was destined to carry the Messiah: "She shall be borne, ready saddled," the old prophecy had gone and this one carried a cavity in the form of a Turkish saddle, swaybacked some of us might have thought, but to Lady Hester, a horse of destiny. There was one mare for the Messiah to ride into the streets of Jerusalem, there was another in her stable on which she would make an entry by the side of the Messiah. She continued to entertain him, and although it was a rich, heady experience De Lamartine did not seem hesitant about removing himself. But they would meet again, she promised, on other journeys and perhaps in strange worlds.

If they met again in that desert in the sky, they probably encountered another delicious traveling and literary eccentric, Lady Mary Wortley Montagu, whose eighteenth-century life and letters were irrepressible.

"Nothing," commented one Victorian writer, writing about her a century after her death, "is so transitory as second-class fame." Then he presumed to make Lady Mary Wortley Montagu completely déclassé but a figure to be reckoned with in the history of her time—a shocking, abandoned period so unlike the Victorian vacuum in which she lost prestige. And yet the names of all who derided her in the nineteenth century are totally unfamiliar to us today, while the cant of the ones who derided her in her own time still is alive and kicking. To have been first a friend and then an

By the middle of the nineteenth century England was mad about traveling. This Cruikshank illustration satirizes this mania.

enemy of Alexander Pope was enough, but she was first a friend and then an enemy of almost everyone. It wasn't hard to see why; she had one of the fastest tongues in England, one of the cleverest wits, and an enormous energy. Gertrude Bell and Lady Hester Stanhope might have traveled for a reason; Mary Wortley Montagu just kept moving.

She sought the limelight; if she did not find it in one country she would gather up her enormous entourage and seek it in another, but the first "limelight" had been her very best. Her father had been a famous man about London. He had inherited dukedoms with an almost careless abandonment; he also acquired a long string of young beauties in his lifetime. But one acquisition, his daughter, Lady Mary, was, in his opinion, at the age of eight, the greatest beauty of them all, and he would show her to that cynosure of the most fashionable world, the Kit-Kat Club. The Kit-Kat Club had been formed in 1700 as a club with a loose organization of political, literary and artistic figures. Here Congreve was known for his spectacular wit and Addison for his mellow drinking. Horace Walpole called it "a fine set of wits." Here Sir Samuel Garth, physician to King George I (who spent many a long evening at the club ignoring his patients), made the comment: "It's no great matter whether I see them tonight or not, for nine of them have such bad constitutions that all the physicians in the world can't save them and the other six have such good constitutions that all the physicians in the world can't kill them."

They drank and toasted women because this was the glorious age of the witty literary woman and the Kit-kat Club, in addition to subsidizing theatrical performances, had an annual ritual of toasting. Exquisite toasting glasses were inscribed with verses for the great female wits and beauties of the day. The witty niece of Sir Isaac Newton, Swift's Stella, and the beautiful daughters of the Duke of Marlborough were all commemorated. Of course it was nonsense, of course it was flippancy, but there was still a charm in this period as the men worked over the various verses that they would propose in the annual toast. Lord Halifax, for example, submitted six such verses in 1703. It's a fair bet that no gathering of men today in their eternal conventions or conferences even consider toasting a lady.

The Duchess of St. Albans.

The line of Vere, so long renown'd in arms,
Concludes with lustre in St. Alban's charms.
Her conquering eyes have made their race complete:
They rose in valour, and in beauty set.

The Duchess of Beaufort.

Offspring of a tuneful sire,
Blest with more than mortal fire;
Likeness of a Mother's face,
Blest with more than mortal grace:
You with double charms suprise,
With his wit, and with her eyes.

The Lady Mary Churchill.

Fairest and latest of the beauteous race,
Blest with your parent's wit, and her first blooming face;
Born with our liberties in William's reign,
Your eyes alone that liberty restrain.

The Lady Sunderland.

All Nature's charms in Sunderland appear,
Bright as her eyes, and as her reason clear;
Yet still their force to man not safely known,
Seems undiscover'd to herself alone.

The Mademoiselle Spanheim.

Admir'd in Germany, ador'd in France,
Your charms to brighten glory here advance:
The stubborn Britons own your beauty's claim,
And with their native toasts enrol your name.

To Mrs. Barton.

Beauty and wit strove, each in vain,
To vanquish Bacchus and his train;
But Barton with successful charms,
From both their quivers drew her arms.
The roving God his sway resigns,
And awfully submits his vines.

Lady Mary's father was seized, as he said, by a "whim" that he would propose his eight-year-old daughter for such a female toast. The members of his club said it was impossible. A woman to be so toasted had to be sixteen, and a beauty that they had not seen they could not elect. "Then you shall see her," he cried. And orders were immediately sent home to have the child dressed as fashionably as any famous society beauty of the day and presented to the group of men. She was in the limelight. Her health was drunk by every cultured gentleman of the club, her name duly engraved on a drinking glass. She was fondled and petted, sat on the laps of the great men of the day, statesmen, poets, the very pride of England. It was one glorious moment in Lady Mary's life that she was never to forget. She admitted that evening was close to ecstacy and that for the rest of her life she was never able to duplicate that glorious moment. The truth was, of course, that except for this one occasion her father had ignored her as he ignored all his other children. But Lady Mary had smelled this sweet breath of attention. She was wise enough to know that, although beauty does not last, brains do, and

229

she applied herself with unbelievable determination to Greek and Latin, French and Italian. She was educated, she said, only by her labors.

We remember her now because of her wonderfully literate letters—and because of two "firsts" that she accomplished. She was the first to ever get inside an Eastern harem, and the first to introduce inoculation into England—both exotic Eastern practices.

American women traveled too, and wrote, but, alas, none could claim to be so colorful. They went forth into strange places, generally as missionaries, publishing endless tracts, establishing schools. Their voices were heard, but then lost. Nevertheless, the woman traveler as a voice has always been appreciated; her books often are controversial, often innovative, often informative, often crusading. Perhaps she could afford to be appreciated for the simple reason that a woman in the desert is less threatening than a woman at the family desk.

10

THOSE EMINENT EDWARDIANS

By the year 1910 human nature began to change.

Virginia Woolf

Amy Lowell leaned back in a big easy chair, puffing one of her Manila cigars. "I have [puff, puff] no patience with the new-fashioned woman [puff, puff] and her so called rights. I believe [and here she drew deep on the cigar] in the old-fashioned woman and all her limitations."

As reported by Heywood Broun

These termagents, these unsexed viragoes, these *bipeds!*

From a sermon against Suffragettes in 1909

How do you do. I forgive you everything and there is nothing to forgive.

Gertrude Stein

T HE old Queen Victoria was in her counting house, counting up her colonies, and the Prince of Wales was at the races, or in bed. It was an age of beautiful, conniving, manipulative women. They bedded themselves down by royal edict and seemed to enjoy it.

It was the dawn of the Edwardian age. Bertie, Prince of Wales, stood in the wings watching his mother, Victoria, tighten the reins on government and society as she commanded, cajoled, and conquered her people. Emerging from a long period of mourning for Albert, and with the nation's increasing alienation, Victoria caught her second wind. Was she not now Empress of India? In addition to all her other, innumerable titles, it was the last touch of command she needed.

She returned to the world. A short, indomitable figure, riding always in a black landau, having nothing to do with the vulgarity of more handsome carriages. Fettered in black, sharp-eyed, she was like a rotund auk, she was the last of a disappearing species. But she was a woman and the women would be heard, if not directly in her court, by involved forms of Court communication. The political hostesses reigned supreme; the great families interbred in and out of Debrett's *Peerage of England, Scotland and Ireland* with the convoluted genealogical lines of good dogs and superb horses.

Far from the Courts with no influence upon the government, the Victorian lady writers sat at their desks probing their psyches, doing good, writing copiously. But their age was drawing to a close, their four-decker novels were piling up on the floor with the spittoon on top. New names were on the horizon, upstarts all of them. Kipling, for one, spitting out his *Barrack-Room Ballads,* his myth of empire, his stories of simple trysts in the Indian hills. In general, voices of women were quiet, subdued and respectable; that is, except for the ones that Bertie knew, the ones shrewd enough to manipulate and be manipulated, rich enough to support his endless demands, narcisisstic enough to never be seen twice in the same gown. The Prince of Wales liked it that way, it was insulting to be in his presence in anything except the newest Parisian gown.

There were exceptions. Margaret Tennant was one; she would appear in the cultural and literary history of the period under the name of Margot Asquith. And for thirty years she was one of the fascinating and compelling figures in the political life of England.

When she met the Prince of Wales at a party in the eighties, she was not in a Parisian dress. It was not her style. Her style was that of "The Souls," a group loosely formed but with a strange adherence for the time to their own beliefs. By the time she was twenty, Margot, the daughter of a rich Scot, knew what she wanted; she wanted not to be bored. She enjoyed hunting and dancing and dressing, but to her own taste. Margot and her friends were the first of the aesthetes of the mid-eighties that would blossom so strongly in the nineties. They were the forerunners of the Bloomsbury group, wherein intellect, instead of the horse, was important; a group fiercely aristocratic, artistic in conscience but with a very slender foothold on religion.

The old-time religion was giving way. An Oxford professor said to Margot, "My dear child, believe in God despite what the church says." She might have admitted to going further. Recognize the prince, but wear what you choose. In such a frame of mind she met him at a party given by Lord Randolph Churchill and beautiful Jennie. With her face, said Margot, she could have governed the world—a forehead like a panther's and great wild eyes. But Margot's extravagant youth gave Lady Churchill a run for her money, even though her dress *was* so simple. Poor child, they said, what a shame with the Prince of Wales coming that it looked like a nightgown. One old gentleman commented, "There is nothing so odd as the passion some people have for self-advertisement." Margot saved her thunder for the Prince of Wales himself. When presented, she said simply with becoming modesty and in a loud voice, "Oh no Sir, I am not dressed at all for the part, I had better slip away. I had no notion this was going to be such a smart party." Bertie, of course.

Miss Ogston defending herself with a whip after heckling the Chancellor of the Exchequer at a Women's Liberal Federation meeting in the Albert Hall, 1908. Drawing by S. Begg, from the *Illustrated London News.*

was enchanted.

Years later Dorothy Parker, another gifted entertainer (as she herself referred to Margot Asquith), commented bitterly upon reading her confrere's *Autobiography*, "Four volumes neatly boxed suitable for throwing purposes. Hers was the poise that should have been on display in the British Museum. The affair between Margot Asquith and Margot Asquith will live as one of the prettiest love stories in all literature." Yet, even Dorothy Parker had to admit there was a desperate gallantry about Margot Asquith. As we look back upon it, there was a kind of precious pride in whatever sort of abortive aesthetic parading was done by the women of The Souls and that other kindred group, the Pre-Raphaelites. Dressed in holly, in white gowns, often barefooted, they trekked through the pages of literary history. On one side there were such women as Margot Tennant, good at the hunt, good at dancing, knowing everyone, her mind, her elbows, her manners and her tongue honed on good conversation and good gentry. On the other hand there was the other type of woman, the intellectual who was making her way sharply and soundly out of the Victorian period.

Constance Black, for example, who had married Edward Garnett and who was one of the greatest translators of the twentieth century, had quite a different upbringing. Raised in a genuinely Victorian household, her mother brewing beer for the clerks of the family's business, she was a typical product of the late Victorian middle class. Not that there weren't connections, mind you, with the literary greats. Her mother, for instance, had known Jane Welsh Carlyle, herself no mean hand at brewing beer. Her grandfather had been a portrait painter for the prince consort. He knew everybody, and Constance and her son David in later years would know "everybody" too. Times had changed. Now there was the possibility of higher education and Constance (who had always been brilliant) had won a scholarship at Newham College, where, naturally women were not given degrees. But they could study under some remarkable persons, none perhaps more remarkable than Jane Harrison, the anthropologist who spoke of freedom and grace in the same sentence.

Edith Wharton. Courtesy, Charles Scribners' Sons.

When Constance married Edward Garnett her circle of friends grew through Edward's friendship with the Rossettis. She met Prince Peter Kropotkin and many other of the Russian political exiles in London and acquired not only a knowledge of Russian, but an extensive interest in Russia itself. Even in those years there was famine trouble in Russia; there were new international feelings and it was Constance Garnett who personally carried money to Russia on behalf of English friends. She visited Tolstoy, sharpened her Russian rather than her wit, and in 1894 published the first of her superb translations. In the United States the world of Constance Garnett and Margot Asquith might rarely meet, but in England of that day everyone eventually met one another and the names of women crop up endlessly in political, social and literary documents.

And then one woman's voice was to be heard no more. In the middle of the South African War, Victoria died, leaving the hands of government in the hands of Bertie. His mother had not read, of course, and she felt that higher education was ruining the health of the higher classes. But Bertie did not have even his mother's accomplishments, had neither been taught drawing by Lear nor had singing lessons by Mendelssohn. The omens were not good, but they turned out to be better than expected. Although he always paled at the memory of his indomitable mother, when Bertie became

Cosmopolitan Society at Deauville, 1906. Drawing by Simont from the *Illustrated London News.*

Edward VII he pulled himself together and began to reign. Despite the fact that such writers as Henry James would complain, "We all feel without a mother, now that we no longer have the mysterious little Victoria, but only the fat, vulgar, terrible Edward," life began to take on a rosy tint.

"By the year 1910," Virginia Woolf said, "the human character began to change." The Victorian age and the Edwardian age were over, and the Georgian years were to come. If not exactly the golden age, with the golden boys and golden girls that we like to envision, it was nonetheless a time of enormous creative social ferment.

There were giants in the land of literature again. Not the towering, abrasive figures that had gone before, but a host of writers trying to understand and experience the new world which they had not made and could do nothing to stop. War was imminent, but one did not recognize that. Revolution was inevitable, and it took all forms. One would not think that one of the greatest revolutionists in the writing of the period would be a woman, second perhaps only to Gertrude Stein in her evolution and changes of the novel and the printed word. Far different from Gertrude, who would stalk her way through the twenties with wonderful arrogance, was Virginia Woolf—commanding, but withdrawn. Subject to terrible mental depressions, indeed insanity, she worked always on the edge of a precipice.

Lytton Strachey, when he first met her family, her sister Vanessa (one of the great beauties of her time), her two brothers and Virginia herself, said that their home life could be summed up simply . . . Vanessa was keeping a tight hand on her three mad children. One, Toby, was to die, making the tight little group even more impregnable and close. Just as there had been Brontës of the moors, this family had the passion of the Brontës, but of the London streets. London was their platform, where they took voice, where they found themselves. London was for them a wild Bloomsbury and from Bloomsbury there emanated myths, stories, tales, truths and reality. Like those other almost-Brontës of the North, the Sitwells, the Stephens (Virginia was at that point still unmarried) would make themselves heard. And particularly Virginia.

Again, like the Brontës and the Sitwells, it had certainly not been easy. All three families had known loquacious, arrogant and yet withdrawn fathers. Ever ready for a lecture or a long series of quotations, Virginia's father, Leslie Stephen, had what the Victorians called "the great sense of preoccupation." This seems to have been a delicate euphemism for rudeness. He went from breakfast to dinner without a word to any of his children. His own dinner parties were never corrupted by the sound of his own voice, and he was not averse to saying before any visitor unfortunate enough to bore him after a short period, "Why can't he go?"

Nonetheless he was well known and influential. He had headed the *Cornhill Magazine* after Thackeray and he was to spend his life in being a true man of letters. He had, too, the Victorian desire for the sound mind in the sound body. This was the age of the amateur mountain climber, and Stephen was a dedicated sportsman. "How could I think mountains and climbing romantic?" Virginia once wrote. "Wasn't I brought up with Alpine stocks in my nursery and a raised map of the Alps showing every peak my father had climbed. Of course, London and the marshes are the places I like best." Stephen's father and grandfather had been strong abolitionists, and

Stephen himself had visited the United States almost on the eve of the Civil War. He was to acquire a host of American friends: Charles Eliot Norton of Harvard, Oliver Wendell Holmes, the autocrat of the breakfast table, a role certainly that Stephen knew well, and James Russell Lowell, who was to become ambassador to Great Britain. It was Lowell who was chosen to be the godfather of that remarkable child, Virginia, a child of Stephen's second marriage. It was, of course, a male-dominated household. The boys went to school, Virginia stayed home reading her father's books. Sometimes precious to the point of pain—she did lack a jolly vulgarity—she would complain, "To think how I was brought up, no schools, mooning alone among my father's books; never any chance to pick up all that goes on in school—throwing balls; ragging, hockey, vulgarity, scenes, jealousies, only rage with my half-brother and being walked off my legs around the Serpentine by my father." He was without doubt a great man, president of the London Library. What more could a daughter want? For one thing, Virginia, as she was growing up, simply wanted a mother. Her mother had died when she was thirteen, leaving pain, anguish and depression with which she coped poorly.

Once Gladstone picked up the ponderous *Life of George Eliot* and remarked that it was a three-volume venture into reticence. Fortunately, the Edwardian and Georgian diaries and letters allow, not the studied portraits of the nineteenth century, but quick-studied snapshots, and often revelations. In some of them we see Virginia Woolf at times as a thoroughly remarkable writer, working with a terrible intensity; at other times one sees her as a terribly lost, often vindictive, miserably jealous girl. Her room was always messy, books were piled up everywhere. She was often unkempt, disliked her own appearance despite her beauty, didn't know how to shop for clothes and didn't want to, wouldn't visit if she didn't have the right hat, longed for friendship, fought it off, treated guests pretty much as her father had. The satirists maintained that she extended two fingers and never smiled at anybody she met. That was a Bloomsbury characteristic: the vacant stare, the arrogant posturing, the retreat, if not into oneself, then into one's little group, and there never was such a group. Ingrown and delighted with their own skill,

239

in love with their own genius, they supported one another, read one another's books. "Wouldn't it be ideal," Virginia wrote at one point, "just to have a magazine to circle among the rest of us?" And in fact, although the magazines they appeared in were perfectly public, it seemed at times that an outpouring of spite was just what their writings were . . . as they were sometimes called.

They called Virginia the Queen of Bloomsbury in the public press, vaguely deriding this hypersensitive, enormously gifted woman, but if ever such an entity as Bloomsbury existed, wrote Clive Bell (later to be her brother-in-law), these sisters with the houses in Gordon and Fitzroy Squares were the heart of it. But did such an entity exist? Yes and no. It was perhaps much more what Virginia said, that human nature had begun to change, or at least the way one looked upon human nature and literature was changing.

It was to be a time of giants. Joyce would burst forth with too much vulgarity, or so Virginia said. Proust would recline into the past. Gide would be heard, and in the wings a whole new generation would sound their voices. The voice of this period immediately before World War I seemed at times the private voice of drawing rooms; wit was in the conversation, gaity was home grown, genius, in the beginning, was for friendship.

It was difficult to be Virginia Woolf's friend, yet her friends were many. Her noble forehead would become lined, her sharp features could take on a harshness, that animated face could become almost wraithlike upon withdrawing into the rage that sometimes came tumbling out in the diary that she kept nearly her entire life. Even her own friends were not safe from her private accusations. Wouldn't T. S. Eliot have made a better branch manager of a bank, perhaps, than a poet? Wasn't Katherine Mansfield just too much? Virginia was inconsistent. When she married Leonard Woolf and they started the Hogarth Press, she published Eliot and Mansfield with enormous satisfaction. But if their books sold better than hers, she was consumed with jealousy.

She was constantly asking questions. What was it that she did wrong? What was the matter with society that it did not understand her? If they liked her current book, certainly they would not like the next one. She began to write a novel just about the time she

240

Fashionable motoring outfits of the Edwardian period. The train and the car were supposed to have "emancipated" women. From the *Illustrated London News*.

decided that human character was changing. *The Voyage Out,* published after the war broke out, seems a period piece today and did not make the impression she wanted. That did not matter. Her friends—they were her friends, weren't they—said they liked it; their opinion was important, wasn't it? Married to Leonard Woolf with small means, she was coddled and protected as she tried to explore other levels of consciousness in the straightforward novel. She tried again in *Night and Day.* It still wasn't quite right—too classical; her friends didn't like the characters. She wasn't too sure she liked them herself.

With her own press, she was free to develop in any way she wished, and that curious sensibility, that thin skin, suddenly made her work take a new turn. Bewildered by time, she began to express the inner consciousness of the society in which she lived. Times were changing, but the past often merged into the present and into the future. There was lost time and found time, and strange states of creative consciousness that could be captured for the first time on paper. Like a somewhat wicked lepidopterist, she caught those moments of consciousness, pinning them to a page where their colors may have faded a little but where they still flutter with life. But her early books also seem impaled as she seemed to have been impaled in her own anxiety and in her own time.

None of the great nineteenth-century women writers thought of referring to themselves as geniuses in public, but in the twentieth century the feminine ego took on new strength. Two towering figures were not likely to keep their lights under a bushel; nor were they to dress conservatively, mind or care "what people thought." They were a striking pair, Edith Sitwell and Gertrude Stein.

"I explained," said Dame Edith, "when I was four years old in my family's drawing room that I intended when I grew up to be a genius. I was banished from the room." But no one could thoroughly banish that provocative child, or the extraordinary woman that she was to become. Indeed, her role was not to *be* banished, but to banish others. She did not suffer fools gladly, poor technique in poetry, critics, contenders or bores of any kind. She did not suffer vulgarity; vulgarity was particularly oppressive to her. Later she was to say that the very Edwardian period was vulgar. All those feathers, curtains, chiffon scarves, all that social climbing, all the screeches of "darling" and "heavenly." All of that was vulgar. A great raconteur and a friend to writers, she explained that vulgarity was nothing but fear in disguise, a fear that did not necessarily extend to the lower classes; in truth she did not consider them vulgar at all. But this was definitely a fear that affected the rich and what she meant by that, of course, was the nouveau riche. She was, after all, a woman of small personal means, but of superb aristocratic heritage. She was never to forget the latter for one moment.

She had been an extremely unhappy child and her feelings were violent. Her parents had their own eccentricities and Dame Edith was always to be very fond of the eccentric. The eccentrics, she explained, were really not mad at all, but had about them a kind of pride and innocence. Both aristocrats and artists were entitled to an eccentricity that the rest of the world was not allowed. One can understand the eccentricity of the artist: it will always exist in part. Dame Edith's joy in the eccentricity of the aristocracy was more distinctly Edwardian. ("Those padded insane asylums, those stately homes of England," said Virginia Woolf.)

Edith Sitwell knew what she was talking about; she had first-hand knowledge. Her father was probably one of the greatest eccentrics in Victorian and Edwardian England. Sir George Sitwell did nothing to encourage his three children to write, nor for that matter did Lady Sitwell. Lady Sitwell informed them early never to put pen to paper, Sir George informed them early it was best never to have friends. But he had been a writer. He wrote one famous book on cultivating gardens, a field in which he was extraordinarily adept. He liked handsome, well-ordered gardens. His private world, as a matter of fact, seemed to be so topsy-turvy he decided that he could impose a topiary form upon nature. He tried to impose the same designs on his children, with far less effect.

With Edith the problems were simple enough. As she said in her own autobiography, in the first place she was in disgrace for being a female; in the second place, she was ugly. She was always referred to as "Poor Little E." Descended from the Plantagenet kings of England, she liked to remind all who knew her that she had inherited their features. They sat poorly on a young child's face in those days when the idealized children of portrait painters were the standard of beauty. Years later she would trade upon those extraordinary features and with aristocratic disdain, with hawk-hooded eyes, look down on the rest of the world from her great height.

As a child her only friends were one of the maids and her beloved peacock. The peacock was one of the denizens of Renishaw, the great ancestral family home of the Sitwells, and he always greeted her early in the morning with a shriek of welcome. It was a liaison that lasted only until the time the peacock found another fine peahen and gave up his Plantagenet princess.

Even as a child she was alert to sounds. The peacock's cry, the sounds of bells, the drone sounds of the country. She remembered them all when she began to probe deeply into the technique of poetry.

She disliked everything that they taught her in what amounted to a schoolroom. It was all middle-class grinders and they would never master her, she said. But her father pushed and pummeled, pressing her even into an orthopedic brace to make her elongated figure assume the stance of a grenadier. It was a weird contraption. She could barely breathe with it, and felt herself imprisoned in what she called a bastille of steel. She escaped into the world of poetry, learning word for word Pope's *The Rape of The Lock*. It was one of the rare works of genius that could be found in the household, she said, and she learned it secretly, taking enormous pleasure in the texture of the words and the structure of the poem itself. She had the satisfaction, however, of having two brothers, both greatly talented. Edith was four years older than Osbert. He was never to say a word against her, but would always be her constant support in the outside world. And in those early years Sacheverell was not far behind.

Actually, all three children banded together, not only against their parents, but against the world; they were known simply as "The Sitwells." There are endless photographs of the three of them together—dramatic, exciting. Edith herself was painted by many important contemporary British painters of the twentieth century. They knew everyone—liked some, disparaged others.

Edith's early life had been spent in baronial halls, but she struggled for personal freedom as well as expression. She became what she called "a ticket-of-leave" woman and was allowed to take a small flat with her old tutor, Helen Rootham. Sir George was notorious for being stingy and she lived on practically nothing. She took a job, but her father urged her to take another with a bankrupt company that he had taken over. She refused. He was to say later to Osbert, "If Edith had done what I told her, she would be earning a thousand pounds a year now." And the old butler was heard to whisper, "Yes, but would she be getting it?" Sir George's comment was, "Leave the room, Robbins." It was obvious that Edith would not have gotten her thousand pounds a year from Sir George.

"Intellectual society at that time," she said, "was divided." There was the bottle-wielding school and then there was Bloomsbury, the home, as she described it, of an echoing silence. She much enjoyed her friend Gertrude Stein's comment that it was the Young Men's Christian Society—with Christ left out, of course. But she admired Virginia Woolf with her transparent beauty.

Edith still derided her own appearance; she was too tall, too ugly, having, she said at that point, the untidy elegance of a tall, thin bird. She scratched for a living and was determined to write. In 1915 she published, at her own expense, *The Mother and Other Poems*, and in December, 1916, she became the editor of a new anthology of poetry, publishing such writers as Aldous Huxley, Nancy Cunard, the fashionable Iris Tree and that superb war poet, Wilfred Owen. It was truly experimental poetry and the poets and Edith were immediately attacked. Attack would never bother Edith. Throughout the rest of her long life she answered them back for what they gave. She was to be silent for a long period and then to speak out again with a new voice during World War II with unforgettable beauty and power. But in those days she played with words, working on such extraordinary pieces as *Facade*. Experiment was important to her; experiments closely related to music, and just as her friend Gertrude would experiment with words in relation to painting, so Edith used words as she might have availed herself of jewels from the family coffers, polishing them until they glistened; shaping new facets, finding the sight and sound as iridescent and

Mr. Asquith intercepted by two suffragettes, 1908. Drawing by S. Begg, from the *Illustrated London News.*

as haunting as the gems of a beautiful necklace. Accused often of being shallow, she would disagree; accused of being the exhibitionist she was, she knew it advisedly. But she was a woman who sensed a great despair in her own time. "This modern world," she cried, "is but a thin matchboard flooring spread over a shallow hell."

Gloomy ancestral halls had produced women poets in the past. There had been, of course, Sydney's great sister, the Countess of Pembroke, and Lady Winchilsea in the seventeenth century, women with enough culture and enough intensity to try to express themselves. They were rare instances, however. In part Edith Sitwell was a continuation of that line, the aristocratic voice trying to be heard in a democratic world. She was attacked in Britain because of her background and tried everything she could to disassociate herself from that ancient lineage, preferring to think that the best of poetry was always democratic, even if the artist was an aristocrat. She was a fine poet, yet she was so pained and troubled by her own lack of traditional education that when she was awarded belatedly a series of degrees of Doctors of Letters, she always inscribed the reverse of her envelopes, Dr. Edith Sitwell, D.Litt., D. Litt.

Diplomas were never to bother her friend Gertrude Stein. She was a wild American maverick and, though born in Pennsylvania, a California Colossus, an Edwardian barbarian. "By combining the functions of critic and poetry," said Laura Riding, "and taking everything around her very literally and many things for granted which others have not been naive enough to do, she has done what everyone else has been ashamed to do. No one but Miss Stein has been willing to be as simple . . . as stupid, as barbaric as simple barbarism demands. Does no one but Miss Stein realize that to be abstract, mathematical, anti-Hellenic, anti-Renaissancist, anti-romantic, we must be barbaric?"

Gertrude Stein expressed some of the tremendous creative ferment that was coming from America. Even as a girl she and her brothers had been bohemians. The famous sandals that she wore through the streets of Paris she donned early in California. As a large girl, she soon discarded any thought of dress and decided instead to be spectacular.

Her wealthy German-Jewish family home had not been as devoid of books as the ancestral British manor houses. She was an assiduous reader: Wordsworth, Scott, Bunyan's *Pilgrim's Progress,* Shakespeare, Burns, the *Congressional Record*—all were grist to the mill. She read history, and, she said, when she wrote her autobiography, "In fact she was, as she still is, always reading." She was caught up very much in the spirit of her time. "Evolution," she said, "was all over my childhood."

She felt desperately the need for direction and in 1893 enrolled herself at the Harvard Annex which would become Radcliffe College. She immediately encountered some great teachers: William James, perhaps one of her most important, whose *Principles of Psychology* had just appeared, George Santayana, Hugo Münsterberg, the great German experimental psychologist. In the *Autobiography of Alice B. Toklas,* her own autobiographical tour de force, she says, "William James delighted her, his personality and his way of teaching and his ways of amusing himself with himself and his students all pleased her. Keep your mind open, he used to say and when someone objected, but Professor James, this that I say is true. Yes, said James, it is abjectly true."

Not only was evolution being discussed but the new concept of "consciousness" was *the* word. James had stated: "Within each personal consciousness, thought is sensibly continuous. Consciousness . . . is nothing jointed; it flows."

The "stream-of-consciousness" novel would involve everyone from Dorothy Richardson to James Joyce. The concept of "the continuous present" and the "immediate existing" would be omnipresent in Gertrude Stein's work.

Suddenly she became extraordinarily popular as a person. Her vitality was overwhelming. She talked superbly, but she also listened and she argued. Argument, she said, is the air I breathe.

As early as 1898 she was writing such reports as "Cultivated Motor Automism; A Study of Character in Its Relation to Attention," which was published in the *Psychological Review.* Her highly original mind appealed to William James and she got away with a great deal, including the famous incident of her examination paper, which she describes:

"It was a very lovely spring day, Gertrude Stein had been going to the opera every night and going also to the opera in the afternoon and had been otherwise engrossed and it was the period of final examinations, and there was the examination in William James' course. She sat down with the examination paper before her and she just could not. Dear Professor James, she wrote at the top of her paper. I am so sorry but really I do not feel a bit like an examination paper in philosophy today, and left.

"The next day she had a postal card from William James, saying, Dear Miss Stein, I understand perfectly how you feel. I often feel like that myself. And underneath it he gave her work the highest mark in his course."

This attitude, the fantasy of every undergraduate, would give her trouble in the future.

James felt she should plan to continue her studies at Johns Hopkins University and acquire a medical education because only that would open the doors to the field of psychology which so fascinated her. Harvard had accepted her early haphazard education. She was to find Johns Hopkins far more structured and far more opposed to women in the schoolroom. Women were suitable as midwives, however, and while she was doing obstetrics she came to discover the life of the blacks in the dirty tenements of Baltimore, a rhythm of life and speech that she would later re-create in *Melanctha*.

Easily bored, she, who was later to be accused of boring others with her repetitive style, soon found that medicine was far too monotonous. She didn't have to worry—she was refused a degree. Some of the professors would have passed her because of her original scientific work, others felt that she was far too much an original; some of her models of the human brain would have taxed even Picasso's inventions. She could have applied herself and she was urged to, particularly by her close friends. "Gertrude, Gertrude," they said to her, "remember the cause of women." Gertrude answered only, "You don't know what it is to be bored."

She had been bored by her own century, but she galloped into the twentieth century, into a new world, with enormous excitement. It was, of course, that famous world, that private salon, that extraordinary meeting place of the twentieth century, 27 rue de Fleurus in Paris. It was a world suddenly of pictures, a world where she could buy a Cezanne and go home to enjoy it. Looking at his pictures, she said, she wrote *Three Lives.* Painters flocked to her house: Picasso, Matisse, Marie Laurencin. The collection of paintings chosen by Gertrude and her brother Leo increased.

When Leo left 27 rue de Fleurus Gertrude's lifelong companion Alice B. Toklas entered her world. Her support was invaluable. Leo and Gertrude had long since drawn apart. He wrote at that time, attacking both his sister and Picasso: "Both he and Gertrude are using their intellects, which they ain't got, to do what would need the finest critical tact, which they ain't got, neither, and they are . . . turning out the most God-almighty rubbish that is to be found."

Many would call her writing rubbish, but others consider her one of the most important geniuses of her time. She would agree with the latter. "If a thing can be done, why do it," she said, "any copy is bad copy." The film was to fascinate her; Cubism was to fascinate her. That time immediately before World War I was like a kaleidoscope slowly turning, she said. And it was filled with her brilliant word pictures; portraits of people she knew. Promoted by such women as Mabel Dodge, "Everybody, just everybody began to talk about Gertrude Stein."

She tried vainly at first to find a publisher. *Three Lives* was published with her own funds. Ahead of her time, it did not matter. Katherine Mansfield, no mean critic, reviewed *Three Lives:* "Miss Gertrude Stein has discovered a new way of writing stories. It is just to keep on writing them. Good Anna is soothing, German life told in the German way, but let the reader go warily, warily with Melanctha. We confess we read a page or two before we realized what was happening. Then the dreadful fact dawned. We discovered ourselves reading a *syncopated time.* Gradually we heard in the distance and coming uncomfortably near the sound of banjos, drums, bones, cymbals and voices. The page began to rock . . . we found ourselves silently singing. Melanctha is Negro music with all its maddening monotony done into prose. It is writing in real ragtime. Heaven forbid Miss Stein should become a fashion." She did not become a fashion, she became an institution. Edith Sitwell and Gertrude Stein were self-proclaimed rebels. They would stand out in any decade, in any crowd, in any history of literature.

Edith Wharton in that period distinctly spoke for the society of her time, and spoke with extraordinary skill and ability. She was the only one too, of the group of women writing copiously in the Edwardian period apparently liberating herself as a woman from the strangulation hold that society had on her. From the time that she had been a little girl in one of those typical brownstone homes of upper-middle-class New York, relegated to below the steps (the only affection she had coming from her nurse), she "made up." Making up stories was the way to ignore the dissension between her parents. Rumor went that her father wasn't her father at all, but some tutor who had once entered the house and then disappeared. Her mother was deeply involved in the fripperies and foibles of social New York. Just as Edith Sitwell had been able to name the lords and ladies in her family, even the kings and queens, Edith Wharton could intone her genealogy: the Schermerhorns, the Pendletons, and the Gallatins, the Ledyards and the Rhinelanders, *the* social coterie of old New York. Edith Sitwell had grown up in a milieu of a dowdy aristocracy going steadily downhill; Edith Wharton came to a maturity in a tight little circle, a circle of "trade." The Victorian fathers and brothers had made their fortunes; some spent their money recklessly, others hung onto it the way a stubborn leaf clings to a New York tree in the fall. Over the hill there was a sinister threat of the parvenu coming up, trying to get into society. Below the uptown brownstones there were other streets, in New York, dark streets of poverty, of crime, of destitution of soul and spirit. Why, Edith remembered one old gentleman who had never been to Europe because he would have to cross from one side of New York city to the other. He would have had to pass the lower regions to reach the docks. The thought was so painful he preferred to stay home.
As a child Edith was not attractive. Terribly shy, at a loss in her own family, she was shouldered with a nickname that was to stay with her throughout her life and, when she was the elegant Mrs.

Reception of the Kaiser by King Edward VII and the Prince of Wales (later George V) at Charing Cross Station, January 20th, 1901, on his arrival for Queen Victoria's funeral. Drawing by R. Caton Woodville.

Wharton, one that hardly fitted her—Pussy Jones. Miserable in her home, she had only one retreat, a refuge for more than one child with literary leanings, the library.

The late-nineteenth-century society in which she grew up never stayed in one place. It floated between New York, Newport and Europe. Financial reverses occurred even in the great families of those days. Europe was a good place to spread one's money a long way; it offered young Pussy a different culture, but at the same time a feeling of displacement. Her novels were always to show this ambiguity.

Bound emotionally and utterly to the conventions of her time, she was always in revolt against her own stiffness. She observed well. She observed, for example, that very few of her family or her friends ever read. Of course there were libraries, but one didn't read in them. Perhaps, if one did read, occasionally Mrs. Browning, but more frequently some popular novel of the day that was read by the elder matrons and then disposed of by the maid. Even such writers as Harriet Beecher Stowe were considered to be in extremely bad taste. The standard classics on the library shelf held some secrets and Pussy wanted to know them. One of her youngest memories was, "I am squatting again on the thick turkey rug pulling open one after another of the glass doors of the oak bookcases and dragging out book after book in secret ecstasy. I say 'secret' for I cannot remember ever speaking to any one of these enraptured sessions. The child knows instinctively when it will be understood. From the first I kept my adventures with books to myself. There was in me a secret retreat where I wished no one to intrude. Words and cadences haunted it like songbirds in a magic wood."

This secrecy in relation to her work was to continue throughout Mrs. Wharton's life. It is almost the kind of secrecy indulged in by Jane Austen or even the Brontës when they began to write. Writing itself implies a secret life. Women writers have been plagued not only by the stereotypes of the "woman writer," but by the very nature of writing which demands a curious intimacy and secrecy that is a further deterrent to accomplishment.

Edith Wharton always regarded herself as having two lives, side by side. One life was the utterly secret one, her creative life. During her long, productive and, in many ways, public life, no one ever saw her write. She wrote in her boudoir. She was never surrounded by a mess of papers, never stained by ink, never frowzy as she wrote and was rarely seen with a hair out of place. When she emerged she was perfectly immaculate, beautifully dressed for the day, or, as they used to say, exquisitely turned out. From then on her working day was over. In her second life she devoted herself with manorial majesty to the large homes that she collected and to her beautifully kept gardens. She maintained a husband for a while and then unconventionally disposed of him.

Great names, famous persons would file through her drawing rooms, but her work was never discussed except, perhaps, with Henry James, or occasionally her lover, Walter Berry. But they were not friends, they were colleagues. For the rest, her writing was a secret. Her very first novel was called *The Cage*, the very title revealing her lot as a woman in a highly structured society. She was in a trap; she could liberate herself. The social traps were tremendously demanding. But she had none of the enormous strength of will of a Gertrude Stein or an Edith Sitwell, to be able to remove herself completely from the chrysalis of her society. That was her advantage and that was her disadvantage. Her advantage was that she was so thoroughly a creature of her own time that she could speak for it; her disadvantage was that she could rarely transcend the world in which she lived, but she tried from the very first time she put pen to paper.

In typical Fanny Burney fashion (a writer she admired), she began to write early. Even Fanny Burney had access to some decent writing paper, but the comparatively wealthy Edith could find only brown paper bags, supplied by the maid. She started a novel on such paper when she was about eleven. It began with the immortal sentences, " 'Oh, how do you do, Mrs. Brown,' said Mrs. Thompkins. 'If I had only known you were going to call I should have tidied up the living room.' " She showed it to her mother, who replied with disdain, "Drawing rooms are always tidy."

It must have been an extraordinary rebuke to the young child, untidied in her emotions, and confused about her future. But one has a feeling throughout all of her books, despite the fact that she was accused of always writing about illicit women (a real shocker for her day), that she was careful in her books to tidy up the drawing room, even if she left the emotions in the bedrooms disordered. She often received such notes as, "Dear Madame, have you ever known a respectable woman? If you have, in the name of decency, write about her."

She was an innovator, one of the great social realists to emerge from that very influential period in the United States, the late nineteenth century. More than any other writer of her time perhaps, she investigated the new standards, the new changes going on through society, best exemplified in the period immediately before World War I.

She carried on, too, an older tradition that so many nineteenth-century women writers had found so successful—that tradition of the supernatural on the hearthside. She saw herself particularly gifted in what she called "spectral straphangers" and wrote an extraordinary series of supernatural stories. They were not symbolic, they were real. She herself thought of herself not as a ghost feeler, but as a ghost seer, explaining that this meant a "person whose extrasensory tentacles are so well developed that they use their sense of sight to submit to the brain presences which otherwise could only make themselves vaguely felt."

Meeting Osbert Sitwell one day, she brooded about it and wrote, "He informed us the other day that ghosts went out when electricity came in, but surely this is to misapprehend the nature of the ghostly. What drives ghosts away is not the aspidistra or the electric cooker; I can more easily imagine them haunting a mean, modern house in a dull, modern street than the battlemented castle with the boring stage properties. What the ghost really needs is not the echoing passages and hidden doors behind the tapestry, but only continuity and silence. It obviously prefers the silent hours when the wireless has ceased to jazz. These hours, pathetically called small, are growing smaller. And even if so few diviners as keep their wands, the ghost may after all succumb first to the impossibility of finding standing room in a roaring and discontinuous universe."

Edith Wharton was a grande dame of literary letters; her American contemporary, Amy Lowell, was also a grande dame, but

In 1909, votes for women was good for a laugh. *Life*, September 15, 1909. Illustration by Power O'Malley. Courtesy, New York Society Library.

had about her a flashiness that tempted Edmund Wilson to include her name in an "all-star literary vaudeville."

Amy Lowell was one of the barons (a title she often employed for herself) of the word in the Edwardian and Georgian periods. James Russell Lowell, Amy's "literary cousin" had been the godfather of Virginia Woolf. It was the closest tie the two ladies were ever to know and we have no record of their ever meeting—probably a matter of their own choice: The Queen of Bloomsbury and the Baron of Boston were a highly unlikely couple, yet both expressed directions the woman writer would follow: Virginia, the loner, the solitary genius, the painfully exquisite writer, the almost-poet, whose literary descendants would be poets as the years moved on: Amy, the public poet, the "operator," whose writing descendants today spend more time in front of a TV camera than at a desk.

Amy had her disabilities. She was very fat, she was very rich, and she was a Lowell of *the* Lowells of Boston. She was never to forget her trio of troubles.

George Eliot had been christened Mary Ann Evans: Amy was christened Amoury, but chose the more feminine form, Amy. Times had changed indeed.

She lived a life rich in ancedotes: There was Amy recklessly driving a four-in-hand as a small child. All Boston knew she was "raised by the coachman, Burns." There was Amy making the grand tour of Europe: turning her pen as a magic weapon upon the Egyptians who did not heed her wishes, hauling up her riverboat herself when they didn't move fast enough. There was Amy summoning the directors of the old Boston Athenaeum for a meeting in her bedroom, shielded by a big black umbrella so that no draft could reach her, clothed only in her old wool nightgown, and smoking a pipe. (The latter is only a rumor. She gave up the pipe because she preferred to write under the blankets and she charred too many holes in the family linen.)

There was Amy, queen of a literary set surrounded by fellow-poets and her seven large English sheepdogs, each guest with a large, clean bathtowel—with the Lowell monogram—spread across his knees. A thoughtful gesture on the part of Amy to protect her visitors from the "affectionate" mouthings of the dogs.

But best of all, Amy sitting on a stone wall, having just commanded a carriage mechanic to fix her car. Carrying no money (paying her bills only once every three years), when asked for identification, she says, "Call my brother, the president of Harvard."

President Lowell queries: "What does she look like?"

"She's big, and fat, sitting on a wall, smoking a cigar."

"Yes, that's my sister."

In 1913 Amy Lowell invaded England. The world of letters was seething with activity—little movements, big movements, new anthologies, new words, *imagism*, for one. *Les Imagistes*, as Pound said, had the future in their keeping. Amy attempted to take over the movement with the élan she used as a chatelaine of her Brookline mansion, Sevenels. Amy had heard of the *vers libre* that was freeing French poetry: it was just her cup of tea—she had been writing free verse since she had dictated to her mother at the age of three. But Amy had not reckoned with Ezra Pound, also an American, and as much of a "character" as she. In terms of poetry Amy had to take a back seat. It was an uncomfortable chair and, although Amy Lowell of Boston continued to write poetry to general acclaim, continued to lecture, continued to be a public personality, she was never to be the "first rater" that Pound became.

And there were first-rate women writers emerging in that prewar London: H. D., the beautiful girl from Pennsylvania, whose poems were as classical as her features; Katherine Mansfield, a refugee from a bourgeois home in New Zealand; the glorious Dorothy Richardson, whose long, interior monologue on a woman's consciousness, *Pilgrimage*, would predate Joyce's *Ulysses*.

Bryher, who was later to write historical novels, and to earn an invaluable place in literary history as a friend of almost every writer of note, wrote of *Pilgrimage:* "I have always told my friends abroad that if they want to know what England was like between 1890 and 1914, they must read *Pilgrimage*, and Dorothy Richardson has often been more appreciated on the Continent than in her native land. People do not want to know what really happened in that epoch that they persist in calling "'the golden years.'"

"Miriam's England was the England that I saw. I never identified myself with her because she was twenty years older than I was and I was full of the revolutionary spirit of my own generation. We had faced the same reproaches, however, and shared the same fury that social conventions were more important than intelligence. Perhaps great art is always the flower of some deeply felt rebellion."

The women writers now could afford openly to be rebels—they experimented with new art forms and new life styles. There were rebels in the streets as well as at the desks. "Votes for Women" was a rallying cry. It was a "blaze of antagonism" on the part of woman, screamed H. G. Wells. Women had become "wildly exasperated human beings." At least he found them human beings. One minister simply declared them "termagants, those unsexed viragoes, those *bipeds.*"

The world and the woman, like the title of one of the literary magazines, were ready to *blast* with World War I.

Lady Gregory's famous autograph tree at her home, Coole. The initials of Shaw, G. B. S., Yeats, A. E. and O'Casey are cut deep into the wood.

11

THE HIGH STYLE OF CATHLEEN NI HOULIHAN

Always visit criminals in your best clothes.

A request from Constance Markievicz in prison

It is only tradespeople who are respectable. We are above respectability.

Speranza (Lady Wilde)

In military uniform, some enacted the part of Brunnhilde with a brilliance that rivalled any stage artist. It is impossible to over-estimate the influence the dramatic genius of Irish and Anglo-Irish women has had over Irish life. One thinks of Countess Markievicz, "Speranza" (Lady Wilde), Lady Gregory and many more. We would not now have a Republic in the south if it had not been for the woman. When I say dramatic gifts, I do not mean insincerity. I mean the aptitude for a gesture, a word, a striking pose that led men to identify national heroines with the personification of Eire herself.

Olivia Robertson

Women are at once the boldest and most unmanageable revolutionaries.

Eamon de Valera

Y ou ask me to write you details of my experience and of the activities of the women of Easter Week," wrote Countess de Markievicz. "I am afraid that I can only give you a little account of those who were enrolled like me or whom I met during the Week. Some were members of Cuman na-mBan, and others just women who were ready to die for Ireland."

Who was this rebel? What is it in the Irish culture that has produced so many remarkable women, from the legendary Queen Maeve down to Bernadette Devlin, the firebrand of today who knitted herself a red minidress for her own release from prison? Extolled, jailed, adulated and condemned, Irish literature is filled with their voices and Irish history peopled by their dreams. The beautiful Maud Gonne, the indefatigable Lady Gregory, the flamboyant Speranza, the dedicated Constance de Markievicz, the minirebel Bernadette Devlin. At home in drawing rooms, hovels, tenements, many of them knowing the inside of prisons, they wove, each of them, endless patterns in the Irish tapestry.

So Constance de Markievicz—first, not because she was the greatest, the most vehement, or the most learned, but perhaps because she showed more than any other that curious passion that burns slowly and then bursts into flame like an Irish peat fire.

Who was she? You can see her statue in St. Stephen's Green; you can walk through her great house, Lissadell, in Sligo. She seems to haunt those rooms; large, baleful rooms filled with Victorian curios, faded photographs, stuffed birds and windows that open onto the garden where Yeats loved to walk. This is Lissadell, and she was one of the "two gazelles" described by Yeats, those young, beautiful Gore-Booth sisters. But they were more than gazelles. Yeats knew. The sisters, he said, belonged to an inflammable family; they were ready to take up new ideas and new things.

Lady Gregory. Portrait by J. B. Yeats
(the father of William Butler Yeats).
Courtesy, National Gallery of Ireland.

Constance Gore-Booth was far different than the Bernadette Devlin of today, a tenement child with a kind of tenement terror and a tenement dedication. For Bernadette, Irish issues seem clearly cut. For Constance, things were a little more complicated. Lissadell was a great house, Sligo was a poor county. Back in the nineteenth century there was a kind of torture and depression on the land, but long afterwards, when Constance had turned her back on her class, the Anglo-Irish gentry, and had become a revolutionist and a new voice of Ireland, she associated her past with a kind of romantic charm. "We lived," she said, "on the beautiful, enchanted west coast where we grew up intimate with the soft mists and the colored mountains, and where each morning you awoke to the sound of the wild birds."

In those mountains they will still point out to you the cairn of Queen Maeve. They will show you one legendary, mythological spot after another. Oppressed with both the past and the future, the countryside is as commanding and as intricate as the interior landscape of the remarkable woman who became Countess de Markievicz. What turns a debutante into a rebel, a beauty into a woman grown work worn and harassed in prison? The end of the last century could barely have predicted it. Then the master of the Sligo hounds gave great fancy balls in the Sligo County Courthouse. It is now a dark, cavernous building with draughty lecture rooms, darkened

263

"Speranza" (Lady Wilde, the mother of Oscar Wilde) in 1848. Speranza, a pen name, wrote nothing until she was eighteen. "Then one day a volume of *Ireland's Library* issued from the 'Nation's' office, happened to come my way. I read it eagerly, and my patriotism was enkindled. Until then I was quite indifferent to the national movement, and if I thought about it at all, I probably had a very bad opinion of the leaders. For my family was Protestant and Conservative, and there was no social intercourse between them and the Catholics and Nationalists. But once I had caught the national spirit, all the literature of Irish songs and sufferings had an enthralling interest for me. Then it was discovered I could write poetry. In sending my verses to the editor of the 'Nation,' I dared not have my name published, and I signed them 'Speranza' and my letters, 'John Fanshawe Ellis,' instead of Jane Francesca Elgee."

old-fashioned home economics classrooms, and a circular staircase, gloomy and forbidding. It was once a place of life and light and gaiety.

Both there and in Dublin, and in the house Lissadell itself, the Gore-Booth girls danced with a gaiety that could not be suppressed. When not dancing, they rode to hounds; Constance was the finest rider in the countryside, over green hedges, past fuchsia-covered walls, galloping down to the sea. And yet, something was not right. They could not put their hands upon it. There was the poverty, yes—there was the need for cooperative dairies: their family recognized the poverty and cooperated in "good deeds."

But there was something else. There was a growing recognition that the women, particularly the women of western Ireland, had sunk into a kind of apathy, diametrically opposed to the extraordinary picture of Irish womanhood that Irish literature has always portrayed. Because, in the pages of history, in novels, in poems and in plays, Ireland is always a woman. Britain might have been John

264

Bull, the United States, Uncle Sam, but Ireland is always a woman, Cathleen ni Houlihan, the starkly beautiful character that Yeats was to portray; the old sow who ate her young that Joyce was to denigrate; the wild, abandoned strumpet that Shaw was to find. Even today Conor Cruise O'Brien depicts her as a glorious old girl, gone quite seedy, stuck always now in front of a telly and probably eating Cadbury caramels. Dont let him fool you; she's probably got a gun under the rocking chair.

Ireland is a country of contradictions—as contradictory as Constance Gore-Booth at the fancy-dress balls is to the figure of Constance fighting in St. Stephen's Square that Easter Week of 1916, in a kind of a curious Boy Scout uniform of her own design; wearing, too, a green hat with an elegant plume on her head. Perhaps not so contradictory after all, perhaps a kind of masquerade, a fancy-dress ball that was continued throughout all her life. But her scenes shifted, her drives turned differently; as a woman she began to speak out for not only Ireland, but also for all women. She became a suffragette and with her sister tried to awaken the women of Ireland; not an easy task, they liked to sleep late. Those girls who enjoyed fancy-dress balls started simply enough. Wasn't the suffragette movement rather like a ball, a fair, a local bazaar? They would make posters and decorate them with evergreens. "Who would be free themselves must strike the blow. No taxation without representation, liberty, justice and equality."

When Constance opened the meeting of what was to be called the Sligo Suffrage Society, a pioneer society in Ireland, her voice rang out in the stirring tones that she would use over and over again: "Now in order to attain to any political reform you all know that the first step is to form societies to agitate and force the government to realize that a very large class have a grievance and will never stop making themselves disagreeable until it is righted. John Stuart Mill said thirty years ago that the only forcible argument against giving women their suffrage was that they did not demand it with sufficient force and noise. Silence is an evil that may easily be remedied and the sooner we begin to make a row the better."

From that point on Constance was rarely silent. Her sister joined the cry: "All of us men and women alike besides our immedi-

St. Stephens Green, Dublin, "held" by the Countess for a day and a night during the Rising.

ate duties to our families have duties to our neighbors and to our country and to society at large." For Eva the world was her oyster and for fifteen years she would work in the north of England in the heavy industrial area, trying to improve the lives of the miserably depressed mill women.

For Constance it was to be different; Ireland would be her world, but she wanted to see the rest of the world—at least Paris where she would paint. She worked at the popular Atelier Julien— never a great artist, not even a good one, but energetic and delightful. Her vivacity impressed everyone, including a young man, the son of a Polish landowner, Casimir Dunin de Markievicz, who had abandoned law and was studying art. They were a handsome couple, the witty Miss Gore-Booth and the charming Polish count. The wedding (it was inevitable that they would marry) was quiet, despite the fact that Casimir was handsomely groomed in the Russian Court uniform, gold braid on collars and cuffs, a three-cornered hat. The bride shone in white satin and old Brussels lace. She carried orange blossoms and myrtle; it hardly seemed possible that as the years went

266

Viceregal Lodge, Dublin, the scene of many a gay ball that the Countess attended before she devoted herself to freedom for Ireland.

by she would carry guns and swords. Their child was called Maeve— who would not call one's daughter Maeve who had grown up in the shadow of that great queen whose cairn one could see from Lissadell? In 1901 they were still in what was called "Castle Society," they were still members of the vice-regal society which was the gay Dublin social center of Anglo Ireland. They made a trip to Poland and by 1903 they were living in Dublin.

Dublin, 1904; the year of James Joyce's *Ulysses.* They knew two different worlds, the Markievicz' and the Joyces. Joyce fashioned a masterpiece from the streets he knew, the happenings of one solitary day, the intensity of talk and excitement; the Markievicz' in the social world could at best fashion a drawing-room play.

It wasn't enough for Constance. There was her painting and they met many painters. They also began to see something of the literary and the political world. Constance met Arthur Griffith and Arthur Griffith had a cause. The cause was Ireland. Griffith, the leader of the Sinn Fein was less interested in her. She remembered later, "I told Mr. Griffith quite frankly that I only just realized that

267

there were men in Ireland whose principles did not allow them to take an oath of allegiance to the foreign king, whose power they were placed to break and overthrow. Mr. Griffith was very discouraging to me and very cautious." Why shouldn't he have been—who was this beautiful woman in her rich gown? "I first thought," she said, "that he merely considered me a sentimental fool. Later on I realized that he had jumped to the conclusion that I was an agent of the enemy. Many years afterwards, it was after my release from prison in 1919, I chaffed him about it. He did not deny it, but laughed heartily and said something to the effect that no one could ever say it again."

Her growing interest in women's rights and her interest in politics made her one of the founding members of a new magazine. It would have some of the great names of Ireland among its contributors, Arthur Griffith and James Connally, Roger Casement and Constance herself who chose to write a column in garden notes as an almost allegorical attack on the British. "It is very unpleasant work killing slugs and snails, but let us not be daunted," she said, "Ireland, like the garden, is sleeping and resting, recuping her vital powers for the struggle that will come. What is Ireland, but a poor wee bulb, buried away in the dust and dirt of English rule and English influence and struggling to gain the light and air?"

She made Ireland wake up. She started with the boys. "I have," she said to her sister "great faith in the young." She formed an organization with a purpose—youth brigades that would fight for Ireland. "We have heard the imperious demand of Cathleen ni Houlihan," she shouted to groups of sniveling youths on camping grounds (she admitted to loathing camping). It was a pompous demand, but she gathered followers with the ease of a St. Patrick's Day parade. Padraic Pearse said before he died in the Irish Rising of 1916 that without Con's boys—the Fianna they were called—there would not have been any Easter Rising at all.

She started cooperatives, developed communes, acted in her husband's plays heavy with theatrical Irish propaganda—it was one of his last gifts to her. After eleven years of marriage the count had finally been exhausted by the "kind, wild girl." Wherever they lived someone on the run from the constabulary would be crawling in a

268

back window during the night. The count loved her and left her. She barely noticed his departure.

Ever alert to the terrible industrial conditions of Ireland in 1913 she organized soup kitchens, grappled with scrub brushes ("No one scrubs a floor as well as I do"), and, on the side was a gunrunner for the Rising that was to come.

The Rising came and fell. Con was sentenced to death for her active role . . . then her sentence was commuted to penal servitude for life "because of her sex." She would, she said, have preferred to die with her friends.

Con, or Madame, as she was now called, seemed to epitomize all those novels that had been written about the "wild Irish girl," starting with Lady Morgan's book of that title in the early nineteenth century. Released from prison, she would be the first woman elected to Parliament, predating Lady Astor, but she refused the appointment and railed against the treaty that allowed Ireland to contain seeds of war again:

"While Ireland is not free I remain a rebel, unconverted and unconvertible. There is no word strong enough for it. I am pledged as a rebel because I am pledged to the one thing—a free and independent Republic. I mean what I mean—a state run for the Irish people by the people." She was not alone.

Despite the rampant Irish antifeminism that was found in Ireland during the nineteenth century, there still existed an almost mythological idealization of what Yeats called "fair, fierce women." In no other country is the landscape peopled with legendary women.

Some are the fabulous creatures of folklore: Red Eva McMurrough of Kilkenny Castle, for example, who was continually at war with neighboring tribes, and, went to her own death defending the border tower built by herself, called Red Eva's Tower. One old volume describes her appearance: "A great cloud of dust shot through with silver sun spoke the approach of Eva Roe. The wind came howling out of Duneen Glen. The cloud of dust ran off shrieking down the glen. Eva Roe, mightiest woman in Ireland trod biggly through the storms. Her armour ran with blood for the hearts of men were stuck on prongs of iron, iron spears that bristled across her heart."

Donegal peasants from whom such women as Lady Wilde (Oscar Wilde's mother) and Lady Gregory collected folklore.

She was supposed to have been extraordinarily tall, some historians saying as high as eight feet. They also talked of her enormous lakes of dark red hair which she braided on either side of her face. She wore them wrapped around her neck like a wimple. When going into battle she was as crafty as a Trojan and braided bits of iron into the coils. When she felt a compassion for an enemy, which was rare, she would simply stun him with one of her braids in which were imbedded the iron rocks that could knock any warrior into an Irish Kingdom Come. One famous story has it that once while her husband, Strong Bow, equally as bloodthirsty as his wife, was having difficulty in battle, she stood high on a battlement and looked at the scene below. She demanded her own armor from her courtier and a two-handed sword. Raising the weapon above her head, she cried out to her husband and jumped. This was the famous Red Eva's Lepp or Leap. They wrote about her afterwards for years. "She lept with a cry in her voice that sounded like a thunderclap. Her red hair streamed out like fire behind her and she sailed through the air like an eagle." She came down on the heads of the small army and such was her weight with her armor that the warriors were driven into the ground like so many spikes. Legends say they sleep there restlessly today, still haunted by the ghost of Red Eva.

She was preoccupied, as almost every Irish woman politician has been, with the idea of annexation; a one Ireland, even if it just meant for Eva, her own domain. She was legendary, unbelievable but, as a historical character, she existed.

Storytellers of the countryside perpetuated these ancient myths. Both Speranza (Lady Wilde) and Lady Gregory were pioneers in the collection of such folklore. Lady Gregory encouraged the young William Butler Yeats to go into the field and make a more extensive collection.

One day he ran across an old lady who told him that she had come face to face with heroic beauty. "That highest beauty," said Yeats, "which Blake says changes least from youth to age, beauty which has been fading out of the arts since voluptuous beauty took its place." The Irish heroine is never voluptuous; she is fierce, fair and wild.

The woman from whom Yeats took down his information said she saw "the finest woman you ever saw travelling right across from the mountain." This extraordinary woman had a sword by her side and a dagger lifted up in her hand and was dressed in white with fair arms and feet. She looked, said the old lady, very, very strong, but not wicked. To the old Irish, wicked was cruel. When the Irish of the nineteenth century went about describing a ghost or a fairy host, they did it with specific realities. This woman "had no stomach armor and was slight and broad in the shoulders and was handsomer than anyone you ever saw. She looked about thirty." The woman knew, of course, who it was. It was the ghost of Queen Maeve who in the west of Ireland often showed herself to the pilots to protect them from the dangerous coast. But there are many of these fair, fierce women in the legends of the West. The old woman said, "Some of them have their hair down; those with their hair up are like this one. The others have long white dresses, but those with their hair up have short dresses, so that you can see their legs right up to the calf." They evidentally wore some kind of boots, but "they are fine and dashing, riding the horses in two's and threes on the slopes of the mountains with their swords swinging." In the countryside they used to say, "there is no such race now living, none so finely proportioned." One of the old women who had seen such apparitions said to Yeats: "The present queen (meaning Queen Victoria) is a nice, pleasant-looking woman, but the fair, fierce women are not like her at all."

Old women, too, in the south of Galway had seen Queen Maeve and described her with perfect clarity: "Queen Maeve was handsome and overcame all her enemies with the hazelstick for the hazelstick is blessed and the best weapon that can be got. You might walk the world with it." An old man that Yeats met said that when he had been young he had met once "a queenly, fair, fierce woman who had called herself Maeve" and she had asked him if he would have money or pleasure. He said he would have pleasure and then she gave him her love for a time and then went from him and ever after he was very mournful. He could remember her song of lamentation; it was very mournful and he called her 'the beauty, beauty of all beauties.' "

Yeats collected these tales and published them in 1902, but he had met his own fair, fierce beauty much earlier. In 1889, as a matter of fact, and not in Ireland, but in London. Her name was Maud Gonne. She was to be as legendary in the Irish cause and as an Irish literary figure (although she wrote little herself), as any queen of the Sidhe, or queen of the fairies, had ever been. Indeed later in Donegal when she worked among those who were always in a constant state of famine, Maud Gonne was called Queen of the Sidhe.

Yeats never forgot that meeting in London, but it had so little reaction on Maud Gonne that when she wrote about their first meeting she placed it far later.

That first memory stuck with Yeats and her personality haunted him for the rest of his life. She haunted Ireland, too. Some disliked her. Miss Horniman, who was one of the first to start the Abbey Theater in Dublin—she had the money and Lady Gregory had the brains—said that whenever she thought of Maud she recalled only "a beautiful woman shrieking from a cart." Speak she did, all over Ireland, all of Europe, but it was not a shriek; she had a voice that had been trained for the theater and, as Yeats said, she could speak effortlessly, even in the open air. A creature of the open air, she also loved crowds.

She enmeshed herself in causes. Willy always sat on the out-skirts writing about them, but it was Maud's enthusiasm and beauty that often inspired him.

Maud Gonne had been born in Aldershot, England, where her father was an officer. In 1882 the colonel was posted to Dublin and Maud joined him. She acted properly for her age. At sixteen she was duly presented at court and danced like a goddess with the Duke of Clarence at the great court ball in St. Patrick's Hall. He danced badly, she remembered, and trod excrutiatingly on her satin-slip-pered toes. But she still had some respect for royalty. The then Prince of Wales, the duke's father, led her to the royal dais, but he was never to lead her to a royal bed. Maud Gonne knew just where she was going. She knew, too, about her beauty, having learned the secret of growing older gracefully from her aunt. "Women are fool-ish," she had been told, "to pretend they are young. Every age has its beauty if you accept it." And Maud Gonne was beautiful until the day she died.

She had a good ear and she kept it attuned to her times. She could hear Dublin beneath all the fashionable talk of the court life—tales of evictions, of reprisals, of the formation of a Land League Ireland. Parnell, the great hero (who fell because of his love for Kitty O'Shea), had a sister Anna, who had been one of the first to start a feminine branch of the Land League. But even the great Parnell had laughed at his sister's efforts. No one was going to laugh at Maud Gonne. She was aided in some of her understanding of Ireland by her own father. Once, as they stopped and watched a Land League procession in opposition to the practice of absentee landlords in Britain, he turned to her and said, "The people have a right to the land."

Maud was delighted that he felt as she did. She did not have his support for long. He died of typhoid and she took off on a peripatetic journey to France where she would start her life of always being on the move. In France she supported General Boulanger, the "new Napoleon," and joining in all political conversations she began to see herself as the Joan of Arc of Ireland. She must return home and find some place in the Nationalist struggle.

She soon became a famous figure around Ireland, she and her

W. B. Yeats. From the portrait by Charles Shannon. Courtesy, National Gallery of Ireland.

enormous Great Dane dog, Dagda. She looked far different from most other Irish women. Her clothes were the smartest that Paris had to offer and she had a sense of authority that was unrivaled. Soon she was a legend. The dog that accompanied her everywhere was a mean-spirited beast and often demands were put upon her, as she dined at a restaurant or took a train, to dispatch the dog. Maud had only one comment, "Remove him yourself, then." Needless to say, he stayed with her.

Later they would remember her walking the streets of Ireland, not only with a dog, but with birds flying around her head and a hawk or two in a basket. She traveled with such an entourage everywhere. Yeats used to think of her as a goddess with the birds flying around her head. But she was woman, and a very determined one.

One of the first subjects she began to write about and to involve herself actively in was the problem of political Irish prisoners, both in Ireland and in England. She was haunted by the way they were treated. They were never allowed to see their families. Somehow or other she was able to gain permission to see prisoners whose families had heard nothing about them. She promised them release and she managed to gain enough public support to assure their release. She went to Britain to try to release the men in Portland Jail. She lectured in America to try to obtain money. She talked and shouted and "shrieked" from carts. But she grew more depressed by the evictions that were still going on.

The immigration ships were still off the coast of Sligo and off the coast of Cork; the homes of the landless Irish were often battered to the ground. But nothing daunted her. She would collect a group of the strongest men, rebuild the cabins and defy the removal of any of the families.

By that time even the British police in Ireland had "stomachs turned against these terrible afflictions" and they used to stand at the side while she rebuilt cottages. Many families, having secreted themselves in other homes, would return to their cottages bearing torches in the night and crying the good graces of the Queen of the Sidhe, Maud Gonne. She would be a creature of literature.

The Irish Revival was on full tilt. The old Irish legends had gone underground and now there was a desire to draw on that literature so that it might express the new Ireland; give it a new vitality. For Ireland the turn of the century was not the end of the Victorian age, as it was for Britain, but the beginning of a new age, and one that produced one of the greatest literary outpourings that any country has ever seen. It seemed for a while that everyone wrote. The magazines had articles and poetry by many women appearing in their pages. Maud Gonne wrote no poetry; she seemed to have lived it and if she did not live it, she inspired it.

From that very first day Yeats had been in love with Maud Gonne. She appears never to have taken him very seriously:

"You make beautiful poetry out of what you call unhappiness," she told him once, "and you are happy in that. Marriage would be such a dull affair. Poets should never marry. The world should thank me for not marrying you."

He was just "dear Willie" and that was enough for her. For Yeats it meant that she was a creative presence always, an inspiration, a muse; she was a force in Ireland as well. There was a quality about her that no one could deny. Yeats immortalized her in a play, *Cathleen ni Houlihan*, in which she was the symbol of Ireland. "If only," Yeats said to her, "we could make contact with the hidden forces of the land, it would give us strength for the freeing of Ireland."

"Most of our talk," she said, "centered around this. It led us both into strange places."

Willie might have had a piece of her heart, but for the rest she gave it to the true radicals, the journalist, Arthur Griffith, and revolutionary labor leader, James Connelly. Her health was poor, however, and with her desire to move about, she would often disappear from Dublin to return to Paris, only to be bored or haunted. Again she would return to Dublin. She felt that the time had come for a revolutionary woman's society. Sixteen years before the Easter Rising, she formed the Daughters of Erin. But she had a strong streak also of the cloak-and-dagger mentality. She joined the Irish Republican Brotherhood.

She made a mark wherever she went. When men and women did her bidding, Yeats wrote, they did it not only because she was beautiful, but because her beauty suggested joy and freedom.

She became irritated with Yeats; he talked too much and did too little. Despite the fact that *Cathleen ni Houlihan*, she thought, was the most beautiful play that had ever been written, she warned Willie and his other friends that they were dreaming too much, perhaps, in what was the Celtic twilight, but which Joyce would call later the Cultic toilet.

"All I want of you" she wrote to Yeats, "is not to build up an imaginary wall of effort between yourself and life—for the rest the gods will arrange—for you are one of those they have chosen to do their work. As for the possible chance of danger which you speak of for me, I am under the great shield of Lugh." (Lugh being the great sun god in Gaelic mythology.) "The day I am no longer protected, if that day comes, my work for Ireland will be over. I should not need and could not accept protection from anyone, though I fully realize and understand the generous and unselfish thoughts which are in your heart and I love you for them. I am in my whirlwind and in the midst of that whirlwind is dead quiet calm which is peace too."

One night she played her own role, the young girl "with walk of a queen" in *Cathleen ni Houlihan*. "She played it magnificently," said Yeats, "and with weird power. She could scarcely be said to act the part, she lived it. When she came into the firelit room there came with her a sense of tragedy and a passion of deathless endeavor."

Her private sense of tragedy also continued. She had had a French lover in Paris and a child by him. Now, with Yeats still asking her to marry him, she met a man whom she felt was as active and dynamic as she was, John MacBride, who had been a hero in the Irish Brigade in the Boer War. They warned her not to marry him, her friend Griffith saying, "For your own sake and for the sake of Ireland to whom you both belong, don't get married."

It would be an impossible marriage, but they undertook it. It was a strange wedding, the best man carrying the green flag of the Irish Brigade, and the bridesmaid the blue flag of the Daughters of Erin. Almost all the shamrocks in Ireland were plucked for the breakfast table. The priest at the wedding breakfast said the bride was one of those women who rise scarce once in a century to sacrifice themselves for their country; the bridegroom, he has seen enduring the hardships and dangers of the battlefield with all that courage and gaiety which has long been traditional with Irish man in whatever clime he has had to fight.

Only a short while later she was seeking a civil dissolution of her marriage. Divorce, of course, was impossible and once again, as Ireland always has, it turned against its heroine. She was afraid that she could not get custody of her children. She now had two, Isault, the daughter of the French lover, and Sean, the son of John Mac-Bride.

She took a small house in France and there began to write articles on the terrible problems of the working-class men and women in Ireland. If she could not return to what she felt was her home, at least she could have something to say. She was not back in time for the 1916 Rising, but she wrote from France, "Tragic destiny has returned to Ireland." She never missed a single Irish newspaper. John MacBride had returned and had died a hero in front of the British firing squad. From then on she often wore widow's weeds and a flowing black veil. She was not, however, in mourning for MacBride, she often said, but in mourning for Ireland itself.

She returned to Ireland and threats of "German plots" were rampant, or thought to be, and by May, 1918, the British govern-

Malahide Castle, Dublin.

ment imprisoned her along with the Countess Markievicz. Maud Gonne could never take her imprisonment with any sense of resignation. All she could do was talk to her canary in a cage. "She was like a caged wild animal herself, like a tigress, endlessly prowling up and down."

Because of her ill health, she was sent to a sanitorium from which she escaped. She went to work fiercely during the Black and Tan war, setting up relief stations, but when the Free State Constitution was formed, under conditions to which she could not agree and Yeats became senator, she quarreled seriously with the poet. It was all Ireland or nothing for her. She was arrested once again when the Cosgrave government came into power.

But her health was so precarious that Yeats had to implore the Irish government not to let Maud Gonne die. She was carried out of the prison with wild cheers from the crowds that were with her wherever she went.

"Ranges of mountains lay like great rows of sphinxes against the sky and shut us off from the rest of Ireland." Constance Gore-Booth (Countess Markievicz) writing about her childhood in Sligo. This is Lough Gill around which she often rode with, as Yeats said, "all youth's lonely wildness stirred."

She grew old. Her beauty was now, her contemporaries said, "heroic, cavernous, made somber by the customary black drapery that she wore. But it was also illumined by a gentleness and humor. She had what now seemed a faint faraway amusement at life. "Still," she admitted, "It's so awful to be old and not to be able to do anything."

She had done enough. She lived out her time until 1953, and all Dublin turned out for the funeral. She always, as Willie said, attracted a crowd.

If Maud Gonne was almost legendary, Lady Augusta Gregory was plodding and patient. Constance Markievicz . . . Maud Gonne . . . Lady Augusta Gregory. Perhaps of the three, Lady Gregory has had the greatest staying power. The pen has always had greater respect and accuracy in Ireland than almost any other country. Since the time of Speranza, later Lady Wilde, women have written not

The Countess on her way to jail to serve a life sentence, May 6, 1916. She deeply regretted not being executed for her part in the Easter Rising. She was saved, she said, only because of her sex.

Maud Gonne. From the portrait by Sarah Purser. Courtesy, National Gallery of Ireland.

only to free Ireland, but to give it an identity. Lady Gregory gave
it more; she gave it the Abbey Theatre—not her money, just her
brains. Her own plays were more effective than all of Con's guns;
her own efforts to record the folklore of her country, more lasting
than the cry of Maud Gonne's voice in the wind. A leading figure
of the Irish literary renaissance, let Sean O'Casey, her protégé write
her epitaph:

"Crying out in her quiet determined way through all the
mumbo-jamboree of twilight that there were things to cook, sheets
to sew, pans and kettles to mend. . . . This woman, who, in the
midst of venemous opposition served as a general runabout in sensible pride and lofty humility; crushing time out of odd moments to
write play after play that kept life to and fro on the Abbey
Stage. . . . In the theater, among the poets and playwrights, herself
a better playwright than most of them, she acted the part of a
charwoman, but one with a star on her breast."

Sheets to sew and plays to write—a requiem for a woman
playwright. But there on the Irish stage the role of the woman writer
had begun to predict the future. If, as Sean O'Casey said, she had
worried less about the sheets, she might have written more, not
necessarily better, plays. And without Yeats she might even have
spoken with a voice peculiarly her own. In the meantime we know
that certainly she helped Yeats, and often without credit, for even
such a magnificent venture as Yeats' play *Cathleen ni Houlihan* has
upon it not just the concept of the beautiful Maud Gonne, but also
the voice of Lady Gregory. It had been his dream, of course, Yeats
had dreamt "of a cottage where there was a well-being and firelight
and talk of a marriage, and into the midst of that cottage there came
an old woman in a long cloak. She was Ireland herself, that Cathleen
ni Houlihan for whom so many songs have been sung for whose sake
so many have gone to their death." Then, he says, addressing Lady
Gregory in his dedication of the play: "I could not get down from
that high window of dramatic verse, and in spite of all you had done
for me, I had not the country speech. One has to live among the
people, like you, of whom an old man said in my hearing, 'she has
been a serving-maid among us' before one can think with the
thoughts of the people and speak with their tongue. We turned my

dream into the little play *Cathleen ni Houlihan,* and we gave it to the little theater in Dublin and found that the working people liked it, you helped me put my other dramatic fables into speech."

"A serving-maid amongst us." A curious expression, but one that women of talent had long grown used to—Dorothy Wordsworth, for example, the constant muse of her brother, as was Aspasia of Pericles, who, legend says, wrote some of his orations; their names are legion. In the Gregory household, it was believed that Lady Augusta had more than a minor role in writing *Cathleen Ni Houlihan,* but Lady Gregory was a lady. It was Willie's greatest popular success. Let him have it. She was the last of the serving maids; the twenties had come—women would have not only the vote, but more importantly, a voice of their own.

12

A VOICE OF ONE'S OWN
THE NEW SOUND OF
THE TWENTIES

Way down south in Greenwich Village
Main Street maidens come for thrillage,
From Duluth or Pensacola
To live a la Flaubert or Zola. . . .

Clement Wood, Greenwich Village Blues, 1926

Why, God damn it, Stearns, the gals are doing better than the men.

H. L. Mencken, 1922

We have music by machines, we travel by machines—the American people are so submerged in them that sometimes I think they can only be made to laugh and cry by machines.

Willa Cather, 1922

They were very young, they were very merry. They went back and forth on the ferry, on the trolleys, on the subways, in taxis and limousines. They bobbed their hair and barbed their tongues. They started with red wine in the old speak-easies and ended up with whisky sours for breakfast. They were emancipated, but by God they could write. They had the terrible emancipation of the very young, the whole world was adolescent: Sara Teasdale had one level of skin too little; Elinor Wylie saw herself as a Chinese vase or a piece of Lalique glass; Edna St. Vincent Millay was Byron; Zelda Fitzgerald epitomized the flapper.

Their names became scattered in the newspapers. The world of the fast, the clever, the witty woman had come. Fanny Burney, back in the early nineteenth century, had said it was a world of witlings. Dorothy Parker named the house of a friend Wits End. And indeed the end of the decade would see the decline of all wit and the stockmarket. One could not go on forever doing what was being done: one cannot lunch forever at the Algonquin, even a ferry trip becomes dull, one cannot forever see the renaissance of the world, one cannot forever be young.

Yet the twenties opened with a glorious feeling of youth. Everything was funny. Why not? Hadn't the war erased the past? In Europe Dadaism gave a death kiss to old traditional art forms. Art, like the roses of yesteryear, had disappeared. You made art out of other things now—anarchy, pain, passion. Yet the passion was public, private passion was muted. Who wrote love letters now like the great women of the past? Instead they sat by the telephone or they met someone at a bar, or they talked and were so clever, oh so clever. The salons had changed: they were at Neysa McMein's now, but you went there only after you were tired of the speak-easy or tired of the theater, but never, it appeared, tired of the same voices. It

Gertrude Stein. Portrait by Pablo Picasso. Courtesy, Metropolitan Museum of Art, Bequest of Gertrude Stein, 1946. Gertrude Stein's brilliant innovative novel *Three Lives* appeared in 1910, but it was to take another decade before she was an indomitable literary "character." Her prescience was such that not only such well-known writers as Hemingway (who later literally attacked her) was influenced by her, but black writers as well admired particularly her story of Melanctha. One of the few black women writers of the time, Nella Larson, wrote to Gertrude saying, "I never cease to wonder how you came to write it and just why you and not some one of us should so accurately have caught the spirit of this race of mine." But blacks attacked the book, too, as well as whites, one of the latter being Wyndham Lewis, who complained that *Three Lives* was cold black suet pudding. To which Gertrude answered, "Here I am. Where is everybody else?"

Sylvia Beach standing in front of her bookshop, Shakespeare and Company, in Paris. Sylvia Beach Collections. Courtesy, Princeton University Library.

was an eclectic group. Everyone seemed to know everyone else; everybody thought their friends were the best of all possible friends. Flappers, foolishness and fancies.

So the women of the twenties arrived on the scene already vindicated by themselves. They went to bed with whomever they chose, they drank, whenever and whatever they liked, they said whatever they cared to say. Paris, London and New York, "the big city," was filled with women as personalities, wits wags and, as we look back, peaks of feeling, exultation, and often desperation.

Two immediately stand out, Edna St. Vincent Millay and Dorothy Parker. And as the popular phrase goes today, Whatever happened to Edna St. Vincent Millay, whatever happened to Dorothy Parker? The young know even now. Disregarded by the critics today, the young have sought them out again, heard the romantic anarchy behind the poetry of Millay, the cry of alienation behind the flashing wit of Dorothy Parker. Heard the confusion, bewilderment and rich romanticism of Zelda Fitzgerald, perhaps in time they'll hear the sharper tones of H.D., the trenchant voice of Kay Boyle, the distinctive pathos of Edith Sitwell. It was a time of curious mixing of genius and talent, that sudden and overwhelming emphasis on the identity; the writer had been discovered by the newspaper, the writer was clever and had something to say, the writer was a personality and the woman writer made news.

In the circle of a few New York blocks they sat in restaurants and in offices, enjoying one another's company, their own curious narrow world.

The world had opened up. For the first time the United States had participated in a world war and had learned that there was something besides the American frontier. For the first time New York became a clever town, not just a town that signaled as a beacon to the farm boy, to some poor hopeful from the hinterlands, to somebody who was lost in a world he had never made.

The streets were clean, you could walk forever on Fifth Avenue, there was a champagne smell in the air as you walked down four steps into any speak-easy. Speak-easies came in all shapes and sizes, Irish and Italian, smart or dingy, but always smoke filled and raucous. Nobody really danced on tabletops like Joan Crawford in *Our Danc-*

ing Daughters, but then no woman was so much an identity that gallants drank from her slipper.

The age of gallantry was gone, this was the age of the buddy: America had equalized. Women had achieved those rights that they had cried for, and what did they amount to? It was the adolescence of the vindication of rights for women and like adolescents they stumbled and fell and didn't quite know where they were heading. It was quite simply, as Gertrude Stein said, the "Lost Generation." But Gertrude was another type altogether. It is difficult to think of Amy Lowell, smoking cigars in the perpetual intellectual smog of Boston, as ever being lost.

There were quarrels and feuds and outlets for both: there were magazines for both women and men. No writer exists in a vacuum and for once the literary world filled that vacuum. There was the *Smart Set* and *Vanity Fair,* there was that ultra new magazine, *The New Yorker* with the dandy on the cover recalling the Regency dandy of the early nineteenth century. Indeed, Rea Irwin deliberately modeled his dandy on Beau Brummel, the contemporary of Fanny Burney's. It wasn't that *The New Yorker* was so dandified in clothing, it was just that there were more walking sticks, fedoras, tie pins, sharp dressers, handsome men, beautiful women, maribou, crepe de Chine, voile, hostess pajamas, cloche hats and closed hearts than we were ever to see again. No silent generation for them, just lost—and forever talking.

There were the little magazines with their eye-catching covers and their strange names: *Broom, Transition, Laughing Horse, Dynamo.* The first volume of *Dynamo* carried a poem that said "worker find your poet"; society was changing.

There were exiles, it was a great holiday and where would you spend it? In Paris, of course, but the voices of women writers were being heard in Vienna, Rome, Berlin. They went to the cafés, they heard the music and, if sentimental, they let a tear or two roll down their faces. If one didn't find the literary salon at the speak-easy, one might find it at Mabel Dodge Luhan's—utterly emancipated, utterly fantastic, utterly "modern"; it didn't seem very different from Margaret Fuller's gathering, ladies who deliberately spoke on each subject of the universe seriatim. Mabel quite simply gave each

WHEN LIFE IS VERY STRENUOUS AND SPIRITS ARE WAY DOWN
YOU'D BETTER GO TO POLLY'S IN LITTLE GREENWICH TOWN
FOR THERE THE CLANS ARE GATHERED - ITS THERE YOU'LL FINDE 'EM ALL
THE ARTISTS AND THE WRITERS RANGED ALONG THE WALL.
MISS POLLY TAKES THE MONEY AND MIKE SAYS HE JUST CAN'T
WAIT ANY FASTER ON THE FOLKS IN POLLY'S RES-TAU-RANT
J.T.B
24
GREENWICH VILLAGE _ NEW YORK
JESSIE TARBOX BEALS

Polly's Restaurant in Greenwich Village. Photograph by Jessie Tarbox Beals.
Courtesy, Museum of the City of New York.

speaker a different subject each week. It didn't matter what the
subjects were, Lawrence, women, euthanasia.

It was the age of the personal magazine, best exemplified by
Margaret Anderson's *Little Review* and she left a record rather like
the record that Mary Shelley left about the painful night before the
birth of Frankenstein shot across her brain. Margaret had neither
Mary's stamina, nor her genius, but she too could suffer. She would
suffer for literature. "I've been curiously depressed all day and in
the night I awakened. First precise thought. I know why I'm depressed. Nothing inspired is going on. Second, I demand that life
be inspired every moment, third the only way to guarantee this is
to have inspired conversation every moment. Fourth, most people
never go so far as to have conversation, they haven't the stamina
and there is no time. Fifth, if I had a magazine I would spend my
time filling it up with the best conversation the world has to offer.
Sixth, marvelous idea,—salvation. Seventh, decision to do it. Deep
sleep."

Could life be inspired every moment? They thought it could.
Could conversation be put down in print? They thought it could.
In truth, if we look at the vitality and excitement of the books about

Dame Edith Sitwell. From a portrait by
Pavel Tchelitchew. Courtesy, Humani-
ties Research Center, University of
Texas at Austin, Austin, Texas.

the twenties, it is primarily in the conversation and in the personalities that a new age emerges. Many of their books are as dated as
dusty Victorian tomes, but the *people* endure, living legends, conversing as figures: they have enormous stamina.

Margaret Anderson evolved into a legend. She was never concerned with the critical point of view, as they said about Edward
Gibbon who scribbled, scribbled, scribbled. Margaret would publish,
publish, publish and if she found nothing too exciting she would
bring out an empty magazine. She admitted later that her first
number betrayed nothing but adolescence. "What I needed," she
said, "was not a magazine but a club room where I could have
informed disciples twice a week, that nature was wonderful, love
beautiful and art inspired." The *Little Review* was for feminism:
the *Little Review* for anarchism and Emma Goldman: the *Little
Review* was for lack of compromise: the *Little Review* was for Art
with a capital *A*. But the woman herself was lovely. "She was always
exquisite," said Harry Hanson, "as if emerging from a scented boudoir, not from a mildewed tent or camp where frying bacon was
scenting the atmosphere. She was always vivid and beautiful to look
upon and lovely in her mind. There was a sort of high, windblown
beauty about her, her fluffy hair blows marvelously, her eyes are Lake

290

Michigan's best blue and she is valiant always." Lake Michigan or not, she knew where the action was. It was in Greenwich Village.

For the first time women were living alone and liking it. They came from everywhere. From the far west, from Chicago where life had suddenly erupted into a kind of literary and artistic renaissance, from Philadelphia, from the south, from the north. Edna St. Vincent Millay came from the north, from Maine, from Camden—that beautiful town where the mountains go down to the sea. "All there had been to see," she had said in her very earliest poem, *Renascence* "was the three long mountains in the wood and three islands in a bay."

More than any other woman writer, Edna St. Vincent Millay was the poet laureate of the twenties. Actually, she had started much earlier. That extraordinary poem, *Renascence*, was published when she was seventeen. More than one person had felt extraordinary jealousy at its publication. Amy Lowell blamed her own lack of success in her early years on the fact that "that child's poem" had been published on the eve of her own first book.

Those women who came from the small town brought with them some of the best and the worst of the traits of the villages and towns they left behind. The best was a kind of homogenized feeling for the world, a feeling that they lived and grew up in some place with an identity, a place that one could always look back upon or dream about.

Edna St. Vincent Millay had that extraordinary sense of place. Her dreams had been fostered by her mother: not only fostered, but encouraged. Mrs. Cora Millay would have something else for her children than what she had had. A district nurse, she was often away from home, leaving the three young girls on their own. Edna was the eldest, the gypsy one, but practical enough to know how to clean a house from top to bottom, how to keep a small family together. Her father had taken off after the birth of Edna's sister Kathleen.

The children were inundated in activities. At the age of four Edna began writing poetry. At seven she played the piano. In her early teens she read assiduously. At fourteen, that wonderful magazine, *St. Nicholas,* welcomed her first poem, "Forest Trees." She

Painting by Charles Sims, R. A., of Lady
Astor's introduction to the House of
Commons by Arthur Balfour and David
Lloyd George.

signed herself then E. St. Vincent Millay, not unlike the Brontës,
reluctant to admit their sex in print. But *St. Nicholas* would never
satisfy her. The poetry that generally dries up in an adolescent did
not disappear. She had a great desire, she said, to pierce away into
the world's great heart. And, by 1912, when her mother saw an
announcement of an anthology of poetry to be published called *The
Lyric Year* and, even more exciting, the offer of a prize of five
hundred dollars, Edna was encouraged to send in her poem *Renascence.* Desperately poor, the Millays thought often of that five
hundred dollars, but the competition was incredible. How could one
unknown girl on the coast of Maine even hope for publication in

292

a national contest, let alone ever win the glorious sum of five hundred dollars? The rest is literary history. An editor in New York going through ten thousand manuscripts suddenly came upon those lines that would shake the whole generation, the opening lines of *Renascence.*

Ferdinand Earle was the editor in charge. He had no doubts about that one in ten thousand and he felt the prize should be awarded to Edna. The two other judges disagreed. The poem *Renascence* came in only fourth. But Earle's opinion and Edna St. Vincent Millay's confidence immediately made history. Even the prize winner, Orrik Johns, wrote later that he felt his own reward was unmerited. The mere fact that he had won was an embarrassment to him.

At nineteen, like a young Fanny Burney, Edna St. Vincent Millay was the talk of the literary world. Still penniless, still eager for more traditional education, Edna and her two sisters had a poetry reading in that charming hotel, the White House, in Camden, Maine. They could thank their lucky stars for the presence of Miss Caroline B. Dow, the head of the National Training School of the YWCA. Miss Dow, who was enormously taken by this attractive, red-haired, intensely vibrant girl, arranged for her to attend Vassar.

She was not yet "Vassarized," she wrote in 1914. Some of the restraints put upon this gypsy girl were far too strong. She felt the college was out of *Alice in Wonderland.* "Damn this pink and gray college," she said. She was annoyed that it wasn't on the Hudson. They had claimed it to be. The water was so important to her, and she was filled with such loneliness that she felt every path in the countryside led just to garbage cans.

She who was always wildly appealing to men and liked them too, though sometimes with more than an ambivalent feeling, felt that the few men who ventured on the campus were treated "like the forbidden apple." Writing, however, was not forbidden. She was still publishing outside of the confines of the college, and her teachers appreciated her. She played, too, occasionally in the theater at Vassar, one time playing scenes from Synge's *Deirdre of the Sorrows* and another time playing in the French Club's *Les Romanesques.* She wrote a one-act play that was published in the *Vassar Miscellany*. She almost did not graduate because she overextended her overnight pass. She did graduate finally, but not with her class, receiving her diploma alone.

But she was already the friend of many: of Harriet Monroe, of *Poetry Magazine*, who would pay her sixteen dollars for a poem (and how, how they needed that, she would say); of John Mansfield, who said that she had a quite rare personal gift; of Arthur Davison Ficke and of Witter Bynner. Afterwards she "fled to Maine," but not for long. It was the city that was to call her, as it would to so many young girls of the period. No longer would they need chaperones. No longer would they have to live in, like Margaret Fuller with the Greeleys, or George Eliot with the Chapmans. They could be completely on their own. The place to go was Greenwich Village.

Over 50 percent of American writing during the twenties emerged from the Village. It was to have, in a short space of time, two Pulitzer Prize winners, Eugene O'Neill and Edna St. Vincent Millay. At first she moved to Waverly Place, an area haunted by that other lonely poet, Edgar Allan Poe. She was used to cold, and she was used to being occasionally hungry, and she was used to being alone. But there during one very icebound winter, living on next to nothing, she hugged a fire in a tiny room brooding about her next step.

Perhaps the theater. She had been so successful at college. It was the answer. She always had remarkable presence. The memoirs that one reads always talk about this quality—the intensity, the fire of her presence. She perhaps could have become an actress, and actually she tried her hand at both writing plays and performing in them. But, perhaps there was some basic loneliness that only the poetry could express. Edmund Wilson once made the remark that all poets should have some other occupation. In reality the poets who have been only poets have found it an emotionally exhausting role to maintain. For that reason, Wilson thought that the women poets of the period, who had in some way to bind themselves to reality or even take a job, made better poets than many of the men.

The drama that now interested her seemed to be the drama of her life. "There was an awful drama," Edmund Wilson said later, "about everything she did." Bohemian, yes, but sometimes shy to the point of embarrassment, sometimes arrogant to the point of

Edna Ferber, an example of the popular novelist of the twenties, made it big with *So Big* in 1924. Portrait by George Platt Lynes. Courtesy, Doubleday & Company, Inc.

annoyance. She had an excellent voice for reading poetry, and the look of a muse. She also had the adulation of the reviewers.

Carl Van Doren said, "What sets Miss Millay's poems apart from all those written in English by women is the full pulse which beats through them. . . . Rarely since Sappho has a woman written as outspokenly as this." But she was, as the time was, fickle. Her love affairs were numerous. As one gentleman after another handed over his role in her life to another, he rarely complained. "There should be an alumni of us," said one. She seemed to be mercurial in many ways. When she would read poetry she could be as innocent as a child, the shining Maine sun on her face. When she went on picnics she was freckled and snub-nosed, as fresh as a new spring flower. When she met someone she disliked, she was "horribly Vassar," with abominably overdone manners. She was all things to all men. From a nun to a chorus girl to a Botticelli. Her legend was incredible. She and her mother and her two sisters had a salon in the Village. If earlier centuries had supported a papa, Edna St. Vincent Millay was careful to support her mother. She was always a family girl, intensely involved with her sisters and her mother, and the entire family took on the world. Although she was to become an even more accomplished poet, she was then the voice of her own time.

Edna St. Vincent Millay's extraordinary popularity went with the twenties. Her feelings of disillusion went with the twenties. Often she was too clever, as was Dorothy Parker. In later years Dorothy Parker would say, "I was just a little Jewish girl trying to be clever." Edna St. Vincent Millay never explained and never offered excuses. But she was a symbol of the times, the symbol of a generation of women, Louise Tanner was to say, who for the first time had their own latchkeys. Edna St. Vincent Millay opened up a new world for many young women. They read her poems with avidity. They went to the Village to trace her footsteps. They put her aside eventually the way they put aside their own youth. But Edmund Wilson, one of our sternest critics, realizing her vulnerability as a poet today says that Edna Millay "seems to me one of the only poets writing in English in our time who has attained anything like the stature of great literary figures in an age in which prose has predominated."

Of course, poetry did not "pay." Edna St. Vincent Millay early started to contribute to *Vanity Fair* under the name of Nancy Boyd.

The Victorians left us noble portraits, the Edwardians left slightly browned snapshots, but in the twenties we find our women writers rather dusty clippings from old literary magazines, or that fashionable of all publishing ventures, *Vanity Fair.*

So let us turn some of those dusty pages, the faces looking very sharp (photography had so improved), the hair is slick like Anita Loos's bangs, the language is lacquered. Flaming youth, the age when women or girls having been rather repressed so long, became sappily and deliciously adolescent. Besides, the men liked them that way. Such editors as Frank Crowninshield at *Vanity Fair* had a whole bevy of bright young things. There was Anita Loos, writing on heredity. Women could write about anything now, but it was better if it was formed as a modern fable and was as funny as a fast slapstick comedy movie. Even Gertrude Stein could write in those august pages, opening "Have They Attacked Mary, She Giggled," with the immortal line: "Can you be more confusing by laughing?" It seemed that the decade would endlessly raise that question.

Men and women alike were confused by laughing, confused by movable saloons, confused by changing ethics, confused by that great adventure into self-expression and freedom that had been the result of the war.

There had hardly been a treaty. The twenties was at once the coldest of cold wars laced with wicked wit and sarcasm—and a bathos of sentimentality. *Vanity Fair* promoted such writers as Michael Strange, and who remembers her now? Byronically Garbo, she stares at us with a face haunted by intense introspection. Everybody was Feeling with a capital *F*. (Though Charles Sumner and his vice squad literally made sure no dirty words ever appeared in print.) When one wrote, one wrote about Fate with a capital or Why with an exclamation mark, or Solitude or Sunset, An Impression. The decade seemed to be one long impression and one that was to disappear, leaving nothing except some fossils of humor.

In *Vanity Fair* Amy Lowell was still arranging strange flowers of wax and jade and calling it svelte. She was like some grandmother now with her poetry: look but do not touch. If you did, the words would shatter.

And then suddenly, in 1920, *Vanity Fair* gave Edna St. Vincent Millay a whole page of poetry. They had the other side of her as well. Under the nom de plume Nancy Boyd she gave all sorts of advice to her eager readers, who wanted to be "as emancipated" as she was. To a mythical landlady who might be troubled with indigent artists, she suggested that the landlady have on the table in the hall a placard reading, "Free Thinkers," "Free Lovers" and "Freebooters." If you have any heathen pity in your hearts, drop a nickel in the slot for the starving baby—anarchists of Russia. Who does not contribute to the cause of anarchy is mid-Victorian.

It was a threat not only to be mid-Victorian, but even to be Edwardian or Georgian. The only thing was to be one's own generation. A girl of the Twenties. One of her poems on the pages of *Vanity Fair*, "A Singing Woman from Woods Edge," contained a line, "What should I be, but a harlot and a nun?" For all the glorious freedom of the time, it shocked the readers; the world was not quite ready for even that expression.

In the Hall of Fame of 1920, Lady Astor was nominated in

those pages of *Vanity Fair* with such persons as Rachmaninoff, Franz Lehar, John Masefield and W. B. Yeats. The Sargent picture shows none of her raging acerbity; none of that determination that would make her an influential politician. She was nominated "because she was one of the famous Langhorne sisters of Virginia," but as the first woman M. P. she should have been nominated because she would raise hell.

In 1921 they were singling out American artists who put their art over their popularity. In those pages Willa Cather stares out at us with that midwestern common sense that typifies her writing. And Edith Wharton, described then as "the greatest living American novelist" looks at us with utter disdain, her diamond choker holding up her chin, her mouth taut and her eyes lit with a baleful glare. Perhaps it was justified. She knew what the young thought of her, that her books were filled with nothing but tufted furniture and gas chandeliers. Yet they came to her in Paris where she was living, the Fitzgeralds, for example, having stopped at a few movable saloons along the way, to go to one of the most famous salons in Paris, Edith Wharton's. Zelda fought all the way; she didn't want to meet any such old lady. Scott, well braced, stood up to this formidable, post-Victorian character.

"Mrs. Wharton, do you know what's the matter with you?"

"No, Mr. Fitzgerald, I have often wondered about it, what is it?"

"You don't know anything about life."

Scott muttered, and wept when he returned home. She had "beaten" him.

They were writing parodies of Edith Wharton in *Vanity Fair*, but there were others who seemed to be parodies of the self-poet: Elinor Wylie, with her strange, neurotic novels, and Sara Teasdale, whose sensitivity was attributed to the fact that she was unusually thin skinned.

With alarming regularity there were symposiums of the "Ten Dullest Authors." Elinor Wylie named three women. "George Eliot, because the dark-brown binding got into her style; Selma Lagerlof, because an English lady read her aloud to me; Gertrude Stein, because. . . ." But, as we look back today, Gertrude Stein towered over the decade.

Edna Ferber, the queen bee of what was to be called "the woman's novel" for several decades afterwards, was equally twentiesh about *her* ten dullest books. She reeled off *Plane Geometry, Eat and Grow Thin, The Book of Job, Elsie Dinsmore, Jurgen, The Genius, Pollyanna,* anything of F. Scott Fitzgerald's written since his first novel and first book of short stories, the *Congressional Record,* and *Bleak House.*

By 1923 they were nominating another woman for the Hall of Fame. After all, the literary lights were not only in New York, sitting at the Algonquin; they were in Paris at the Select or the Dome, or the private salons. The Comtesse de Noailles was then called the "most distinguished living woman writer in France." It would be a few years before the title would go to Colette.

By 1924 Edna Ferber was writing with what *Vanity Fair* called "a divine discontent," and Rebecca West was showing that the decade and its women were becoming active politically. She would "stump" in behalf of a cause she believed to be right. But mostly they nominated her to the 1924 Hall of Fame because "for all the richness of her gifts, she remains young, beautiful, brilliant, genuine and feminine." If you were all those things, you couldn't go wrong. Not in the twenties.

By 1925, the decade half over, a group of writers were asked to write their own epitaphs; one that was preserved was Dorothy Parker's:

CI-GIT
DORTHY PARKER,
EXCUSE MY DUST!

The humor was getting a little dusty indeed.

In 1925 there was no woman writer in the Hall of Fame, just entertainers—from Minnie Marx, the mother of the Marx Brothers to Fannie Brice.

Vanity Fair made great copy out of the "ideal woman." "No two men could agree on the perfect woman" said the article and the connoisseurs tried their humor once again. The perfect woman's diamond bracelets never need cleaning, said Chaplin. Day and night

Women writers have always had a gift for mystery and the supernatural. The twenties saw them develop into major craftsmen of crime and character . . . none more perennial than Dame Agatha Christie who published her first book in 1920. She is shown here, in a rare photograph, with her husband the noted archeologist, Sir Max E. Mallowan. Photograph courtesy of Howard Thompson.

elevator service was very helpful, said Ring Lardner. An old-fashioned and wholehearted acceptance of monogamy, said that great lover, Rudolph Valentino. Height 7½ times the length of the head said Flo Ziegfeld, plus native refinement. "Where this exists education is not necessary." A million dollars, said Al Jolson. She must not be afraid of being thought old-fashioned, said Lee Shubert.

Allowing for the entertainment value of all the comments it was a pretty poor ploy. It was a time of "blazing publicity." A lady writer could get it only by being pretty blazing herself. She had a lot to compete with in the pages of the newspaper from Peaches Browning to Queen Marie of Rumania, from Billie Burke to all those glorious expatriates in Antibes, from Marilyn Miller and Clifton Webb to the Fitzgeralds to Lady Mendl and even, mind you, H. R. H. Edward, Prince of Wales, with a line beneath his portrait, "Presenting the apparently fragile, but really indestructible heir to the British throne."

In 1929, that fabulous year, Djuna Barnes appeared in the pages of *Vanity Fair* with one of her rare stories, "A Duel Without Seconds," and there was a spectacular picture of the three Sitwells, Sacheverell, Edith and Osbert—"three porcelain exquisites," they were called. "Perhaps," the caption writer suggests, "they are fabulous comedians; certainly they would resent any accusation of usefulness. But the wonderful and really heartening part of it all is that they always keep perfectly straight faces, so that no one can ever afford to laugh, nor can you and I."

No, indeed, no one dared laugh at Edith, even though they attempted to do so in those days, in the same fashion that they were laughing madly at Gertrude Stein. One laughed at one's betters and one's betters did not care.

By 1929 Virginia Woolf made the Hall of Fame. It is Virginia Woolf's name that stands out in any attempt to examine the woman writer. She alone among critics thought the subject worthy of consideration. She closed the decade with the publication of her famous book, *A ROOM OF ONE'S OWN.*

Virginia Woolf seemed an unlikely contender as a champion of the woman writer. Intensely withdrawn, suspicious of her own sex, a writer who worked in an eclectic vein of her own, the pride and glory of Bloomsbury, she might have been well content to simply explore her own rich vein of genius. She had one of those beautiful, inquiring, nineteenth-century minds, and it was inevitable that she should ask questions. Why was there, for example, no significant writing done by women before the eighteenth century, and then what happened? There seemed to be a flowering. The flowering was in fiction, of course. But what particularly happened to women that they began to write as freely, or at least, as copiously as men?

She had to grudgingly admit that there was a sore point in her own personal history, that the history of England had certainly been a history of the male line, not the female. It wasn't simply a question of the Victorian father, though Virginia had had more than enough of that, but the father in English history was distinctly a man of distinction.

If we look at the overall role of the woman in American history, despite that patriarchial symbol of Uncle Sam, woman has had more significance. In a pioneer society she had to. It was the mother who rocked the cradle, the mother who raised the child, but in England the mother didn't even have that particular role. Her children were assigned to nannies and governesses. She was assigned to ride in her carriage into society. America has a tradition that was quite different from the one that Virginia Woolf knew, and she made no attempt to understand any woman writer of America. Indeed, she was more than a little suspicious of American writers in general. But, she was obsessed with her own tradition. She was to demand, in print, *A Room of One's Own.*

What had mothers been, she asked? They were for her, and for many in the age in which she grew up, just a tradition. Perhaps if she had known her own mother more intimately, less as a fabulous beauty who had died young, but as a more concrete figure, she would have felt happier within herself, perhaps been even more assured of her own femininity. For some curious reason, she associated femininity with a kind of weakness, a suffering, a misery—not an unusual concept when women were supposed to swoon easily and still sway men. So what were they to her? Just stories one heard at the nurse's knee. A beautiful grandmother, someone with red hair, another woman who had been kissed by a queen. Yes, she admitted, one knew the number of children they had, but for the rest, one knew little about them.

The very title of this book denotes that most of the women who found their way to paper, in their own way to self-identity in one way or another, were extraordinary women. But Virginia Woolf made the astute remark that the extraordinary woman depends on the ordinary woman. "It is only when we know what were the conditions of the average woman's life, the number of her children, whether she had money of her own, if she had a room to herself, whether she had help in bringing up her family, if she had servants, whether part of the housework was her task—it is only when we can measure the way of life and the experience of life made possible to the ordinary woman that we can account for the success or failure of the extraordinary woman as a writer."

And yet, even knowing all this, what do you have? You have great silences between women writers. Genius, even talent, is inexplicable. Oh, of course, there was Sappho and the gods know what they had to blame on her. Then about 1,000 A.D. there was Lady Murasaki, courtly, majestic, writing one of those strange, isolated novels of genius in Japan.

It is fascinating to pick up book after book of English literary criticism—even to pick up a contemporary book, such as *Eight Great Writers*, and find no woman's name among them—not even Virginia Woolf, who certainly should be there.

Virginia mused that women's voices had been dumb for ages. In the Elizabethan age, for all the glory of the queen, their voice was heard but rarely inscribed on paper. Then suddenly, the eighteenth century draws to a close, and women go to a desk, if not a desk, to a kitchen table. Or they sit with a pad on their knees, often surrounded by relatives or children, getting up more than once to boil water, to calm a child, to dig eyes out of potatoes, to try to combine the ordinary and extraordinary life. Because the woman writer is perhaps only extraordinary to the extent that she can combine two roles which the world had decided long before could not be so combined—one in which she expressed herself as a continuum of the human race, the other in which she could express herself. So what happened? Suddenly there was the end of the eighteenth century and the beginning of the nineteenth century, a very distinct flowering, the flowering within a sense we have not seen in literature since. A great deal had happened since the time woman was completely a chattel, when she could be married without consent to any man who was chosen for her. She had some of the few basics, a little leisure, some education, a bit of self-assurance to understand what even talent, let alone genius, demands of one.

Quite frankly, as Virginia Woolf said, an abnormal effort is required to produce a work of art. Woman should have been content then just to produce a child, a natural form of creativity. And yet, what is that wierd desire on the part of many women, including those who have produced innumerable children, for a voice of their own, which is even more necessary than the constant cry of Virginia

Virginia Woolf. Courtesy, Harcourt, Brace and Jovanovich.

Woolf for a room of her own?

Virginia Woolf had more than a reasonably happy marriage—of her own kind. She played many roles—printer, publisher, superb conversationalist, hostess, friend, companion. But her role as a wife obviously filled her with a kind of hysterical, sexual anxiety. One doesn't know what her fears were but they were certainly elaborate, and it was often commented upon by her friends that the sensual or sexual sides of marriage alarmed her. She substituted for bodily indulgences the sensuality of words. Yet she could not be blamed for her own deprivation because a marriage that is maintained in such a fashion is sanctioned by both parties. Quite obviously Bloomsbury had a low sexual burning point. It is difficult to look upon any of the Bloomsbury characters, despite their many books and documents and their occasional forays into homosexuality, as a hot-blooded, passionate group. They seemed more given to conversational, intimate encounters, and yet they demanded and even forced upon others their own particular eclectic privacy.

Virginia Woolf then had a husband, of the kind particularly acceptable to her and to the role she had to play, but she had, of course, no child. She often pointed out that the four great women novelists, Jane Austen, Emily Brontë, Charlotte Brontë and George

Eliot, never had children, and the two of them, Jane Austen, a born maiden, and Emily Brontë, a born pagan, had never married. Those four women were extraordinarily unlike each other, and yet all became novelists. Their training was certainly different from the training of a man. If anything, a woman almost unconsciously absorbs some of the ingredients that make fiction. Virginia Woolf felt that it had been even important that these women had been forcibly withheld from most outside experiences. All their experience had been confined to a middle-class drawing room—sometimes not even that. It's an unfair comment, of course. Who can imagine confining Emily Brontë anywhere when there was the moor outside, calling? Or, for that matter, Jane Austen, who explored a social world so filled with do's and dont's in a hierarchy of persons and places with an ungovernable wit. Or George Eliot confined to a drawing room, lusting for a man's world, not a part of it, in those glorious days. Or Charlotte Brontë . . . perhaps she would have been confined by nothing, but felt that she had to be, and built up a fabric of respectability, painfully around her. Or Virginia Woolf herself. One had the feeling that the wicked wit, a general hostility to the outsider was not necessarily the product of a middle-class drawing room. It was something quite different. So Virginia Woolf tells us and does not tell us in the same breath, explains and does not explain, because there is no complete explanation of any writer, woman or otherwise.

But certainly the needs flowered, and even the subject matter of novels changed. One began to hear the woman's voice. One was conscious that a woman was doing the writing. There was a voice pleading for some recognition in those pages. Often a grievance. Some kind of cry that made Virginia Woolf feel that the mediocre writer was distorting what she had to say by her own particular demand to be heard, as any minority group would be heard—the working man, the black one who was conscious of a disability.

And certainly they had their disabilities, the cantankerous do-gooders of the nineteenth century. Harriet Martineau was deaf: the Brontës were consumed by disease: George Eliot was hounded by her ugliness; endless women writers saw the tragic disruption of their lives; others, the early deprivation of mothers or fathers; yes, all were disabled, yet all were entitled to a voice.

By the end of the twenties, the woman writer had extended herself in all phases of the literary life. She was active in publishing, on newspapers, muckraker as well as moralist. She no longer had to be "clever"; she could, as Virginia Woolf said, begin to write "naturally."

Virginia Woolf pointed the way to the present when she spoke to a group of young women at the end of the decade:

"I would ask you to write all kinds of books, hesitating at no subject, however trivial, or however vast. By hook or crook, I hope that you will possess yourselves of money enough to travel and to idle, to contemplate the future or the past of the world, to dream over books and loiter at street corners and let the line of thought dip deep into the stream. For I am by no means confining you to fiction. If you would please me—and there are thousands like me— you would write books of travel and adventure, and research and scholarship and history and biography, and criticism and philosophy and science." They have. And they will.

SELECTED BIBLIOGRAPHY

Compiled with the Assistance
of Mrs. Clara Pye.

Adams, Samuel Hopkins. *A. Woollcott: His Life and His World.* New York: Reynal and Hitchcock, 1945.

Adcock, A. St. John. *The Booklover's London.* London: Methuen, 1913.

Adelphi Monthly. Edited by John Middleton Murry.

Alcott, Louisa M. *Jack and Jill: A Village Story.* Boston: Little, Brown, 1926.

Alcott, Louisa May. *Life, Letters and Journals.* Edited by Ednah D. Cheney. Boston: Roberts Brothers, 1890.

Allen, Walter (ed.). *Writers on Writing.* New York: E. P. Dutton, 1949.

Allott, Kenneth and Miriam. *Victorian Prose, 1830–1880.* Harmondsworth, England: Penguin Books, 1956.

Alpers, Antony. *Katherine Mansfield.* New York: Alfred A. Knopf, 1954.

Altick, Richard D. *The Scholar Adventurers.* New York: Macmillan, 1960.

Altick, Richard D. *Lives and Letters.* New York: Alfred A. Knopf, 1966.

Anderson, Margaret.*Strange Necessity: The Autobiography, Resolutions and Reminiscence to 1969.* New York: Horizon Press, 1969.

Anderson, Margaret (ed.). *The Little Review Anthology.* New York: Hermitage House, 1953.

Les Années Vingt, Les Écrivains Américains à Paris et Leurs Amis. Paris: Centre Cultural Américain, 1959.

Ariés Philippe. *Centuries of Childhood: A Social History of Family Life.* Translated from French by Robert Baldick. New York: Alfred A. Knopf, 1962.

Armstrong, Margaret. *Trelawny: A Man's Life.* New York: Macmillan, 1940.

Arnold, Arnold. *Pictures and Stories from Forgotten Children's Books.* New York: Dover Publications, 1969.

Arvin, Newton. *Hawthorne.* New York: Russell & Russell, 1961.

Ashton, John. *Social Life in the Reign of Queen Anne.* London: Chatto and

Windus, 1883.

Asquith, Lady Cynthia. *Diaries, 1915–1918.* Edited by E. M. Horsley. New York: Alfred A. Knopf, 1969.

Austen, Jane. *Collected Works.* New York: Pantheon Books, n. d.

Austen, Jane. *Pride and Prejudice.* New York: Dell, 1959.

Austen, Jane. *Lady Susan, the Watsons' Letters.* Part I. Edited by R. Brimley Johnson. New York: Frank S. Holby, 1906.

Ausubel, Herman. *Late Victorians: A Short History.* New York: D. Van Nostrand, 1955.

Bagnold, Enid. *Autobiography.* Boston: Little, Brown, 1969.

Bailey, J. O. *Pilgrims Through Space and Time.* New York: Argus Books, 1947.

Balakian, Nona and Simmons, Charles (eds.). *The Creative Present.* New York: Doubleday, 1963.

Ball, Albert H. P. (ed.). *Selections from the Paston Letters.* London: George G. Harrap, 1949.

Barlow, S. L. M. *The Astonished Muse.* New York: John Day, 1961.

Barnes, Djuna. *Nightwood.* New York: Harcourt, Brace, 1937.

Barnet, Sylvan and Berman, Morton and Burto, William (eds.). *The Genius of the Irish Theater.* New York: Mentor Books, 1960.

Bayne, Peter. *Two Great Englishwomen.* London: J. Clarke, n. d.

Bayne-Powell, Rosamond. *The English Child in the Eighteenth Century.* New York: E. P. Dutton, 1939.

Beam, Philip C. *Winslow Homer at Prout's Neck.* Boston: Little, Brown, 1966.

Beebe, Lucius. *Boston and the Boston Legend.* New York, London: D. Appleton-Century, 1935.

Bell, Clive. *Old Friends.* New York: Harcourt, Brace, 1956.

Bell, Florence, Lady (ed.). *The Letters of Gertrude Bell.* Vol. 1, vol. II. Harmondsworth, England: Penguin Books, 1939.

Bennett, Joan. *George Eliot.* New York: Cambridge University Press, 1962.

Benson, E. F. *Charlotte Brontë.* London: Longmans, Green, 1936.

Besant, Walter. *Fifty Years Ago.* New York: Harper and Brothers, 1888.

Bigland, Eileen. *Mary Shelley.* London: Cassell, 1959.

Bindoff, S. T. *Tudor England.* Harmondsworth, England: Penguin Books, 1950.

Blackwood's Edinburgh Magazine. Vol. 80, July-December, 1856. New York: Leonard Scott, 1856.

Blunden, Edmund. *Shelley: A Life Story.* London: Oxford University Press, 1965.

Bourne, Randolph. *The History of a Literary Radical and Other Papers.* New York: S. A. Russell, 1956.

Bowen, Elizabeth. *Collected Impressions.* London: Longmans, Green, 1950.

Bowne, Eliza Southgate. *A Girl's Life Eighty Years Ago.* New York: Charles Scribner's Sons, 1887.

Briggs, Asa. *Victorian People: A Reassessment of Persons and Themes, 1851–67.* Chicago: University of Chicago Press, 1955.

Bibliography

Brinnin, John Malcolm. *Third Rose: Gertrude Stein and Her World.* Boston: Little, Brown, 1959.

Brontë, Charlotte. *Shirley.* London: T. Nelson and Sons, n. d.

Brontë, Emily. *Wuthering Heights.* Harmondsworth, England. Penguin Books, 1954.

Brontë, Emily Jane. *Gondal's Queen.* Arranged by Fannie E. Ratchford. Austin: University of Texas Press, 1964.

Brooks, Van Wyck and Bettman, Otto. *Our Literary Heritage.* New York: E. P. Dutton, 1956.

Brooks, Van Wyck (ed.). *Writers at Work: Second Series.* New York: Viking Press, 1965.

Brown, Arthur W. *Margaret Fuller.* New Haven, Conn.: College & University Press, Twayne Publishers, 1964.

Brown, E. K. and Edel, Leon. *Willa Cather: A Critical Biography.* New York: Alfred A. Knopf, 1953.

Browning, D. C. (ed.). *Everyman's Dictionary of Literary Biography: English and American.* London: J. M. Dent & Sons, 1958.

Browning, Robert and Elizabeth Barrett. *Letters 1845–1846.* Vol. I, vol. II, New York: Harper & Brothers, 1899.

Bryant, Arthur. *The Age of Elegance, 1812–1822.* London: Collins, 1950.

Bryce, James. *Studies in Contemporary Biography.* London: Macmillan, 1903.

Bryher, *The Heart to Artemis: A Writer's Memoirs.* New York: Harcourt, Brace and World, 1962.

Burke, Thomas. *Living in Bloomsbury.* London: George Allen and Unwin, 1939.

Burnet, John. *Early Greek Philosophy.* London: A. and C. Black, 1930.

Burnett, B. Constance. *Happily Ever After: A Portrait of Frances Hodgson Burnett.* New York: Vanguard Press, n. d.

Burney, Fanny. *Evelina.* London: J. M. Dent and Sons, 1931.

Butts, Mary. *The Crystal Cabinet: My Childhood at Salterns.* London: Methuen, 1937.

Cameron, Kenneth Neill (ed.). *Shelley and His Circle, 1773–1822.* Vol. I, vol. II, Cambridge, Mass.: Harvard University Press, 1961.

Cameron, Kenneth Neill. *The Young Shelley: Genesis of a Radical.* New York: Collier Books, 1962.

Campbell, Olwen. *Mary Kingsley: A Victorian in the Jungle.* London: Methuen, 1957.

Carrington, Dorothy. *The Traveller's Eye.* London: Readers Union with the Pilot Press, 1949.

Carson, Rachel, *Silent Spring.* Greenwich, Conn., Fawcett Publications, 1964.

Cary, Richard. *Sarah Orne Jewett.* New Haven, Conn., College University Press, 1962.

Cassell's Encyclopedia of World Literature. Edited by S. H. Steinberg. Vol. I, vol. II, New York: Funk & Wagnalls, 1954.

Cecil, David. *Early Victorian Novelists.* Harmondsworth, England: Penguin Books, 1948.

The Century Illustrated Monthly Magazine. Vol. 23, Nov. 1881–April 1882. Vol. 45, Nov. 1892–April 1893. Vol. 46, May 1893–Oct. 1893. New York: Century, 1893.

Chambers, R. (ed.). *The Book of Days.* Vol. I, vol. II. London: W. & R. Chambers, 1869.

Chapin, Anna Alice. *Greenwich Village.* New York: Dodd, Mead, 1917.

Chapman, Maria Weston (ed.). *Harriet Martineau's Autobiography.* Vol. I, vol. II. Boston: Houghton, Mifflin, 1885.

Churchill, Allen. *The Improper Bohemians.* New York: E. P. Dutton, 1959.

Clemmer, Mary. *Poetical Works of Alice and Phoebe Cary.* New York: Hurd and Houghton, 1876.

Cockery, Daniel. *The Hidden Ireland.* Dublin: Gill and Son, 1967.

Cole, Margaret. *Beatrice Webb.* New York: Harcourt, Brace, 1946.

Colum, Mary. *Life and The Dream.* London: Macmillan, 1947.

Connely, Willard. *Adventures in Biography.* New York: Horizon Press, 1960.

Cooper, Lady Diana. *The Light of Common Day.* Boston: Houghton Mifflin, 1959.

Cooper, Lady Diana. *The Rainbow Comes and Goes.* Boston: Houghton, Mifflin, 1958.

Cooper, Diana. *Trumpets From the Steep.* London: Rupert Hart-Davis, 1960.

Cowley, Malcolm. *Exile's Return.* New York: Viking Press, 1962.

Coxhead, Elizabeth. *Daughters of Erin.* London: New English Library, 1968.

Coxhead, Elizabeth. *Lady Gregory: A Literary Portrait.* New York: Harcourt, Brace & World, 1961.

Creegar, George R. (ed.). *George Eliot: A Collection of Critical Essays.* Englewood Cliffs, N.J.: Prentice Hall, 1970.

Cunard, Nancy. *Grand Man: Memories of Norman Douglas.* London: Secker and Warburg, 1954.

Curtis, Edith Roelker. *A Season in Utopia: The Story of Brook Farm.* New York: Thomas Nelson & Sons, 1961.

Daiches, David. *Virginia Woolf.* Norfolk, Conn.: New Directions Books, 1942.

Daiken, Leslie. *Children's Games Throughout the Year.* London, New York: B. T. Batsford, 1949.

Davis, Elizabeth Gould. *The First Sex.* New York: G. P. Putnam's Sons, 1971.

Dawson, William J. and Dawson, Coningby W. *The Great English Letter-Writers.* Vol. I, vol. II, New York, London: Fleming H. Revell, 1908.

Dean, Leonard F. (ed.). *Essays.* New York: Harcourt, Brace, 1953.

Decter, Midge. *The Liberated Woman and Other Americans.* New York: Coward, McCann & Geoghegan, 1971.

Deiss, Joseph Jay. *The Roman Years of Margaret Fuller.* New York: Thomas Y. Crowell, 1934.

Bibliography

Denson, Alan (ed.). *Letters From AE.* London: Abelard-Schuman, 1961.

Dodds, John W. *Age of Paradox: A Biography of England, 1841–1851.* New York: Rinehart, 1952.

Dolmetsch, Carl R. *The Smart Set: A History and Anthology.* New York: Dial Press, 1966.

D'oyley, Elizabeth (ed.). *Great Travel Stories of All Nations.* London: George G. Harrap, 1932.

Dufferin, Lord. *Letters From High Latitudes: Some Account of a Voyage in 1856.* Boston: Ticknor and Fields, 1859.

Durrell, Lawrence. *Key to Modern British Poetry.* London: Peter Nevill, 1952.

Dyer, T. F. Thiselton. *The Folk-Lore of Plants.* London: Chatto and Windus, 1889.

Earle, Alice Morse. *Customs and Fashions in Old New England.* London: David Nutt, 1893.

Earle, Alice Morse. *Two Centuries of Costume in America 1620–1820.* Vol. I, vol. II. New York: Dover Publications, 1970.

Edes, Mary Elisabeth and Frasier, Dudley. *The Age of Extravagance: An Edwardian Reader.* New York: Rinehart, 1954.

Edgeworth, Maria. *Castle Rackrent.* London: J. Johnson, 1801.

Eliot, George. *Scenes of Clerical Life.* Boston: C. C. Brainard Publishing. n. d.

Ellis, Amanda M. *Rebels and Conservatives: Dorothy and William Wordsworth and Their Circle.* Bloomington: Indiana University Press, 1967.

Elwin, Malcolm. *Lord Byron's Wife.* New York: Harcourt, Brace and World, 1962.

Emerson, Edwin Jr. *A History of The Nineteenth Century Year by Year.* Vol. II. New York: P. F. Collier and Son, 1902.

Emerson, R. W., Channing W. H., and Clarke, J. F. *Memoirs of Margaret Fuller Ossoli.* Vol. I, vol. II. Boston: Roberts Brothers, 1874.

Ervine, St. John. *Parnell.* London: Ernest Benn, 1925.

Ewing, Juliana Horatia. *A Flat Iron for Farthing.* New York: Frank F. Lovell, 1891.

Ewing, Juliana Horatia. *Jackanapes: Daddy Darwin's Dovecot.* New York: Thomas V. Crowell, 1893.

Fairclough, Peter (ed.). *Three Gothic Novels: The Castle of Otranto,* by Horace Walpole, *Vathek,* by William Beckford, *Frankenstein,* by Mary Shelley. Harmondsworth, England: Penguin Books, 1968.

Falk, Robert P. (ed.). *The Antic Muse: American Writers in Parody.* New York: Grove Press, 1955.

Farjeon, Eleanor. *Portrait of a Family.* New York: Frederick A. Stokes, 1936.

Feinberg, Leonard. *The Satirist: His Temperament, Motivation and Influence.* New York: Citadel Press, 1965.

Ffrench, Yvonne. *Mrs. Gaskell.* London: Home & Van Thal, 1949.

Fields, James T. *Yesterdays With Authors.* Boston: Houghton, Mifflin, 1899.

Follett, Mary Parker. *Dynamic Administration Collected Papers.* Edited by Henry Metcalf and L. Urwick. New York, London: Harper and Brothers, 1940.

Ford, Boris (ed.). *From Blake to Byron. Guide to English Literature.* Vol. V.

England: Penguin Books, 1961.

Forster, E. M. *Abinger Harvest.* New York: Meridian Books, 1955.

Franzero, Carlo Maria. *Beau Brummell, His Life and Times.* New York: John Day, 1958.

Froebel, Friedrich. *Pedagogics of the Kindergarten.* Translated by Josephine Jarvis. New York: D. Appleton, 1906.

Froude, A. James. *Thomas Carlyle: A History of the First Forty Years of His Life, 1795–1835.* London: Longmans, Green, 1890.

Froude, A. James. *Thomas Carlyle: A History of His Life in London, 1834–1881.* London: Longmans, Green, 1890.

Fuller, Margaret. *Memoirs.* Vol. I, vol. II. Boston: Roberts Brothers, 1874.

Gaskell Elizabeth C. *Cranford.* New York: Home Book, Dresden Edition, n. d.

Gaskell, Elizabeth C. *Life of Charlotte Brontë.* London: J. M. Dent and Sons, 1941.

Gentleman's Magazine Library: A classified Collection of the Chief Contents of The Gentleman's Magazine, 1731–1868. Edited by Sir George Lawrence Gomme. London: Elliot Stock, 1883.

George, Daniel. *A Book of Anecdotes.* England: Pitman Press, 1958.

Gerin, Winifred. *Charlotte Brontë.* London: Oxford University Press, 1967.

Gilder, J. L. and J. B. (eds.). *Authors At Home.* New York: Cassell, 1888.

Gloag, John and Walker, C. Thompson. *Home Life in History, Social Life and Manners in Britain 200 B. C.–A. D. 1926.* New York: Coward-McCann, 1928.

Goodrich, S. G. (ed.). *Robert Merry's Museum.* Vol. III. Boston: Bradbury, Soden, 1842.

Goodwin, Michael. *Nineteenth Century Opinion.* Harmondsworth, England: Penguin Books, 1951.

Grant, Arthur. *In the Old Paths: Memories of Literary Pilgrimages.* London: Constable, 1913.

Grant, Joy. *Harold Monro and The Poetry Bookshop.* Berkeley and Los Angeles: University of California Press, 1967.

Green, Roger Lancelyn. *Authors and Places.* London: B. T. Batsford, 1963.

Greenslet, Ferris. *The Lowells and Their Seven Worlds.* Boston: Houghton, Mifflin, 1946.

Gregor, Ian (ed.). *The Brontës: A Collection of Critical Essays.* Englewood Cliffs, N.J.: Prentice-Hall, 1970.

Gregory, Lady Augusta. *Poets and Dreamers: Studies and Translations from the Irish.* Dublin: Hodges, Figgis, 1903.

Gregory, Horace. *Amy Lowell.* New York: Thomas Nelson & Sons, 1958.

Gurdjieff, G. *Meetings With Remarkable Men.* New York: E. P. Dutton, 1963.

Gwynn, Stephen. *The Life of Mary Kingsley.* Harmondsworth, England: Penguin Books, 1940.

Hamel, Frank. *Famous French Salons.* New York: Brentano's, 1909.

Hanaford, Phebe A. *Daughters of America or Women of the Century.* Augusta, Me.: True, 1882.

Bibliography

Hanscom, Elizabeth Deering (ed.). *The Friendly Craft: A Collection of American Letters.* New York: Macmillan, 1909.

Hapgood, Hutchins. *The Spirit of the Ghetto: Studies of the Jewish Quarters of New York.* New York: Funk & Wagnalls, 1902–1965.

Harper's Round Table. Harper's Young People. New York: Harper and Brothers, 1895.

Harrison, Jane Ellen. *Ancient Art and Ritual.* New York: Henry Holt, 1913.

Hawthorne, Julian. *Nathaniel Hawthorne and His Wife: A Biography.* Vol. I. Boston: Houghton, Mifflin, 1896.

Hays, Elinor Rice. *Lucy Stone: One of America's First and Greatest Feminists.* Tower Publications, 1961.

Hemingway, Ernest. *A Moveable Feast.* New York: Charles Scribner's Sons, 1964.

Hemlow, Joyce. *The History of Fanny Burney.* Oxford: The Clarendon Press, 1958.

Herbert, Mrs. S. *Child-Lore: A Study in Folk-Lore and Psychology.* London: Methuen, 1925.

Herford, C. H. *The Age of Wordsworth.* London: G. Bell and Sons, 1911.

Herold, J. Christopher. *Mistress to an Age: A Life of Madame De Stäel.* New York: Bobbs-Merrill, 1958.

Hochfield, George (ed.). *Selected Writings of the American Transcendentalists.* New York: New American Library, 1966.

Hoffman, Frederick S.; Allen, Charles; and Ulrich, Carolyn. *The Little Magazine.* Princeton, N.J.: Princeton University Press, 1946.

Hole, Christina. *English Home-Life, 1500 to 1800.* London: B. T. Batsford, 1949.

Holman-Hunt. *My Grandmothers and I.* New York: W. W. Norton, 1960.

Holmes, Oliver Wendell. *Ralph Waldo Emerson.* Boston: Houghton, Mifflin, 1886.

Hone, Joseph. *W. B. Yeats. Eighteen Sixty-Five to Nineteen Thirty-Nine.* London: Macmillan, 1967.

Howe, George and Harrer, Gustave Adolphus (eds.). Revised edition by Epps, Preston Herschel, *Greek Literature in Translation.* New York: Harper and Brothers, 1948.

Howe, Marie Jenney (ed. and tran.). *The Intimate Journal of George Sand.* New York: John Day, 1929.

Hubbard, Elbert. *Little Journeys to the Homes of Famous Women.* New York: G. P. Putnam's Sons, 1897.

Hurll, Estelle M. *Child Life In Art.* Boston: L. C. Page, 1898.

Ingoldsby, Thomas. *The Ingoldsby Legends.* London: Macmillan, 1906.

Janeway, Elizabeth. *Man's World, Woman's Place: A Study in Social Mythology.* New York: William Morrow, 1971.

Jeffares, A. Norman (ed.). *A Review of English Literature.* London: Longmans, Green, 1963.

Jefferson, D. W. (ed.). *Eighteenth Century Prose 1700–1780.* Harmondsworth,

England: Penguin Books, 1956.

Jenkins, Elizabeth. *Jane Austen.* New York: Grosset and Dunlap, 1949.

Jewett, Sarah Orne. *A Country Doctor.* Boston: Houghton, Mifflin, 1884.

Johnstone, J. K. *The Bloomsbury Group: A Study of E. M. Forster, Lytton Strachey, Virginia Woolf and their Circle.* New York: Noonday Press, 1954.

Jolas, Eugene (ed.). *Transition Workshop.* New York: Vanguard Press, 1949.

Josephson, Matthew. *Life Among the Surrealists.* New York: Holt, Rinehart & Winston, 1962.

Jullian, Phillippe. *Edward and the Edwardians.* Translated from the French by Peter Dawney, New York: Viking Press, 1962.

Kain, Richard M. *Dublin In The Age Of William Butler Yeats And James Joyce.* Norman: University of Oklahoma Press, 1962.

Kamm, Josephine. *Gertrude Bell, Daughter of the Desert.* New York: Vanguard Press, 1956.

Keats, John. *You Might As Well Live: The Life and Times of Dorothy Parker.* New York: Simon and Schuster, 1970.

Kellogg, Grace. *The Two Lives of Edith Wharton: The Woman And Her Work.* New York: Appleton-Century, 1965.

Kendall, Paul Murray. *The Art of Biography.* New York: W. W. Norton, 1965.

Knight, Damon. *In Search of Wonder.* Chicago: Advent Publishers, 1967.

Knoll, Robert E. (ed.). *McAlmon and the Lost Generation: A Self-Portrait.* Lincoln: University of Nebraska Press, 1962.

Kraditor, Aileen S. (ed.). *Up from the Pedestal: Selected Writings from the History of American Feminism.* Chicago: Quadrangle Books, 1970.

Kronenberger, Louis. *Marlborough's Duchess: A Study in Worldliness.* New York: Alfred A. Knopf, 1958.

Lamb, Mary and Charles. *Poems: Letters and Remains.* Edited by W. Carew Hazlitt. London: Chatto and Windus, 1874.

Lane, Margaret. *The Brontë Story.* New York: Duell, Sloan & Pearce, 1953.

Lane, Margaret. *The Tale of Beatrix Potter: A Biography.* Harmondsworth, England: Penguin Books, 1962.

Langbaum, Robert (ed.). *The Victorian Age: Essays in History and in Social and Literary Criticism.* Greenwich, Conn.: Fawcett Publications, 1967.

Langdon-Davies, John. *A Short History of Women.* New York: Viking Press, 1927.

Lord, Walter. *The Good Years: From 1900 to The First World War.* New York: Harper and Brothers, 1960.

Larousse Encyclopedia Of Mythology. New York: Prometheus Press, 1959.

Laski, Marghanita. *Mrs. Ewing, Mrs. Molesworth and Mrs. Hodgson Burnett.* London: Arthur Barker, 1950.

Laver, James. *Clothes.* London: Burke Publishing, 1952.

Laver, James. *Edwardian Promenade.* Boston: Riverside Press, 1958.

Leavis, F. R. *The Great Tradition: George Eliot, Henry James, Joseph Conrad.* New

York: George W. Stewart, 1947.

Lehmann, John . *In My Own Time: Memoirs of a Literary Life*. Boston: Little, Brown, 1969.

Leslie, Frank. *Christmas Box*. New York: Frank Leslie's Publishing House, 1880–1881.

Leverson, Ada. *The Little Ottleys*. New York: W. W. Norton, 1962.

Lucas, E. V. *The Colvins and Their Friends*. London: Methuen, 1928.

Lynd, Robert. *Dr. Johnson and Company*. Harmondsworth, England: Penguin Books, 1946.

Lyon, Peter. *Success Story: The Life and Times of S. S. McClure*. New York: Charles Scribner's Sons, 1963.

Macaulay, Rose. *Life Among the English*. London: William Collins, 1942.

Macdonald, Dwight. *Against the American Grain: Essays on the Effects of Mass Culture*. New York: Vintage Books, 1965.

Madison, Charles A. *Critics and Crusaders*. New York: Henry Holt, 1948.

Madison, Charles A. *Book Publishing in America*. New York: McGraw-Hill, 1966.

Manley, Seon. *Nathaniel Hawthorne: Captain of the Imagination*. New York: Vanguard Press, 1968.

Manley, Seon. *Rudyard Kipling*. New York: Vanguard Press, 1965.

Mannin, Ethel. *Confessions and Impressions*. England: Penguin Books, 1937.

Manning-Sanders, Ruth. *Seaside England*. London: B. T. Bayford, 1951.

Mansfield, Katherine. *The Letters of Katherine Mansfield*. Edited by J. Middleton Murry. New York: Alfred A. Knopf, 1936.

Marreco, Anne. *The Rebel Countess: The Life and Times of Constance Markievicz*. London: Transworld Publishers, 1969.

Marshall, William H. *Byron, Shelley, Hunt, and the Liberal*. Philadelphia: University of Pennsylvania Press, 1960.

Martineau, Harriet. *Autobiography* (see Chapman, M. W. ed.). Vol. I, vol. II. Boston: Houghton, Mifflin, 1885.

Marwick, Arthur. *The Deluge: British Society and the First World War*. Boston: Little, Brown, 1965.

Matthews, T. S. (ed.). *The Selected Letters of Charles Lamb*. New York: Farrar, Straus and Cudahy, 1956.

Maurois, André. *The Edwardian Era*. Translated by Hamish Miles. New York: D. Appleton-Century, 1933.

Maxwell, Constantia. *Dublin Under the Georges (1714–1830)*. London: George G. Harrap, 1946.

Mayhew, Henry. *Mayhew's London: London Labour and the London Poor*. Edited by Peter Quennell. London: Spring Books (first published 1851).

McHugh, Roger. *Dublin, 1916*. New York: Hawthorne Books, 1966.

Mead, Margaret. *Male and Female: A Study of the Sexes in a Changing World*. New York: Dell Publishing, 1970.

Mendilow, A. A. *Time and the Novel*. London: Peter Nevill, 1952.

Meynell, Viola. *Alice Meynell: A Memoir.* New York: Charles Scribner's Sons, 1929.

Mill, John Stuart. *The Subjection of Women.* Philadelphia, J. B. Lippincott, 1869.

Millay, Edna St. Vincent. *Letters.* Edited by Allan Ross Macdougall. New York: Grosset and Dunlap, 1952.

Miller, Betty (ed.). *Elizabeth Barrett To Miss Mitford.* New Haven: Yale University Press, 1954.

Mitchell, Donald G. *English Lands, Letters and Kings: Queen Anne and the Georges.* New York: Charles Scribner's Sons, 1895.

Mitchell, Edwin Valentine. *Adrift Among Books.* New York: Farrar & Rinehart, 1929.

Mitford, Mary Russell. *Our Village.* Chicago: Belford, Clarke, 1880.

Mitford, Mary Russell. *Recollections of a Literary Life.* Vol. I, vol. II. London: Richard Bentley, 1853.

Moers, Ellen. *The Dandy: Brummell to Beerbohm.* London: Secker and Warburg, 1960.

Moore, Thomas. *Letters and Journals of Lord Byron. With Notices of His Life.* Vol. II, vol. III. London: John Murray, 1833.

Moore, George. *Hail and Farewell.* New York: D. Appleton, 1912.

Morgan, Robin (ed.). *Sisterhood Is Powerful: An Anthology of Writings from the Women's Liberation Movement.* New York: Vintage Books, 1970.

Morison, Samuel Eliot. *The Intellectual Life of Colonial New England.* Ithaca, N.Y.: Cornell University Press, 1965.

Morrell, Lady Ottoline. *Memoirs.* New York: Alfred A. Knopf, 1964.

Mosher, Thomas B. (ed.). *The Bibelot: A Reprint of Poetry and Prose from Scarce Editions,* vol. VIII. New York: Wm. H. Wise, 1902.

Moss, Arthur and Marvel, Evalyn. *The Legend of the Latin Quarter: Henry Murger and the Birth of Bohemia.* New York: Beechhurst Press, 1946.

Muir, Edwin. *An Autobiography.* New York: William Sloane, 1954.

Murasaki, Lady. *The Tale of Genji.* Garden City, N.Y.: Doubleday, 1955.

Neagoe, Peter (ed.). *Americans Abroad.* The Hague, Holland: Sevire Press, 1932.

Nevins, Allan and Barker, Ernest (eds.). *Golden Ages of the Great Cities.* London: Thames and Hudson, 1952.

Newton, A. Edward. *The Amenities of Book-Collecting and Kindred Affections.* Boston: Atlantic Monthly Press, 1924.

Norman, Charles. *Mr. Oddity: Samuel Johnson, LL.D.,* Drexel Hill, Pa.: Bell Publishing, 1951.

O'Casey, Sean. *Autobiographies, vol. II. Inishfallen, Fare Thee Well, Rose and Crown, Sunset and Evening Star.* London: Macmillan, 1963.

Oliphant, Margaret O. *The Literary History of England.* Vols. I, II, III. London: Macmillan, 1889.

Our Young Folks. An Illustrated Magazine edited by J. T. Trowbridge and Lucy Larcom. Vol. VIII. Boston: James R. Osgood, 1872.

Bibliography

Ossoli, Margaret Fuller. *Woman in the Nineteenth Century, and Kindred Papers.* Boston: John P. Jewett, 1855.

Parker, Dorothy. *The Portable Dorothy Parker.* Introduction by W. Somerset Maugham. New York: Viking Press, 1970.

Parker, Dorothy. *Constant Reader.* New York: Viking Press, 1970.

Perrin, Noel. *Dr. Bowdler's Legacy.* New York: Doubleday, 1971.

Peterson, Virgilia. *A Matter of Life and Death.* New York: Bantam Books, 1961.

Phillips, William (ed.). *Art and Psychoanalysis.* New York: World Publishing, 1963.

Quennell, Peter. *Victorian Panorama: A Survey of Life and Fashion from Contemporary Photographs.* London: B. T. Batsford, 1937.

Radcliffe, Ann. *The Mysteries of Udolpho.* New York: Derby & Jackson, 1861.

Rader, Dotson (ed.). *Defiance no. 2.* New York: Paperback Library, 1971.

Rayne, Mrs. M. L. *What Can a Woman Do?* Pittsburgh, N.Y.: Eagle Publishing, 1893.

Reid, T. Wemyss. *Charlotte Brontë: A Monograph.* New York: Scribner, Armstrong, 1877.

Richardson, Dorothy M. *Pilgrimage II, The Tunnel, Interim.* New York: Alfred A. Knopf, n. d.

Riding, Laura. *Anarchism Is Not Enough.* Garden City, N.Y.: Doubleday, Doran, 1928.

Riding, Laura. *The World and Ourselves.* London: Chatto and Windus, 1938.

Robinson, A. Mary. *Emily Brontë.* Boston: Roberts Brothers, 1896.

Roe, Ivan. *Shelley, The Last Phase.* London: Hutchinson, 1953.

Rogers, Agnes. *Women Are Here to Stay.* New York: Harper and Brothers, 1949.

Rogers, W. G. *Wise Men Fish Here: The Story of Frances Steloff and the Gotham Book Mart.* New York: Harcourt, Brace & World, 1965.

Rugoff, Milton (ed.). *The Great Travelers.* Vol. I. New York: Simon and Schuster, 1960.

Russell, Bertrand. *Autobiography.* Boston: Little, Brown, 1967.

Saint-Beuve, C. A. *Portraits of the Eighteenth Century.* Translated by Katharine P. Wormeley. New York and London: G. P. Putnam's Sons, 1905.

Saint Nicholas. Vol. XV, part I, Nov. 1887 to Apr. 1888; *Vol. XXI, part 1,* Nov. 1893 to Apr. 1894. New York: Century, 1888, 1894.

Saint Nicholas. Vol. XXVII, May, 1900 to Oct. 1900; *vol. XVIII,* May, 1891, to Oct., 1891. New York: Century, 1891.

Salmon, David and Hindshaw, Winifred. *Infant Schools: Their History and Theory.* New York and Bombay: Longmans, Green, 1904.

Sanborn, Kate. *The Wit of Women.* New York: Funk & Wagnalls, 1885.

Sappho. *Poems and Fragments.* Translated by Edward Storer. Hampstead, England: Richard Aldington, n. d.

Scarborough, Dorothy. *The Supernatural in Modern English Fiction.* New York: Octagon Books, 1967.

Scherman, David E. & Wilcox, Richard. *Literary England, Photographs of Places*

Made Memorable in English Literature. New York: Random House, 1943.

Scribner's Monthly, 1871. New York: Charles Scribner's Sons, 1971.

Scribner's Magazine. Vol. VIII, July–December, 1890. New York: Charles Scribner's Sons, 1890.

Shannon, David A. (ed.). *The Great Depression.* Englewood Cliffs, N.J.: Prentice-Hall, 1960.

Shelley, Mary. *The Last Man.* Lincoln: University of Nebraska Press, 1965.

Shorter, Clement. *Charlotte Brontë and Her Circle.* London: Hodder and Stoughton, 1896.

Sinclair, May. *The Three Brontës.* London: Hutchinson, 1911.

Sitwell, Edith. *English Eccentrics.* New York: Vanguard Press, 1957.

Sitwell, Edith. *Selected Letters, 1919–1964.* Edited by John Lehmann & Derek Parker. New York: Vanguard Press, 1970.

Sitwell, Edith. *Taken Care of: The Autobiography of Edith Sitwell.* New York: Atheneum, 1965.

Sitwell, Osbert and Barton, Margaret. *Brighton.* London: Faber and Faber, 1935.

Sitwell, Sir Osbert. *Tales My Father Taught Me.* Boston: Little, Brown, 1962.

The Smart Set. Anthology. New York: Dial Press, 1966.

Smith, Page. *Daughters of the Promised Land.* Boston: Little, Brown, 1970.

Snelling, Vera (ed.). *Victorian Byeways.* London: Staples Press, 1949.

Somerville, E. OE and Ross, Martin. *Irish Memories.* London: Longmans, Green, 1933.

Somerville, E. OE and Ross, Martin. *Some Experiences of an Irish R. M.* Harmondsworth, England: Penguin Books, 1938.

Somerville E. OE and Ross, Martin. *Some Irish Yesterdays.* London: Longmans, Green, 1933.

Speranza, Lady Wilde. *Poems.* Dublin: M. H. Gill and Son, n. d.

Sprigge, Elizabeth. *Gertrude Stein Her Life and Work.* New York: Harper and Brothers, 1957.

Stanley, Lady Augusta. *Later Letters 1864–1876.* Edited by the Dean of Windsor and Hector Bolitho. New York: Jonathan Cape & Harrison Smith, 1929.

Starling, Elizabeth. *Noble Deeds of Women.* Boston: Phillips, Sampson, 1850.

Stedman, Edmund Clarence and Hutchinson, Ellen Mackay (eds.). *A Library of American Literature from the Earliest Settlement to the Present Time.* Vol. XIII. New York: Charles L. Webster, 1890.

Stein, Gertrude. *Two: Gertrude Stein and Her Brother.* New Haven, Conn.: Yale University Press, 1951.

Stein, Gertrude. *Four Americans in Paris,* The Collections of Gertrude Stein and Her Family. New York: Museum of Modern Art, 1970.

Stein, Philip Van Doren (ed.). *Selected Writings of Thomas De Quincey.* New York: Random House, 1937.

Stoddard, R. H. *Poet's Homes.* Boston: D. Lothrop, 1877.

Strachey, Lytton. *Books and Characters, French and English.* London: Chatto and

Windus, 1922.

Strahan's. *Boys' and Girls' Annual.* London: Strahan & Co., 1878.

Szladits, Lola and Simmonds, Harvey. *Pen & Brush, the Author as Artist.* New York: New York Public Library, 1969.

Tanner, Louise. *Here Today.* New York: Dell Publishing, 1963.

Targ, William (ed.), *Bibliophile in the Nursery.* Cleveland, New York: World Publishing, 1957.

Thackeray, Smith, Beckett, Mayhew (eds.). *The Comic Almanack.* London: Chatto and Windus, 1835–1843. Second Series, 1844–1853.

Tharp, Louise Hall, *The Peabody Sisters of Salem.* Boston: Little, Brown, 1950.

Thaxter, Rosamond. *Sandpiper.* The Life of Celia Thaxter. Francestown, N. H.: Marshall Jones. 1963.

Timbes, John. *Clubs and Club Life in London.* London: Chatto and Windus, 1899.

Todd, Rutheven. *Tracks In the Snow: Studies in English Science and Art.* London: Grey Walls Press, 1946.

Trask, Georgianne and Burkhart, Charles (eds.). *Storytellers and Their Art.* New York: Doubleday, 1963.

Trevelyan, George M. *A Shortened History of England.* New York: Longmans, Green, 1942.

Treves, Giuliana Artom. *The Golden Ring: The Anglo-Florentines, 1847–1862.* Translated by Sylvia Sprigge. London: Longmans, Green, 1956.

Trilling, Lionel (ed.). *The Selected Letters of John Keats.* New York: Farrar, Straus and Young, 1951.

Trollope, Frances. *Domestic Manners of the Americans.* Edited by Donald Smalley. New York: Vintage Books, 1960.

Tryon, W. S. *Parnassus Corner.* Boston: Houghton Mifflin, 1963.

Tuchman, Barbara W. *The Proud Tower.* New York: Bantam Books, 1970.

Tuer, Andrew W. (ed.). *Stories From Old-Fashioned Children's Books.* London: Leadenhall Press, 1899.

Untermeyer, Jean Starr. *Private Collection.* New York: Alfred A. Knopf, 1965.

Untermeyer, Louis. *Lives of the Poets.* New York: Simon and Schuster, 1959.

Van Doren, Carl. *Swift.* New York: Viking Press, 1930.

Van Thal, Herbert (ed.). *Victoria's Subjects Travelled.* London: Arthur Barker, 1951.

Van Voris, Jacqueline. *Constance De Markievicz in the Cause of Ireland.* Amherst: University of Massachusetts Press, 1967.

Vanity Fair, 1920–1929. Greenwich, Conn.: Condé Nast.

Wallace, Irving. *The Square Pegs: Some Americans Who Dared To Be Different.* New York: Alfred A. Knopf, 1957.

Ward, Mrs. Humphry. *A Writer's Recollections.* New York, London: Harper and Brothers, 1918.

Wardle, Ralph M. *Mary Wollstonecraft: A Critical Biography.* Lawrence, Kans.:

University of Kansas Press, 1951.

Ware, Caroline F. *Greenwich Village, 1920–1930.* New York: Harper & Row, 1965.

Waugh, Arthur (ed.). *Georgian Stories, 1927.* New York, London: G. P. Putnam's Sons, 1928.

Webb, Beatrice. *My Apprenticeship—I.* Harmondsworth, England: Penguin Books, 1938.

Webster's Biographical Dictionary. Springfield, Mass.: G. & C. Merriam, 1970.

Wells, Carolyn (ed.). *A Parody Anthology.* New York: Charles Scribner's Sons, 1904.

Wells, H. G. *Experiment in Autobiography.* New York: Macmillan, 1934.

Wharton, Anne Hollingsworth. *Colonial Days and Dames.* Philadelphia: J. B. Lippincott, 1895.

Whicher, George Frisbie, *This Was a Poet: Emily Dickinson.* Ann Arbor: The University of Michigan Press, 1957.

Whipple, A. B. C. *The Fatal Gift of Beauty: The final years of Byron and Shelley.* New York: Harper and Row, 1964.

Whipple, Edwin Percy. *Recollections of Eminent Men.* Boston: Ticknor, 1886.

White, Newman Ivey. *Portrait of Shelley.* New York: Alfred A. Knopf, 1959.

White, Terence DeVere. *The Parents of Oscar Wilde. Sir William and Lady Wilde.* England: Hodder and Stoughton, 1967.

Wickes, George. *Americans in Paris.* Garden City, N.Y.: Doubleday, 1969.

Wilson, Edmund. *The American Earthquake.* New York: Doubleday, 1958.

Wilson, Edmund. *Classics and Commercials: A Literary Chronicle of the Forties.* New Yok: Farrar, Straus, 1950.

Wilson, Edmund. *A Literary Chronicle 1920–1950.* Garden City, N. Y.: Doubleday, 1952.

Woollcott, Alexander (ed.). *As You Were.* New York: Viking Press, 1943.

Woolf, Leonard (ed.). *A Writer's Diary.* New York: Harcourt, Brace, 1954.

Woolf, Leonard. *Growing: An Autobiography of the Years 1904–1911.* New York: Harcourt, Brace & World, 1961.

Woolf, Virginia. *Granite and Rainbow.* New York: Harcourt, Brace & World, 1958.

Woolf, Virginia. *A Room of One's Own.* New York: Harcourt, Brace & World, 1957.

Woolf, Virginia. *The Second Common Reader.* New York: Harcourt, Brace, and World, 1960.

Woolf, Virginia. *The Waves.* London: Hogarth Press, 1931.

Wright, Julia McNair. *Practical Life; or, Ways and Means for Developing Character and Resources.* Philadelphia: McCurdy, 1882.

Wykes-Joyce. *Triad of Genius: Part I, Edith and Osbert Sitwell.* London: Peter Owen, 1950.

Wyndham, Violet. *The Sphinx and Her Circle: A Biographical Sketch of Ada*

Bibliography

Leverson. New York: Vanguard Press, 1963.

Yeats, W. B. *Autobiographies.* London: Macmillan, 1966.

Yeats, W. B. *Letters on Poetry from W. B. Yeats to Dorothy Wellesley.* London: Oxford University Press, 1964.

ACKNOWLEDGMENTS

WE ARE deeply grateful to the organizations and individuals who were helpful in the course of writing this book. We would like to thank in particular: the Amherst College Library, Doubleday and Company, Inc., Eighth Street Bookshop, the Gotham Book Mart, the Greenwich Book Store, the Greenwich Library, Harvard University Library, the Metropolitan Museum of Art, the Museum of the City of New York, National Portrait Gallery (London, England), National Gallery of Ireland, Princeton University Library, Charles Scribner's Sons, the Sou'Wester Bookshop, Bellport, N.Y., University of Texas Humanities Research Center, Vassar College Library, Walker Art Gallery (Liverpool, England) and Wellesley College Library.

Individuals who offered inspiration as well as concrete assistance were many, but we'd particularly like to single out: Dr. Edith Beck, Mrs. Chaucy Bennets, Mr. Donald Cameron, Mr. Arthur R. Cleverly, Margaret Du Bord Givens, Mrs. Marie Pettit, Mrs. Gogo Lewis, Miss Elizabeth Powers, Miss Luberta McLean, Mr. John F. Marion, Dr. Geraldine Pederson-Krag, Mrs. Clara Pye, Mrs. Betty Shalders, Miss Katie Siafaca, Miss Margarita Siafaca, Miss Frances Steloff and Mrs. Alice Walter.

And a special note of thanks, of course, to our husbands, Benjamin M. Belcher, Jr. and Robert R. Manley.

322

Index

Chesterfield, Lord, decree on women, 8

Child, Lydia, 142

Children, 18th Century, 95, 96

Children's literature, beginnings, 176

Churchill, Lady Jennie, 233

Churchill, Lord Randolph, 233

Claire (Jane) Byron's mistress, 35, 50-52, 54, 55; attacks on Mary Shelley, 56; pregnant, 55-56

Clarence, Duke of, 273

Coleridge, Samuel Taylor, 5

Colette, 299

Connally, James, 268, 276

Constant, Benjamin, 77

"Conversations," Bronson Alcott's, 163; introduced by Margaret Fuller, 141

Cornhill Magazine, 238

Cowley, Hannah, 5

Crowninshield, Frank, 296

Cunard, Nancy, 245

Dadaism, 284

Darwin, Dr. Erasmus, grandfather of Charles, 63-65; *Botanic Garden*, 64; on health, 65; *The Loves of the Plants*, 65

de Markievicz, Casimir Dunin, 266

de Markievicz, Constance, 262-69; developed communes, 268; elected to Parliament, 269; marriage, 266-67, 269; painter, 266; sentenced to death, 269; started cooperatives, 268; suffragette, 265

De Quincey, Thomas, 103; on Hannah More, 86, 89-92

Devlin, Bernadette, 262-63

Dr. Johnson's Wits, 92

Dodge, Mabel, 250

Dow, Caroline B., 293

Du Maurier, Daphne, 49

Earle, Ferdinand, 293

Edgeworth, Maria, 106-07; *Castle Rackrent*, 107; father of, 106-07

Edgeworth, Richard Lovell, 106-07

Edward, Prince of Wales, 300

Edward VII, King of England, 237

Edwardians, the, 231-59

Eliot, George, 298; in Chapman ménage, 195; early life, 193-94; editor, 195; and Herbert Spencer, 197; and Lewes, 198; translation of *Jesus*, 195

Eliot, T. S., 240

Elliott, Sir Gilbert, 101-02

Emerson, Ralph Waldo, 68, 141; helps the Alcotts, 163; on Margaret Fuller, 133-36, 138-39

Emma, 83

Encyclopedia Britannica, 8-9

Etiquette, subject for women writers, 171

Evans, Mary Ann. See Eliot, George

Evelina, 58, 67-68

Family Shakespeare, 102

Ferber, Edna, 299

Fianna, the, 268

Ficke, Arthur Davison, 294

Fire Island, 19th Century, 132

Fitzgerald, F. Scott, 284, 298, 300

Fitzgerald, Zelda, 287, 298, 300

Frankenstein: film, 32; popularity, 49

Fruitlands, farm of the Alcotts, 158

Fuller, Margaret, 131-50; "Conversations," 141-42; death, 150; early life, 136-37; editor of *The Dial*, 142; editor of New York *Tribune*, 143; father's death, 138; foreign correspondent, 144; friends, 133-35; on George Sand, 148-49; and human liberation, 142; and James Nathan, 143-44; linguist, 137; in love, 149-50; and Nathaniel Hawthorne, 135; obsession with death, 137; at school, 137; scoffed at, 136; superstitions, 136; and Thomas Carlyle, 144-47; toured the country, 142; and Transcendental Club, 140-41; trunk of letters found, 133; on woman's rights, 143-44

Fuseli (Fuzeli), Henry, 18-19

Garnett, Constance. See Black, Constance

325

Index

Index

ABOUT THE AUTHORS

SEON MANLEY, who has published over thirty books, has had long experience in the literary world. In addition to her biographies of writers, she was an active editor in publishing circles and a keen observer of the frustrations and rewards of the writer as well as some of the foibles and follies of literary life.

She is married to Robert Manley, and is the mother of Shivaun. The Manleys live in Greenwich, Connecticut.

SUSAN BELCHER, born and educated in Toronto, Canada, was introduced early to the works of the women writers of the nineteenth century in a fashion that gave them a living immediacy. A researcher on many books, this is her first full collaboration with Mrs. Manley.

She is married to Benjamin Moore Belcher, Jr., and is the mother of two young children, Allyson and Jamie. The Belchers also live in Greenwich, Connecticut.

Seon Manley and Susan Belcher have collected an extraordinary portfolio of rare prints of women writers, their friends and times, from which they have drawn many illustrations for this book.